THE 1968 WORLD SERIES

The Tigers-Cardinals Classic as Told by the Men Who Played

Brendan Donley

SPORTS
PUBLISHING

Visit our website at www.sportspubbooks.com.

10 9 8 7 6 5 4 3 2 1

Library of Congress Cataloging-in-Publication Data is available on file.

Cover design by Tom Lau and 5mediadesign
Cover photos credit: AP Images

ISBN: 978-1-68358-354-7
Ebook ISBN: 978 1 68358-203-8

Printed in the United States of America

For my grandfather, Edward Donley

CONTENTS

PREFACE

WHEN YOU ASK an old ballplayer about their playing days, they tend to show you things. In Lancaster, the heart of Amish country, Don Wert showed his glove, his cap. In Cincinnati, Jon Warden showed his old No. 39 jersey. In Akron, Hal Naragon showed Johnny Sain's "baseball spinner"—a ball on a stick, drilled through with a wooden handle attached. Rotating in the palm of his hand as his fingers flicked the ball forward with the spins of a slider, a fastball, a curveball.

Tim McCarver, on a sunny morning in Florida, showed his collection of bats. His closed left-handed batting stance that George Crowe had taught him. His damaged left catching hand—and what it was that Bob Gibson did to it: "I've told him," he said, "I think about him every day of my life. Because when I get up, my hand hurts. It's hurt for twenty years."

Mickey Stanley showed his four Gold Gloves, from center field, next to an array of framed photos. He showed his workshop, his woodworking, his golf cart, the land he'd bought and developed into subdivisions. He took me around in his truck, and performed what must be his favorite stunt—driving past the garage, across the lawn, a panicked look on his face, arms locked against the steering wheel, the truck rolling steeply down a slope until he turned, ten yards from the edge of a pond. Chuckling all the way back up.

He showed the still-crooked knuckle of his fourth finger on his right hand, an injury that never quite healed. He showed a big smile, excusing his memory—"Hell," he said, "I don't remember *shit*!"—before recalling to perfection the details of the center-field flagpole in Tiger Stadium, of Dick McAuliffe turning a double play, of Lou Brock slapping the first ball of the World Series right to his feet.

Umpire Bill Haller showed his old high school, in Joliet, Illinois. His lunch group at Thayer Bros. Deli, on Ruby Street.

Jim Price, in the Tigers' radio broadcast booth, showed an old picture: Tiger Stadium, 1968—Denny McLain pitching, Price catching, Mickey Mantle at bat, connecting on his 535th career home run.

Fred Lasher, in northern Wisconsin, showed a grin, calling his granddaughter over, at the sight of World Series film he'd never seen before. "Get in here—come see your grandpa pitch!" He showed his right arm, and where it sometimes still hurts, years later.

In California, Orlando Cepeda showed a shelf that used to hold his jazz albums. "They're all packed up," he said. "See those boxes? I'm moving. Moving *out*."

Dick "Ducky" Schofield let his cell phone ring—a "quack-quack" tone repeating on the kitchen counter. He showed his baseball room, photo albums for each season. Caps of each team he'd played for. He showed, half-smirking, the promotional give-away bobblehead of his favorite Washington National: his grandson, Jayson Werth.

John Hiller showed his home in the woods, in Michigan's upper peninsula, with deer standing a few arms' reach away, approaching the salt licks he'd set up around the yard. He showed his old jersey, his ring, his flannel Tigers "Yooper" hat.

In Plano, Texas, Julián Javier took me out for tacos with his extended family—the first days of his visit from the Dominican Republic.

And in Michigan, his lifelong home, Willie Horton showed his old game-used glove. His awards and plaques. Framed photos covering the walls of his basement. A scale model of Tiger Stadium he'd been given—a painted wood replica about four feet by four feet.

"That *whole* thing lights up," he said. "I've got a black light, the whole thing lights up if you turn the lights off—there's a mini Ernie Harwell hanging out of the booth, calling the game. Some of my grandkids took some of the lights and flags off it—it had flags on top of the roof, there. But all of that, if you want to talk about *beauty*... if you cut all these lights off and put that blacklight on it, those people will be *cheering* and everything. All that stuff lights up."

They like to show you things, these old ballplayers.

And I hope through this that they show something else:

What it was like, in their heads, in their recollections, in their bones, to be a Detroit Tiger. A St. Louis Cardinal. What it was like to play a World Series, fifty years on.

This is a book about them, their stories, how it was back then—in the World Series of 1968.

In November 2016, my hometown Chicago Cubs won the World Series. I was there, at Game Seven. Cleveland. The first fall classic of my life. Thinking only one thing as the ballgame began: *The World Series. The World Series. Holy cow, the World Series...* Seeing something distinct, from those summer afternoons at Wrigley Field. A new baseball language, hardly intelligible at first sight. With awe in everything—awe in the infield grass, awe in the eyes of each fan. Awe passed out in little pieces around the ballpark—in the programs, the ticket stubs, in the red towels us Cub fans weren't meant to take. Feeling, in every moment, that this World Series thing was different. Baseball, the World Series. A planet and then its moon. Lit up in the night with nothing else around.

Twenty-four years earlier, I was born. And twenty-four years before that, exactly to the day, the Tigers and Cardinals played a ballgame in Detroit, Michigan. October 7, 1968. Game Five. The Tigers down three games to one. The day Willie Horton gloved a line drive off the left-field grass, planted his left foot, released a cannon toward home, Lou Brock charging around third, and—well, history happened.

I sometimes wondered, driving across the roads of the Midwest, if my age would pose a problem. If, in sitting down with someone far younger, they might feel unable to relate, recalling years and players completely intangible to me.

"You obviously weren't there," Denny McLain said, stopping in the middle of a story. "How old are you?"

"Oh Jesus, God. I'm *ten* times older than you are!"

But then, his story would resume. And then another began. And another. He talked, and he talked, and he *talked*. Generously, as they all were, spending an afternoon remembering a time they never seem to have fallen far out of touch with.

When this project began, it was no certain thing that a single player would participate at all, let alone tell me the kinds of "unscrupulous," in John Hiller's words, activity that goes on in a twenty-three-year-old ballplayer's life in the late '60s.

The first get was in doubt, as was the second, the third, and—until, at some point, the doubts succumbed to something more promising, suddenly materializing: a nearly complete roster of voices, telling a nearly complete story of baseball past.

But, you realize you won't get them all.

That you *can't*, in fact, get them all.

Norm Cash, 1961 American League batting champion, has been gone since 1986. Roger Maris, since 1985. Curt Flood, 1997. Eddie Mathews, 2001. Jim Northrup, 2011. Dick McAuliffe, 2016. Ten years ago, Bill Freehan was diagnosed with Alzheimer's disease.

So this is, in the end, an imperfect record. In part by circumstance, in part by design. We lament their absences, but hope those absences form a kind of resonance. A reminder of the time that's passed.

You could produce a more complete record, perhaps, some other way. Gathering quotes and records from newspapers then and since. From the books these players have written over the years.

But that would mean something different.

I hoped to capture something else entirely—to see what stories stood out fifty years later. What do they remember *now*? What they remember, in feeling and in memory, from a week of baseball in the days they were young. What remains, and what doesn't.

On that note, I would be remiss not to mention a rather important thing: the absence of one Mickey Lolich, outright hero of the '68 Series (he's still very much alive).

The odyssey to find him went something like this:

You wait, saving the best for last, to interview each of his teammates before reaching him. You wait, you interview, and you progress one by one. Then, you write a letter. You talk to Mickey Stanley, who pays him a phone call. You hear that Lolich just had surgery, figuring it best to wait a while longer. You write another letter.

Then, after weeks go by, you get in your car. You drive across the state of Michigan, from Chicago. You show up at a house, unsure if you've got the right one.

You see a woman in the front yard, tending the garden. You button your jacket, re-comb your hair, stride across the street, somewhere distant from hopeful. You carry with you a list of completed interviews—the entire team but him.

You've prepared a gift—a 45 rpm record from 1968: "Roly Poly Mickey Lolich" by The Fans.

You introduce yourself to Mrs. Lolich, in your Sunday best, giving the gift with a handshake. You get an answer, quicker than expected.

"Sorry," she says. "But he's writing his own book."

You smile, sort of, understandingly. *His own book. His own book… Now?*

"I'll see what he says—but I don't think it's going to happen."

And so, the Mickey Lolich story. The Mickey Lolich non-story. The Mickey Lolich story that won't be in this story. The story that would have to be told some other way, of Detroit's unsung number-two starter of 1968, who pitched *three* complete games to win the World Series.

The story that will be told through a teammate. Another teammate. Every one of his teammates. His opponents. His *frustrated* opponents, who each described one thing:

"Mickey Lolich—*he* was the guy."

A story almost told not at all—plotted and mapped out after a week of "Cancel the whole book!" blues subsided.

The same approach was taken with Bob Gibson, who also declined an interview. On the last-ditch attempt, after a series of turn-downs, an email ask to his nephew Fred came back like this:

"I can't give out his number. He would *execute* me if I did."

Even before, I'd considered that an hour-long interview might not do it justice, Gibson's 17-strikeout performance in Game One. That you could write an entire book about it—and, in fact, he has. Gibson's *Pitch by Pitch*, in 2016. More than 250 pages retelling every moment, every pitch of that first game. The kind of detail a single interview, even if granted, would not come close to matching.

So, a different tack was taken: Could the legend of a Bob Gibson be better captured another way? A group of hitters, a still-intimidated group of Tigers hitters, reminiscing on and on in panoramic agreement: he was the *best* damn pitcher they'd ever seen.

Inside this book are their voices, their words.

Their voices, their memories—no more, no less.

Recalling what they can about a week in October 1968.

They expressed great nostalgia for the past, frustration at the base-ball of today. A simple joy for the way things were. They spoke about each other as if handing off a baton—beginning stories and stopping like they'd planned it, in wait for another to conclude, months and many miles away. A disjointed chorus that would sync, accidentally, into occasional harmonies. "Al Kaline will probably tell you this," they would say. "When you talk to him."

They spoke in the past tense, and then the present—nearly inter-changeably. As if the old team were still playing out there, somewhere, set for an afternoon start.

In April 2017, the very week this project began, my grandfather passed away—a boy from the Detroit of the 1920s. From Highland Park, then a farm at 29 Mile and Gratiot. Who saw Tiger Stadium in its hey-day—Hal Newhouser pitching and Joe DiMaggio batting. Who knew nothing about baseball, but kept one sole photo to prove he was there. The green beams and railings, the umpire's bubble chest protector, the 15-cent cap on the hot-dog vendor. The worn dirt track from the pitch-er's mound to home.

The old ballpark at Michigan and Trumbull is long gone, of course. The green seats and walls taken out for blue and orange, then none at all—replaced a mile down the road by the giant, flattened-out Comerica Park, built like a model of Tiger Stadium's opposite.

You can still see it, if you look hard enough. Through a construction fence (as of 2017) propped up where its walls once stood, the packed-in seats and the overhanging upper decks. Quick flashes of a bat, the roar of the crowd within. A flickering, in the shadows, of strikeouts and double plays and home runs and wins and losses and—*baseball*.

The stadium that held the great ones, the Ty Cobb Tigers of the 1910s and '20s, to the Greenberg and Gehringer years—and then to the Kalines, the Hortons, the Northrups, the McAuliffes. Mickey Lolich. Norm Cash. Denny McLain and his 31 wins. The 1968 Detroit Tigers, champions of baseball.

And a Series of seven games. A Series of Hall of Famers—Al Kaline, Eddie Mathews, Bob Gibson, Lou Brock, Steve Carlton, Orlando Cepeda. The last true Series before the playoff system began. Before free agency. Before the designated hitter, the pitch count, ear flaps on the helmets, swooshes on the shoes.

A stadium gone, with its '68 season now fifty calendars in the past.

And the life of that Series endowed to the voices left to tell of it. In their own words, their memories—telling what they know of a legend.

In 1965, Lawrence S. Ritter published likely the greatest of all baseball books, *The Glory of Their Times*, for which he spent three years traveling the country in search of the old-timers of baseball's Deadball Era. And which formed the inspiration for this very book. With a title, like many others, taken from *Ecclesiastes*, which says, in one of its verses:

"To every thing there is a season, and a time to every purpose under the heaven: A time to be born, and a time to die; a time to plant, and a time to pluck up that which is planted."

October, then—a time to play baseball.

The *World Series*. Harvest festival for the summer game.

This is a book about what it was like to win a World Series, fifty years after it was played. What they remembered, what they felt, what they saw. What it was like, down to the most precise details, to play ball in the 1960s. To wear a Tigers uniform, a Cardinals uniform. To face Bob Gibson at his best, to face Mickey Lolich. To come back, down three games to one.

To *win*.

In St. Louis, and Detroit. October 1968.

BRENDAN DONLEY
February 2018

LIST OF INTERVIEWS

DETROIT TIGERS

Al Kaline
Willie Horton
Denny McLain
Mickey Stanley
Don Wert
Jim Price
Fred Lasher
John Hiller
Tom Matchick
Dick Tracewski
Jon Warden
Hal Naragon

ST. LOUIS CARDINALS

Tim McCarver
Orlando Cepeda
Julián Javier
Mike Shannon
Ray Washburn
Dick Schofield
Johnny Edwards
Bobby Tolan

ADDITIONAL INTERVIEWS

Tony Kubek
José Feliciano
Pat Freehan
Bill Haller
Mel Butsicaris
Mary Ann Peacock
Sherry Gaston-Caldwell

Conducted between June 2017 and February 2018

1968
WORLD SERIES
ROSTERS

DETROIT TIGERS

1 Dick McAuliffe	2B	**Pitching Staff / Bullpen**
2 Mickey Stanley	SS	Mickey Lolich
3 Al Kaline	RF	Earl Wilson
4 Norm Cash	1B	Joe Sparma
5 Willie Horton	LF	Pat Dobson
6 Jim Northrup	CF	Daryl Patterson
7 Bill Freehan	C	John Hiller
8 Don Wert	3B	Fred Lasher
9 Denny McLain	P	Don McMahon
		Jon Warden

Bench

Eddie Mathews
Gates Brown
Ray Oyler
Tom Matchick
Jim Price
Wayne Comer
Dick Tracewski

Manager / Coaches

Mayo Smith
Wally Moses
Johnny Sain
Tony Cuccinello
Hal Naragon

ST. LOUIS CARDINALS

1 Lou Brock	LF	
2 Curt Flood	CF	
3 Roger Maris	RF	
4 Orlando Cepeda	1B	
5 Tim McCarver	C	
6 Mike Shannon	3B	
7 Julián Javier	2B	
8 Dal Maxvill	SS	
9 Bob Gibson	P	

Pitching Staff / Bullpen

Nelson Briles
Ray Washburn
Steve Carlton
Joe Hoerner
Ron Willis
Wayne Granger
Mel Nelson
Dick Hughes
Larry Jaster

Bench

Ron Davis
Phil Gagliano
Johnny Edwards
Bobby Tolan
Dave Ricketts
Ed Spiezio
Dick Schofield

Manager / Coaches

Red Schoendienst
Joe Schultz
Billy Muffett
Dick Sisler
Bob Milliken

BROADCASTERS

Harry Caray
Curt Gowdy
George Kell
Tony Kubek

Denny McLain:

We *knew* we were going to win the World Series. They had one fucking pitcher. *One.* If we couldn't beat the other fuckin' stiffs, then we weren't anywhere near as good as we thought we were.

They had one pitcher, they didn't have anybody else worth a shit. They had *one* guy. And he pitched the game of his *life* that day—which we all do, from time to time—but he picked the day to be on the biggest stage to do it. A lot of people just remember *that* game… but a lot of them don't remember who *won* the Series, you know?

We *won*. No matter what, we *won*—fair and square.

Julián Javier:

We were supposed to *win* in 1968—and we were ahead 3–1! But, you know how baseball is… We say: "*Viene en una caja cuadrada. La bola es redonda, y viene en una caja cuadrada.*"

The baseball is round, but it comes in a square case. No? So, you know how baseball can be that way. Anything can happen.

La bola es redonda, pero viene en una caja cuadrada.

Al Kaline:

I had played in a lot of All-Star Games, and with a lot of press and stuff like that, but *nothing* like the World Series.

And every year before that, I always said, "I'm not going to go to a World Series, unless I play in one." It's probably a stupid comment, but I wanted to *play* in one, I didn't want to just go sit and watch it. That was the statement I made: "I'm not gonna go to one unless I play in one."

So, fortunately I was able to. You got a chance to play in the biggest game of all for a baseball player—and that's what you play for. Everybody wanted to be a world champion, or at least get a chance to play in play in the *big game*.

The World Series.

GAME ONE

Busch Stadium | October 2, 1968

Mary Ann Peacock:[1]

I don't really know how it came about, but I was four, and I guess being the United Way "Poster Child," my parents must have arranged it.

But, somehow, I got to throw out the first pitch.

And when I got to the stadium, I was *enthralled* with all the people. I just couldn't believe there were that many people there. I think that might've been my *first* baseball game, so when I got to the stadium I knew it was a big deal. I thought the field was pretty, I remember thinking that. It was amazing, it really was. But beforehand, my mom only told me that I'd be throwing a baseball. But I didn't really realize how big it was going to be until, like I said, I got to the stadium and all these people... I was just *enthralled*.

And I remember, at the time I didn't know who was holding me—but later on my mom told me [Cardinals owner] Mr. Busch was holding me! And I just remember that I kept saying, "Do it myself... do it myself." Because my mom had told me that I could throw out the first pitch. And I thought she meant, you know, without any help, so I wanted to do it without help, because I wanted to do it by myself.

And I remembered the catcher, I don't remember the catcher's name, but I remember the catcher, you know, getting in and out of his stance. He must've done it at least three or four times. I remember looking at him, and he got out of his stance at least three or four times. And they were just laughing at me, shaking their head! But I held on to the baseball, because I wanted to "do it myself."

And then Mr. Busch got mad at me, and he took my arm with the baseball, and *threw* it! I just remember the feeling of him throwing the baseball with my arm.

And then, finally, the World Series started.

HARRY CARAY: A little tension now, builds up around this beautiful ballpark. In any World Series, the first game is important, but perhaps never quite as important as *this* year.

CURT GOWDY: Of course, the Cardinals have been made the favorites. But sport has a precedent sometimes, of not coming out the way it was supposed to.

	1	2	3	4	5	6	7	8	9	R	H	E
Tigers										0	0	0
Cardinals										0	0	0

Denny McLain: 31-6 (1.96 ERA) Bob Gibson: 22-9 (1.12 ERA)

Hal Naragon:

I was on three World Series teams. And you can't imagine how, you can't express how you really feel. At least it's hard to. Here you are, you know, I'm at the *World Series*, and when you were a kid you dreamed of this and you dreamed of that, and did it come true? It's just hard to think about it—is this really happening? When you see players jumping up and down, and even just winning the American League flag is a *big* deal. Here you are, and you've got a chance to be one of the best in the world!

Baseball… there's nothing like the game of baseball.

Dick Tracewski:

All we knew was that it was a big ballpark, it wasn't like Tiger Stadium. It was a big ol' ballpark, it even looks big, doesn't it? You gotta hit a legitimate home run to knock it outta that park. We knew that, but we didn't worry about the ballpark much. We worried about the Cardinals. Because they were *good*. They had a solid club all around. They had a hell of a ballclub, they were an aggressive team.

And we knew that it was a good field, the surface was a good field. The grass was good, the infield was good. That's the first thing as an infielder I'd go out on the field and I'd check the infield. Because if you're out there playing, you don't wanna play on a cow pasture! So you look, and the field was *good*. And it was on the fast side. Because they had a lot of speed. Just like when I was with the Dodgers, we played on a *fast* field. And we'd go to San Francisco, and they'd have all those thumpers up there. They would come and put three inches of dirt on the field, and it would be a lot of dirt and it was slow. And they wanted that, that's the way they doctored it. But the Cardinal field was *fast*.

And, you know, we were playing all day games—that was taken for granted, playing day games. We didn't even think about that, we were playing day games! In St. Louis, he ballpark would be filled, and televisions on around the country, everybody would be watching.

And that's the way it was.

Orlando Cepeda:

Well, playing in the World Series, it used to all be day games. The sun was shining. It's much different now. I mean, I don't take anything away from night games, but baseball is meant to be played as a day game. I remember it was a *lot* of white shirts—the background. And all the white hats, too.

And I have to say that they are the best fans in baseball, Cardinals fans. Still today. They packed in every single game. And even though I played out here, my best days in the game of baseball were in St. Louis.

Johnny Edwards:

Well, the only difference is, when you play in the World Series, there's so many newsmen around, that it's *unbelievable*. In the locker room and clubhouse. During the season, you might have six or seven, but during the World Series you've got thirty and forty. And *all* looking for a scoop of some sort, something different.

Al Kaline:

The World Series was *so* big, and—of course, the Cardinals were World Champions in '67, and they were the odds-on favorite to beat us.

Denny McLain:

You know, you looked forward to it; it was going to be a great time. Win lose or draw—you don't think about losing—but what you really hope for is the ability to pitch well that day. Win lose or draw, you wanna *win*. But you don't wanna embarrass yourself, you don't want to make many mistakes, and you only hope that with the club you're representing on the mound, that you're doing the most you can do on that particular day. And with our club, I think our guys proved themselves pretty well for those seven days.

And the club, *because* of all the media attention, we were used to it. You know, *nothing* was gonna bother those guys. We'd been through it, we'd seen it, I mean we had *three* managers in one year die. And who the fuck kills three managers in one year? Dressen, Swift, and Frank Skaff. We killed three of them in one season... I kept thinking I was gonna get accused of murder! It was unbelievable.[2]

But, it was a very intense Series, it was talked about coast to coast for at least eight or nine days, with the days off, and it was just a great time. And I don't think anybody who saw that World Series will ever forget it.

It was one of the great World Series of all time.

Al Kaline:

Facing Bob Gibson, none of us had ever faced him before. And he was *really* special. He was special his whole career, but that game he was just painting the corner. He was a little mean, pitching inside and every once in a while the ball would get away from him, and that was *quite* a day, to face a man like that.

Tim McCarver:

He was, as everyone knows, a *relentless* competitor. The combination of athletic ability, violence in his delivery, explosive pitches, and that's why it was almost unfair for a team that had never faced him to face him for the first time in the World Series. I don't know whether these guys had ever faced him.

Al Kaline:

We didn't have scouting reports, you had to ask players that had faced him before—what's he throw, what's his best pitch, what does he like to throw in tight situations, and that's what you had to go by.

Mickey Stanley:

It's not like today, it's not entirely as hi-tech—shit, there was nothing! You know, quite honestly, it might've been just the players talking about it. You know, we'd see games—we had TV back then, believe it or not. We could see a few things that he had done. And you've only got to watch an inning, and you know what he's got.

Willie Horton:

I knew how they pitched… spring training, you know how they pitched. You keep up with stuff like that. Every pitcher has got certain things they like to throw. So, if you don't do your homework, I think that's where guys struggle a lot, they don't do that. With the scouting report, I'd incorporate that into the way I hit, and I adjust to that. But really, the only thing I ever wanted to know about a pitcher was, "Is he *on* or *off*?" If he's *on*, I know what part he likes—middle of the plate up, or wherever.

Dick Tracewski:

I'd faced Gibson—I'd seen him in the minor leagues. He was a two-pitch pitcher. Great movement on his fastball, and an unhittable breaking ball. And he got it over. And he could throw it, he could take you three-and-two and throw you a breaking ball, you know, he was that kind of pitcher. But he was aggressive. And he was a mean guy. He'd pitch inside, he was a tough guy, he really was. He was a menacing guy.

But before Game One, we didn't care, we beat everybody. We didn't care, there was a lot of guys like Gibson in the American League, and we handled them.

Al Kaline:

Bob, he sort of *stared* all the time. Well, what I didn't realize was—I got to know him a lot at the Hall of Fame—and he says, "You know, I had bad eyes, *that's* why I was staring all the time… Everybody thought I was mean!"

But he was on his game that day—and he took it right to us. He was fantastic. I'm glad I didn't have to face Bob Gibson for a long period of time, all those years.

Willie Horton:

I didn't even think about it, facing him—it's just another game. We're playing in the World Series, and we had to go through the emotion of thinking about all the people around the world watching, and you want to do well for that. But in your mind, you go out there and you know what you have to do.

See, I ain't seen a pitcher yet I didn't want to face. I ain't never had that attitude—I just kept that same approach. That's a mode I guess I got in when I was young, I respect every pitcher, whether you're a 20-game winner or a 20-game loser, or what. Because, if he couldn't pitch, he wouldn't be out there. Some of them gave me more trouble than the other, but I'd never think like that. I always thought every day I was up to the challenge. To go out there and say I didn't want to face somebody, I never had a feeling like that. Because, I always kept the game fun, you know, just have *fun*. I see some guys chewing their nails and all this kind of stuff... and I see some guys that'll be *praying*. And I told them, I said, "God loves that pitcher too—hell, we ain't never gonna finish the game!" I said, "He loves *all* of us!"

So I ain't *never* been intimidated. Gibson always stared at the hitter, but stuff like that never bothered me, because other pitchers did that—Luis Tiant, and Catfish Hunter.

But this particular day when Bob was out there, as the game went on, it proved that he could've whupped *anybody* that day. That was his day in the sun. And all I remember through that whole game was that he was just telling Tim McCarver, "Give me the ball." He was always one of the greatest pitchers there ever was, but that day there, he took it to another level.

Denny McLain:

We knew Gibson was going to be tough. And he *was*.

But, you know, there wasn't much talk. I mean, we both knew what we had to do, and if I had good stuff I knew we would win. If I didn't have good stuff, I thought we'd *still* win.

The one game he pitched—anybody could've pitched the fourth game, I mean, Jesus, they scored ten runs. But the first game he pitched a career game, and no one could ever deny that wasn't a career game.

Mickey Stanley:

I can feel like we got overmatched. And, not only, it *looked* like it was overpowering—I didn't feel like he was overpowering—but between the control and the power, it made him a pretty awesome pitcher. You know? He had *both*. He had great control. We knew what he had. I mean it's pretty obvious, he just pounded everything. And he had good control, he could get both pitches over… I mean, three-and-two, it wasn't like he had to go to the fastball.

He threw hard, but he wasn't like Ryan. Ryan was overpowering, I mean, that was just *Let's hurry up and get this thing over with*. That was a mismatch.

But you know, I hit three or four balls decent off Gibson, a couple were caught. I felt like I had a chance. I didn't get many hits, but it didn't feel like he could throw it completely by me on a consistent basis.

And I remember getting the first hit off Gibson. I can *still* see that base hit.

CURT GOWDY: …there's a line drive into left field, in front of Brock—and there's the first base hit of the Series. Stanley's on.

Mickey Stanley:

I think I remember Curt Gowdy saying, "Stanley bloops one to center." But that wasn't a bloop—that was a hanging slider, and I hit it pretty good! I don't like that, Gowdy said it was a bloop!

But Gibson… well, I'd heard a lot about him, I knew he was a real competitor. And if you hit a home run off him, you didn't wanna show him up. Which, none of us guys did that back then anyway. But it was a challenge. I was a fairly good fastball hitter, so I figured I had a chance to put the ball in play against him, and I think I got a hit on three-and-two.

Mickey Lolich used to say about me, "Thou shalt not pass." Because when I'd go, I always I swung at the first pitch and everything. I didn't like striking out, so I figured the more times I swung, the better chance I had of putting the ball in play. So Lolich used to say, "Thou shalt not pass, Stanley!"

But I think that base hit, I worked him to a 3-2 count, which is surprising. And it was a slider. You know, I think he was tougher on right-handers than left-handers. I'd rather have been a left-hander off him any day. You can pick the ball up better. Instead of the ball coming *behind* you, it's coming—I just think it would be a lot easier.

But he threw everything hard. It wasn't like a flopping changeup or flopping curveball that you had to worry about with him. You just had to get it geared up for something *hard*. Other than Jim Palmer, Nolan Ryan, Gibson probably threw the hardest. But there were a lot of guys in the American League who threw *close* to him. Tiant could throw pretty good, Dennis Leonard, there were some guys that threw hard. But, he didn't have—he didn't throw a changeup. At least, I wasn't aware of it. Or a big floppy curve. So, all you had to worry about was one thing: something *hard*. So that helped me. Not that I hit him that well—I hit the ball fairly decent off him, but…

He was a *good* competitor. Probably the best!

CURT GOWDY: Al Kaline, who has been an outstanding performer for the Tigers, for sixteen years. Has always had the dream of playing in the World Series, and realizes his goal right now… he steps in.

And—there goes the runner! The throw down, and Stanley is… *out!*

Tim McCarver:

Well he was *safe*.

Mickey Stanley:

Son of a *bitch*!

The throw beats me—but it was close.

I didn't go on my own, we weren't given the "Go on your own" order. Or I probably wouldn't have gone. Actually, I'm surprised I was stealing in the first inning, off Gibson. Because I'm sure he had a good move. You know, he was a good athlete; he wouldn't have taken a long stride or nothing. I'm surprised I was going! I was the second hitter. No, I was the leadoff hitter—I led off against right-handers. You know what, I think I was second. But during the season, I led off against—maybe I've got it messed up. Maybe I led off against lefties. It was one way or the other!

But, you know, as fast as Gibson pitched, if you're going to steal, that third-base coach better hurry up and flash that sign! Cuccinello would get the sign from Mayo.[3] Brush the thigh. Most teams are the same. Everybody uses pretty much the same cadence: take, bunt, hit-and-run, steal. You might have a different area, but ours was *take, bunt, hit-and-run, steal.* Work your way down. "*Take*" was the hat. Take, bunt, hit-and-run, steal. If you go to the Yankees, it might be "take, bunt…" but it's all that order. I mean, players remember the signs— take, bunt, hit-and-run, steal. Indicator might be: none of it means anything until I go to my nose. First sign after I go to my nose. And they wouldn't change it, you know, we weren't smart enough for that.

One time back in the minors, we were playing at Duluth, Minnesota. Our manager was Al Lakeman. People called him "Big Stoop." And *everybody* was missing signs. And this one guy, Rufus Anderson, nice kid from Valdosta, Georgia. He says, "Rufus, you missed so many steal signs—from now on, when you can see my face between my legs…" The manager was the third-base coach. He bends over, he says, "*That's* the steal—when you can see my face!" Can you believe that!? Isn't that funny, you remember stuff like that? He says, "When you can see my face, that's the steal." Big Stoop. Big boy, from Spartanburg, South Carolina, or wherever the hell it is.

Tony Kubek:[4]

One interesting thing, too, is: I don't think Detroit, off the top of my head, I don't think they had a stolen base in that World Series. I think there was one caught stealing, it might've been Mickey Stanley—and this is off the top of my head. Meanwhile, you know, the Cardinals were running, running, running, but they also got five guys thrown out as I recall, too. What that might've done to the outcome of the game, if they hadn't lost those baserunners, *and* lost that out? Who knows—that's kind of the unpredictability and things you can speculate about.

Mickey Stanley:

You know, isn't that funny? If I'm safe there, how much that makes a difference in a manager's mind the rest of the Series? And that's more or less maybe he's afraid of the press. Because none of us had blazing speed. McAuliffe was a better basestealer than I was. Northrup. All three of us were close, in speed. Northrup, McAuliffe, and me. Gates was the fastest guy on the team, but you know, he was a pinch-hitter. And *Willie* was fast. I'd say all of us were close.

I was quick, but I wasn't that fast. I think one year I had ten triples, which makes you think you're fast, but you can get triples because you hit a little blooper to right and it bounced over the right fielder's head, you know what I mean? Center field at Tiger Stadium was 440, I think. And 365 to both right- and left-center, as I recall.

Julián Javier:

That was quick! I remember that.

You know what happened? McCarver, he was *quick* on that play. Look at McCarver—look, look, see? He just threw the ball; he didn't wait long to throw the ball. He threw the ball quick. He didn't have a great arm like Johnny Bench or those guys, you know, but he threw very good. He was a very good defensive catcher.

So, I say, every time they throw the ball, "I gon' be there." That's why they call me "the Phantom," too, because you throw the ball to the base, I'm gonna be there. For a double play, or steal, or anything. And sometimes, you know, I don't even have to touch the guy to have the umpire call him out. It looks like I didn't touch the guy! Look. Look. See the glove? I got it right in front, you know, but it doesn't look like it touched!

I told the guys, the shortstop, the third baseman—"Throw the ball there—I gon' be there. Just throw the ball." And they never touched me. Never, never touched me. Twelve seasons, nobody touched me. I got to the base, and got out right away. And Detroit—they didn't have that many good runners, we didn't expect them to be stealing. They didn't steal too much.

Tim McCarver:

I didn't have a strong throwing arm. Strong enough to win three pennants, though!

You know, baseball can be a very callous, individual sport. We don't have a hole to open, for instance, as running backs. We don't have a guard or tackle pulling or trapping, or what you might have. We have: when the pitch is made to me, and the runner runs, I have to throw the ball quickly, release it with something on it... And Bob was right—I mean, my arm was not, if my arm had been better, I'd have been a much better catcher.

But they didn't have a Lou Brock or a Curt Flood. They had *some* speed, Mickey Stanley.

And he certainly was a story in that Series. The guy had never played shortstop...

Dick Tracewski:

What Stanley did in the World Series, I never heard of that before. And I got thirty-five years in the major leagues. To take an outfielder and put him in the World Series?

We were shocked! That's still the strangest thing I've ever seen in baseball, Mayo taking Stanley in from center field to shortstop. I mean, he was physically equipped to do that, because he was a great athlete—he was a *superlative* athlete, so if anybody could he could. But to do it in the World Series? I could see him doing it in June. But in the *World Series*? Game *One*?

Here you're talking about the most important defensive position on the field, other than maybe a catcher, and you're gonna put a novice there. It just didn't make sense.

I remember guys snickering, everybody laying around the training room, and saying "Can you imagine what's going on here?" But Matchick and Ray Oyler and myself, we all played shortstop—and we're looking at each other thinking, "You've gotta be kidding me, he's gonna play shortstop?" We thought maybe we didn't have a chance to win.

But you couldn't take Northrup out of the lineup, or Kaline. And Horton led our team in RBIs. Still, we're thinking, "If we're going to do this, you know—how could Mayo do this?" But he did it. And it *worked.* To this day, I don't ever remember a move by any manager that's as shocking.

But it worked.

Mickey Stanley:

We were in Baltimore, and Mayo Smith called me up to the hotel room. Which, I'd never been called to the manager's room in my life. I had no idea what it was about. First thing he says—*first* thing out of his mouth—"You're gonna be our shortstop in the Series." I said, "Holy shit… so that's what I get for taking all those ground balls with Oyler." You know, and then *boom*, it clicked. Right then I remembered Cash saying something about, "You could play there." So I think he might have come up with the idea to Mayo in the first place.

And I knew Mayo was serious. So I said, "Well what are the other guys gonna think? I'm kind of concerned how they're gonna feel." He says, "Don't worry about them." He says, "I know you can do it!" Well, what could I say? Back then, you didn't tell people when you were hurt, unless you were *dead*. And I'm not going to say, "I'm not gonna do it." I didn't have an answer. I mean, what man would say, "Well, I'd rather really not." Could you imagine somebody doing that, if you're a competitor? I didn't have a choice, but I didn't like the choice. I mean, I never bitched about it, but it just wasn't fun.[5]

Willie Horton:

Stanley was the best athlete on the team, he could play anywhere—he was a hell of an athlete. So I remember me, and him and Northrup were talking, and Jimmy said, "Well Stanley, what do you think about doing it?"

Al Kaline:

Well, in 1968 I got hit by a pitch and broke my wrist. In Oakland, Lew Krausse was pitching. And so Jim Northrup, he filled in for me on a regular basis that summer. He would split with Stanley. Right-hander, left-hander. So he had a chance to play a full year—well, five straight weeks—and he did a wonderful job, he really stepped up. He doesn't get the recognition that he should've.

So for the World Series, I would've felt very—I don't know how to explain it—but I would not have been comfortable had Mayo placed me in the outfield instead of Northrup.

And so Mayo called me into his office one day, and I told him, "You can't take Northrup out of the lineup, he's done too much." And, I mean, I didn't know what his plans were, if he'd have Northrup and Stanley split, or what he was thinking. And so I told him, I said, "Mayo… I want to play, but you can't take Jim Northrup out—he was spectacular all year long." And that's when he told me, he says, "Well, why don't you start taking some ground balls at third base?" So, that's what I did, one or two days. But then all of a sudden Horton got hurt for a time, and they had to make a change—Northrup had to go to left, and I went to right. And I got really hot at the time, really started hitting the ball well.

And *that's* when he made the decision about Mickey moving in to shortstop.

Around that time, when I was still getting back into shape, Mayo Smith called four of us veteran guys into his office. It was Bill Freehan, Norm Cash, myself, and I think it might've been Eddie Mathews—I'm not really sure who it was. And Mayo says, "I'm thinking about moving Mickey Stanley to play shortstop in the World Series." And we all went like... But then we all said, "Well, hell—he's the best athlete on our club!"

So then, of course they moved me to right field, and moved Northrup to center. And that's how I really got a chance to play in the World Series. Otherwise, I had to be at third, because I would've done anything to play, but I would've been uncomfortable. So I'm glad it didn't happen—because I might've made the error that cost us the World Series!

And to this day I keep thanking Mickey Stanley for accepting to do that, at shortstop. Because the *pressure* that he would've had... Now, I could understand if it was the regular season, you bring somebody in to play shortstop during the regular season. But the *World Series*? What if he made an error that lost the whole Series?

So, to this day, I keep thanking him, for accepting the responsibility of playing shortstop. And I got a chance to play in the World Series.

My only World Series.

Tony Kubek:

Mayo Smith at one time was an advance scout for the New York Yankees, and having been a part of our organization, I think he learned a little bit from watching Casey Stengel. Casey used to platoon, but some of it was just to give some of the other players rest. So I think Mayo said, "You know, I don't have to play the same eight guys every day." And I think Mayo Smith may have also learned that, "You know what? I've gotta get somebody that'll maybe give me a little more pop at shortstop, and I think I'm gonna be OK in center field—Northrup or somebody else." So he put Stanley there! I think he maybe learned some of that from Stengel.

And I'm pretty certain that it was Wally Moses, their hitting coach, that said, "You know, Kaline's still your go-to guy. He still should be your number-three hitter, even though he's had some problems this year with the arm and some other things." And so he put Kaline in there, and Kaline came through for them in the Series, batting in the three spot.

And I think it was unusual putting Mickey Stanley in the two spot, too. But Mayo Smith was a gambler—I mean, his reputation got around when he was a Yankee. He was a guy who invested in real estate in Florida before anybody had heard of it—and did *real* well in real estate in Florida. And he was just that kind of guy who was always a gambler.[6]

Mickey Stanley:

They say it was to get Kaline's bat in the lineup. And he had been around for fifteen years or so at that time, and they wanted him to play in the Series. He'd been injured most of that summer. But they could've sat me down and they'd have had Kaline's bat in the lineup. I guess if I was calling the shots, I'd say, "Well, put Kaline in" and then I'd play against left-hand pitchers and Northrup plays against righties, or something like that. I mean if I was one of our pitchers, that's what I would have rather seen. Because Oyler, shit, he was like—he *never* made an error! And how many more hits was I going to get than Oyler?

I had a better bat than Oyler, but is it worth that gamble? One boot is a game. You don't want to give runs away. You'd think a manager would go the other way. So I don't know—I know Wally Moses liked me. Shit, everybody liked everybody on that team!

Actually, you know what I think it was? I think they'd have felt pretty bad about me, because I had a good year. I think they'd have felt pretty bad not letting me play.

Dick Tracewski:

They did it for Kaline. They didn't do it for the club, they did it for Kaline. Because Kaline was a great player, great guy. Hall of Fame guy.

Fabulous person, unbelievable, and really a team player. But you had to use him. You gonna put him on the bench?

Mickey Stanley:

Every day during batting practice, when I wasn't hitting, when the scrubinis were, I'd go to shortstop, take ground balls. Then when we hit, as soon as I got through hitting, I'd grab my glove and go shag in the outfield. And I'd kick the pitchers out of the way so I could get my share. Pitchers always shag during batting practice, and Hiller loved to shag. So, if I kind of made him go away, he didn't like that!

I always had a lot of nervous energy, just like now. I get up in the morning, I'm raring to go do something. I'm seventy-five—and that used to seem old! Shit, I still feel like doing stuff. But during batting practice, you'd go to the outfield, and you know, you'd see *one* ball in five minutes. So, I'd take ground balls with Ray Oyler. Every day. And I loved it. I'd beg some pitcher to go to first base and take throws—because usually when you take ground balls you'd throw back to the fungo guy. So, I'd get a pitcher go over there so I can do the real thing.

I loved doing it—I just loved to fuck around, having fun. And I loved doing it at shortstop because it was a further throw, I can show off my arm! But that throw from shortstop is a little more three-quarters. An outfield throw, you throw overhand and more of a long-arm, so the ball carries. You stretch it. And an infielder short-arms it a little, instead of three-quarters. Especially on a double play. You've got to make a quicker throw, you don't have the time to make that long throw.

But I only had five games to prepare. I never played shortstop in my life. In center, I felt like I was as good as anybody. I mean I got Gold Gloves, four of them, so I must've been—I mean, I was 100 percent comfortable. I felt like I could catch anything I touched. I felt like I could catch *anything* I touched. And in the infield, I could catch anything, too, in non-game situations. I think my hands were as good as anybody's. It was just, the fact of fucking up. You know, which should've been easy for me, because I'm playing out of position. You know, I get to the World Series, and I can't play where I'd play. And I'd never played there.

So I had five games to prepare during the regular season, because we clinched the pennant early in September. I had those five games to prepare, and I was pretty darn nervous.

I had five days. That's how much time I had to prepare.

And actually, I used Bobby Christian's glove for those five games in September.[7] And then I used it in the Series. Because it was smaller. He was an outfielder-infielder, he had two gloves, so I used his. He wasn't eligible for the Series, but he played with us some that year. I used my outfield glove, my normal glove for infield practice the rest of the year. But Bobby Christian's was definitely smaller than my outfield glove.

And when it came time to play, I didn't know I knew all the positioning, but I did know it. I didn't know I knew it, until it happened, and I just did it. Because I saw it so many times. I was worried about that, but when it came up, I just went to the right place. We never talked about cutoffs—in fact, that was one of my big concerns, when I started playing shortstop. Because, would I be in the right place at the right time? But that never became an issue. I saw those plays develop so many times in front of me, playing center field, that I just went to the right place. And, you know, when the ball's hit, there's an image in your mind of where you're supposed to be. So I just went to the right place.

Nobody gave any indication that they were concerned about it. But they *should've* been! I mean, if I was a pitcher—just think if you're a pitcher. You know damn well Oyler catches everything and never makes a bad throw.

Willie Horton:

Well Ray Oyler, he couldn't hit nothing, but he was about the best fielder I'd ever seen in my life! I mean he'd make plays... I'd wonder how he'd catch the ball—I ain't seen nobody yet do that.

And when we made the switch, Ray didn't care—all he wanted was to *win*. That's how we all thought. Because, see, that year Al was having an off-and-on bad year. He didn't play that much, and every time he was out there, we didn't do too well. He hurt his hand, and it was just one of those years. But when he left me, Stanley, and Northrup out there in the outfield, that's when we took that lead for the American

League pennant. And then we got in the World Series, and, you know, of course we *wanted* Al to play. He's the oldest Tiger, *great* Tiger, a leader, and we wanted him in there. And so we discussed making that change.

But Stanley, he *had* to play—he was one our key players! And so Ray, he didn't give a shit. Ray just wanted to win. You give him a Budweiser and a Marlboro and he's straight! That's the type of team we had—we sacrificed for each other. These guys played *team* ball. *Sacrifice* ball. *Commitment* ball. It's not about them, it's about their *teammates*. It's about the W.

Denny McLain:

Oyler, he was a wonderful guy, but he had a little bit of a problem, he was an alcoholic. And I always used to tell him, I said, "If you just have two or three less drinks on the day of a ballgame, you might be able to see which fuckin' ball you're supposed to hit!" And it was funny stuff. And he'd come to me during the game, and say, "Hey roomie, which ball am I supposed to hit—the top one or the bottom one?"

He was a wonderful guy, just had a horrible, horrible, horrible problem. 'Course, we had a couple guys had horrible problems on that club, which I won't name. But, you know what, that's life. We didn't have any more alcoholics than society has percentage-wise.

Tom Matchick:

Oyler was our shortstop, and he could *pick 'em*. He was really good defensively, you know. But Ray, they had him in about twenty different batting stances and he still couldn't make contact. Oh my God, he was 0-for-August, and 0-for-June, 0-for-July. We tried everything. But, I remember when Oyler hit a triple one time, and he slid into third base. Well, he went to *second*, and Cuccinello kept calling him to third base. They overthrew the ball to third base against the wall, and came back out. And so Ray took off from third base, he was going home, and Cuccinello says, "Get back, Oyler, get back!!"—and he just got back in time. He just got in before the tag at third base, and he's laying down on the ground, he looked up at Cuccinello, and he said, "Cuch—I could've made it home! What'd you send me back for!?" Cuch looked down and said, "Oyler, it took me four years to get you to third base, you want me to kill you sending you home?"

Mickey Stanley:

Before Game One, at night, when I had to go to sleep, I thought, "OK... I'm gonna be the shortstop tomorrow..." You know? The pressure's there.

So I just thought, let's get this over with, so I can get relief! It was just pure tension; it was not fun. Would you have fun? Put yourself in my boots. Just think about it. In fact, before we took the field, Norm Cash came up to me, he said, "I bet they couldn't pull a pin out of your ass with a tractor right now, could they!?"

But the *first* ball, Lou Brock hit me a ground ball! Sharp ground ball, but no bad hops.

GOWDY: Mickey Stanley with his first chance—throws him out. That'll help Stanley, he's got that first one out of the way!
CARAY: You think that Brock deliberately tried to test him, on the very first time up?

Mickey Stanley

It looked like it hit to me on purpose. To me, it looked like he took a little inside-out swing, but I don't know that.

Tom Matchick:

Best thing that ever happened to him was Lou Brock starts the ball-game, ground ball to Stanley, he threw him out. Mickey said—his butt was so tight, he says, you couldn't stick a needle up his butt. That's what he said! So that was the best thing that ever happened to him, that first ground ball. And *boom*, he threw Brock out.

Denny McLain:

That was the biggest play of the World Series for us. Mickey Stanley playing shortstop for the first time in his major-league career, first ball of the game is hit to Mickey Stanley—it took *all* the edge off. And then he was ready to *play*.

The best thing that could've happened is a hard-hit ball to Stanley at shortstop because we were all holding our breath. And Mickey made it look like he'd been there fifty years.

Al Kaline:

It all worked out, because the first ball hit, Lou Brock hit a one-hopper to Mickey Stanley and he made the throw. So that had to be a sigh of relief, getting that first ground ball and getting that out.

Dick Tracewski:

Mickey went in there and he played very well. But he hated it. He *hated* it! Can you imagine him sleeping? How could he!? He hated it, but he did it.

I know Mickey didn't enjoy it. He's human, and he couldn't enjoy that.

For many years, when I was with the Dodgers, I used to do this: in the eighth and ninth innings, I'd go in and play shortstop, I'd go in and play second base. And that's no fun. I played the last inning of Sandy Koufax's perfect game. Defense. You don't wanna do that! You think I wanna do that? Go and play in a perfect game, play second base? All you can do is screw up. If you catch the ball, well you're *supposed* to! And if you screw up, well, you screwed up. So it's not easy. Just to go in there to play defense? That's tough, and you don't wanna do it.

Mickey Stanley:

I was kind of relieved when it was all over, because I was just waiting to screw up, at shortstop. You know what I mean? It just, it wasn't fun. You know, I felt like I was a good center fielder, and I knew I had good hands, I knew I could catch ground balls as good as anybody. But I didn't know if I could do it in the World Series, you know? And it was just—not fun! Constant pressure. So I was really glad it was over.

And to be honest, it didn't seem fair, for me to play out of position. I mean, such a big difference. Now if they said, "Go play left field or right field," sure, but to go play shortstop? I mean, who would want to do that? I mean, that's no fun. When you don't have confidence, you know? If I'd played there for half a season or a season, even *then* that's inexperience.

I mean, I wasn't pissing and moaning, I was glad to be playing. If they gave me a choice, "Do you want to play shortstop, or just sit and watch?" I don't know what choice I would've made.

And you want to know something? I wasn't going to bring this up, you brought it up. I think about that once in a while, because every night I watch major-league baseball. It doesn't bother me, I'm not envious, but I said, "God, maybe I wasn't as special as I thought." I've never heard *one* mention of it, and I've been watching this for years. I've never heard *one* mention of that move. I have never once heard about it, I thought, "God darn—I know damn well that was not easy." And you know, I haven't seen anybody else do it! But it's funny, I have never *once* heard any announcer mention it.

Jon Warden:

Actually, Peter Gammons talks about that almost every year. He'll say, "Well one of the craziest things that ever happened in World Series history, was Mayo Smith moved Mickey Stanley, a Gold Glove center fielder, to shortstop." They *still* talk about that. Imagine that today. Bryce Harper. "Hey Bryce, we need you to play short, man, just for the Series." "*What*?" Not gonna happen.

Mickey Stanley:

Well, after all that, it actually took an effect on my arm. At the end of the Series, because I took a lot of ground balls and stuff—I could feel the effects on my arm. I can't honestly tell you where it was bothering me, but it was definitely different.

Because then at spring training in '69, I was going to be the shortstop. I can remember this like it was yesterday. Dick Tracewski hit his first fungo of the spring, and I was going to field my first ground ball of the spring. Well he hit a horseshit fungo, a little high chopper to my right—and, like a dummy, I charged it and threw off the wrong foot like it was do-or-die. There was nobody running, it was just fungoes! And it hurt my arm, the *first* ground ball. And then that ruined baseball for me, for the rest of my career. I couldn't throw well any more. I played there part of the season, but I didn't start, I couldn't throw well. Had several cortisone shots, did no good. Then they moved me to the outfield, and Tom Tresh came in to play short. I'd skip infield practice sometimes, just because I didn't want people to see I couldn't throw.

But, you know, I don't want to sound like a whiner. Anybody that knows me know I'm not a whiner. It's just—in the World Series I'd have preferred to play center field, is all.

	1	2	3	4	5	6	7	8	9	R	H	E
Tigers	0									0	0	0
Cardinals										0	0	0

CURT GOWDY: Thirty-one-game winner, Denny McLain, on the mound.

HARRY CARAY: Curt Flood batting now—ball one.

Denny McLain:

Where the hell was *that* pitch?

It was all high fastballs—that was the way I pitched. I was jamming everybody right then. Hard stuff, *good* high fastballs, pitching up, where it's supposed to be. And none of them were on time at that point.

But there—that's a little curveball. In fact, it may have been a slider. It was right in on the hands. *See?* Right on the hands. Never got the bat out.

Jim Price:

You knew, going in, what they liked to hit. You know, like nowadays, they have hot spots here, cold spots here. I think, to me, that's crazy—in all honesty. You know, high-ball hitter, low-ball hitter, likes the ball inside. Once you play a team a couple games, you know all about them. And we learned more about them during the World Series, we even got better at attacking that.

CURT GOWDY: You know, Harry, he was playing the organ last night. At 11:30, in one of the lounges there, entertaining some of his teammates. He's quite an organ player.

Denny McLain:

"Eleven-thirty" my *ass*, it was two o'clock.

Dick Tracewski:

I remember going to St. Louis when we first got there, and Denny McLain went into the bar the night before the opening game, and it was a day game! He played the organ until God knows what time. But I didn't hear about until I got in the clubhouse the next day. And some other guy says, "You know what Denny did?" "No, what did he do now?" "He played the organ in the hotel bar!"

Jim Price:

Well I know in St. Louis, Denny and some of the boys stayed up playing the piano, and so forth. Just in the lobby!

We didn't change in the World Series—that's the way we were.

Jon Warden:

My birthday's October first. The eve of Game One. I spent my birthday the night before the Series, I turned twenty-two. So actually, all year I was twenty-one playing in the big leagues, and I was the youngest Tiger. And Bobby Tolan was the youngest Cardinal. They had a picture of us together in the paper, said "Youngest from each team" so that was pretty cool.

I had dinner out for my birthday, and when I get back to the hotel, go down the stairs, and all the guys are out for the evening, everybody's at dinner. And they're in the lounge, and there's Denny, playing the organ, you know. And all of a sudden—curfew's like midnight. So I'm thinking, "I'm going upstairs, man, I can't be hanging down here at the bar." I'd drank a little bit, but not much. But I mean, some of those guys—*phew*—Oyler, Cash, oh my God... they were plastered every night. No day goes by that they weren't hammering. Cash used to come into the locker room during the year, he'd be hung over, and he'd walk over to McLain or Lolich or Wilson or whoever, and he'd go, "Hey—hold 'em until about the fifth inning... and when I get done throwing up I'll hit ya a bomb." I don't know how he did it, man. He was an amazing guy.

But, on the road, we weren't allowed to go in the hotel bar—that's the manager's bar. So when you're on a road trip, you go out, because you can't have the hotel bar. But I didn't see Mayo that night, he was probably already passed out. He might've gone somewhere else, or he was up already in his room with Wally and they were popping a few down up there.

So, in this instance, they were in the hotel bar, and they're playing and singing and this and that, and like I said, it's midnight, past midnight. And I went up. Well, they were there till about three in the morning. Northrup's singing, and a bunch of other guys and McLain's *starting* the next day. Day game! But Gibson, we wouldn't have won the first game anyway, didn't matter who pitched. We could've had Walter Johnson pitching, or Cy Young, and I don't know if we would've beat them.

So that was before Game One, and I turned twenty-two the night before.

Julián Javier:

You know, we got all together, too, we had a lot of fun—Stan Musial was there playing the harmonica for the team, before the World Series started. And Orlando, he used to play the bongos. He was good, *very* good. And I can remember Orlando, during the World Series, at the Chase Hotel—he told me to go to the hotel, he said there was some band from the Virgin Islands playing there, steel band. And Cepeda went there, and he played a little bit with them. They didn't have the bongos, but the steel drums, so he was playing that with them. He said, "Hey, let's go—let's go see those guys." So we went there, but we didn't stay too late for the game the next day.

Cepeda and me, we used to play a lot of *Cha-cha-chá*—that's why they called him Cha-Cha, you know?

Mickey Stanley:

McLain, you know, he *did* play at a lot of places. Nightclubs or bars, or lounges. In the winter, in the offseason—you'd see advertisements where he'd be playing, at Joe Blow's joint. But McLain didn't drink, hardly. He'd drink screwdrivers, but not much. And Pepsi, a lot of Pepsi.

Denny McLain:

Never been a drinker. But sure, anytime the group got together, I'd go in and play a little bit, do a little bit of shtick, and I just enjoyed it.

My dad always said, "If you ever had to make a choice, do you want to pitch, or do you want to play piano, you play piano first—that's got a longer lifespan to it than playing baseball." But he never figured that I would be *that* good at baseball, you know. That was the big thing. He never figured that, and neither did I. But it's amazing the way things happen.

And before that first game in the World Series, we were staying near The Gaslight Square or something like that. We were staying near there. It was a big, big old hotel in St. Louis. Beautiful hotel. It was the old hotel with the great big high ceilings, that's what I do remember about it.

And it was probably fifteen of us. Everybody went in, most of us had dinner together in one form or another. We didn't sit together, but we were all over the restaurant, this was early evening. And one thing led to another, all of a sudden Norm Cash wanted to get up and sing—because Norman really thought he was the rebirth of Johnny Cash. So Norman started getting up and singing, and I don't know who was next, so I just played for—hell, I didn't stop playing till almost two o'clock! Organ, they had an organ and a piano there. I played the organ all night. We just had a great time, I mean, we had people coming up from the audience to sing and, you know, fuck around with us. Lot of St. Louis fans, I mean, I think by the time we got through Game One, we had more St. Louis fans pulling for us out at the bars than they had pulling for *them*.

It was a great time. And it was *supposed* to be a great time, it was the World Series! Lot of Detroit fans, absolutely.

But it was only that first night. Fuck, we had to recover from the first night. I mean, listen, a lot of guys were shitfaced that first night. And that's not the reason we lost—I mean, Bob Gibson pitched the greatest game of his career, on the biggest stage of his life. You had to congratulate him.

Orlando Cepeda:

Bob Gibson was *unhittable* that day. He had a great slider, you know. But Bob was unhittable. I'll never forget that.

Al Kaline:

Well, we knew he had a fastball and a slider, or slider-curve, whatever they called it back in those days. And he had such great control, that day, and… he took care of us, that's for sure.

Mike Shannon:

Norm Cash said to me, "It almost looked like a pro pitcher pitching against high school guys." And Norm said to me, "It was *amazing*." Of course, that's when Gibson had that slider, that broke about a *foot*—and he threw it at about 91 miles an hour.

Let me tell you something. When a guy's throwing a 97-, 98-, 100-mile-an-hour fastball, that's one thing. But if he's throwing a 90- and a 91-mile-an-hour slider, and putting it on the black? You might as well take your shit and go home.

There's a lot of guys throwing a 100-mile-an-hour fastball nowadays, and they turn them around like there's nothing to it. But if the guy's throwing a 100-mile-an-hour fastball, and a 90- or 91-mile-an-hour slider, you can take your bat, and your ball, and you can go to any high school you want, and see if you can do any better there. Because that's about the only chance you have.

Willie Horton:

One of our coaches, Wally Moses, we called him "Peep Sight"—shit, he'd make you think all the time. He'd say, "How many hits you gon' get today?" "Well…" "You don't *know*? Shit, *two* ain't a problem, son—two hits shouldn't be a problem off that son of a gun out there." He'd always say that when a pitcher would be pitching a damn good ballgame. He'd say, "He ain't throwing *shit*."

"*Hell*, he ain't throwing shit," Cash would say. "You can't even *see* the goddamn thing!"

Cash was what kept everybody loose on the bench. I remember that first World Series game against the Cardinals, he came back to the dugout, he said, "It's gonna be a short day today—that motherfucker throwing balls out there that look like a gnat-ass! It's gonna be *tough* out there today." But, he kept you loose.

I remember, it was just like Fergie Jenkins. I played against him in the city ball, when he was over there in Canada, he's Canadian. He ain't never threw me a strike his whole life, but he got me out! He'd make balls look big, and make them look like strikes. He did the same thing as a professional that he did in the sandlot. He'd make the ball look big, and then you swing, and you hit it on the end of the bat. I don't know how he'd do it. I'd think I got him, and then I *don't* have him.

So with Gibson, I knew how he'd do—Bob kind of used both sides of the plate. Early in the game, he was more on the outside, and then he'd kind of come in the end of games, going into the later innings, he'd be more inside because the umpire won't give him that much outside. I knew that from studying the game! You've got to have an idea when you go to bat, see. And you've got about a second to get ready—you can't be thinking *too* much. And so, you can't use it all.

But Bob had always been a good pitcher, he'd always come at hitters—he'd throw strikes. Everything he did, he came at you. He'd throw to contact, and not away from contact. When you find pitchers throwing away from contact, they're the ones that don't win. But Bob, he always came right at you. So you had to be ready to hit, and I think we just got tied up these first couple innings right there, like, "We're in the World Series, and all these people watching" and stuff like that.

CURT GOWDY: Orlando Cepeda—ball one. Most Valuable Player in the National League last year.

The 2-2 delivery to Cepeda… he *fouls* it back.

Denny McLain:

Cepeda? First time I faced him in Puerto Rico, in '64, I struck him out four straight times. And Clemente, the same night.

These hitters are thinking: "Try to get on top of it." But they can't get on top of this fastball. They gotta get on top of the ball to hit it hard, and they *can't*. You get a guy seeing *fastball, fastball, fastball,* and you throw a little bit out there—see how far out in front of the ball he was? That's what you call, you know, keeping people off tempo. He's way out in front of the ball.

Orlando Cepeda:

I remember I faced Denny McLain in Puerto Rico, in 1963. He was playing Triple-A ball, for Mayaguez. And I said to myself, "If the guy that I faced today, if he pitch like that, he's gonna win thirty games in the big leagues." Before he went to the big leagues, he was unhittable. His fastball was rising, he had a hell of a curveball, a slider he controlled.

He was like Sandy Koufax—that high fastball. But, a pitcher with a high fastball doesn't last too long.

CURT GOWDY: Now Tim McCarver, batting .253 for the year, five homers, 48 RBI.

Denny McLain:

There's Mr. Asshole.

Come on Northrup, you've gotta catch that fuckin' ball. McCarver hit a *triple*? Hanging curveball...

He wasn't lookin' for that, it was a hanging curveball! Shit, you'd have hit that. Belt high! Belt high, over the plate.

Tim McCarver:

Off of McLain. High curveball. To right-center field. My first at-bat, but I saw him in spring training, I remembered him. Oh yeah, I remembered him. I'd faced him two or three times in spring training. I'd homered off a high curveball, in spring training at Lakeland. I can see it now. I could see it then. In my mind's eye. I knew.

And I had a bad Series in 1967, I was 4-for-24 or something like that, and I was bound and determined not to have another bad Series. So I went out and took extra hitting on that Monday before we played. We opened on a Wednesday, I believe. And that Monday, I hit till my, you know, I had it down. I mean, at least, my approach was right. If I had a bad Series it wasn't going to be for lack of effort. On that Monday, after the season—I came in, and Red said, "No workout." I think we had a mild workout on Tuesday, I'm not sure. But I was the only one at the ballpark on Monday. Dave Ricketts came out and threw to me, he was great. And threw just great batting practice, knew exactly what I wanted. I was weak on balls up and away, so he kept my strength strong.

I put the utmost into that Monday two days before the Series started. And ended up having a good Series. But it was because of my determination and what happened in '67. You know, I was runner-up to Cepeda in the MVP voting in '67, and I was mad at myself for not having a better World Series against Boston. So I was determined not to have another bad Series. And didn't.

Denny McLain:

They had a good hitting club, but not like us. And they had no pitching, with the exception of Bob. And he pissed and moaned all the time about the run support. And you know, other players don't like that. They don't like that. You just need to keep your mouth shut when you're not getting runs because, sooner or later, what goes around comes around. It does come and bite you in the ass. And if you're gonna piss and moan about not getting runs, you need to ask to be traded to go find a club that'll score you more runs.

CURT GOWDY: The Cardinals ahead one to nothing.
And Javier hits it into right field, this'll score maybe two!

	1	2	3	4	5	6	7	8	9	R	H	E
Tigers	0	0	0	0						0	2	2
Cardinals	0	0	0	3						3	3	0

Julián Javier:

I think I hit the ball to the right—he was trying to throw the ball outside. And the infield was in. I remember that, yeah. I can remember I hit it to right field… I don't hit too many balls to right field, but that day I hit one.

We just went out there and tried to hit the ball. We didn't care if he won 100 games or 200 games or 30 games or whatever—we looked for the way he was pitching. And McLain wasn't that kind of great, great pitcher, you know what I mean? But he would throw a good slider outside, and he would throw the ball hard. But all the balls I hit off McLain were to right field. I don't hit so many balls to right field, that was unusual for me. But he was trying to throw a slider outside, and so I'm going to go that way then. If you try to pull it, you're never going to hit it.

And, you know, in the '64 World Series, we played the Yankees. But I didn't play in that World Series, because I got hit on the hip. So they tried every day to see if maybe I can play. But before the game, the manager went to the training room, and they said, "No, he can't do it." The whole week was like that. I played just one inning. I played the inning, you know, but when I go to hit, I can't move. So that's it—one inning.

And then in 1967, I had a good Series.[8] When we won, I played real good in '67, and they had a big celebration in my hometown. The whole town had a parade, they came out to the airport.

And let me tell you something. When I started playing, I didn't know I was going to play in the major leagues or professional ball. But I liked baseball, since I was a little one. My father wanted me to study, but I didn't care—I'd go down to school, and play baseball with the kids. But we played different, you know, like if the ball hits the top of the house, and comes down and we get it, we call them out, you know? We had different rules, when I was a little one. And when I started growing up, I kept playing ball, my father wanted me to study. And I told him one time, when I was about ten or eleven, "Dad, I'm going to make more money than my older brother, and he's going to study medicine." And he was a good doctor, too. But I made more money you know? But... I wish I could be playing *now*. There's a *lot* of money now.

So anyway, I kept going, and I remember my godfather, he told my father to let me play baseball. So he said, "OK, go ahead"—and I went and played amateur ball. And then I signed with the Pittsburgh Pirates. My family was thinking maybe I can't make it, you know? But then they saw I played so good over there, they said, "OK—keep going." Even my father.

There were only a few Latino guys to look up to back then. The Alou brothers. And the guy who started first over there was a guy named Virgil, Ozzie Virgil. Then, the second one was Alou. And I was the third one. Right after the other one. And later Marichal, Matty Alou. Jesus Alou. Manny Mota. And some of the other guys.

HARRY CARAY: Here's Tim McCarver, bottom of the sixth. The new pitcher is Pat Dobson... He's a sinkerballer.

Mickey Stanley:

McLain's arm must've been really bothering him, because if it wasn't, no way he would've come out. McLain would *never* have gone to the trainer or pitching coach. If they asked him, he probably would've told them the truth—so it must've really been bothering him, or you wouldn't get him out. Or Lolich, if they weren't hurt. McLain and Lolich, they did not want out of the game.

And we're not scoring many runs, either. Not that day.

Hal Naragon:

Now, Dobson was a starter, and so in a situation like that, if a manager thought he could get the side out, he'd use him. Got to. Can't wait for tomorrow! Because we were down. We were down, we had to come back.

Jon Warden:

We were down, you had to hit for him. Get him out of there, and just figure, hey, why try to burn him another two innings. I think Denny was like a 1.79, and Gibby 1.12. And just, that was the call. I mean, if you go by the stats, what you should've done or should do, you pinch-hit for him after seven. We were down.

So Dobson came in—and he was a pretty seasoned veteran, and they probably wanted to get him on the mound, let him get some work. To me, that was probably the obvious call. And they were predominantly a right-handed hitting team. Cepeda, Javier, Maxvill, Shannon, Flood. And Brock's lefty, Brock and McCarver.

So that was pretty on par, for Dobson to be the guy. And from then on, it was our bullpen.

And for them, it was Gibson.

	1	2	3	4	5	6	7	8	9	R	H	E
Tigers	0	0	0	0	0	0	0			0	4	3
Cardinals	0	0	0	3	0	0				3	3	0

Johnny Edwards:

I'll tell you—one of the things Bob Gibson was noted for was how *fast* he pitched. You know, we'd go over the hitters, and then he'd say, "I don't know if I'm gonna win or lose, but the game's gonna be over in two hours!" And he used to *really* get upset that somebody backed out of the box and didn't get right back in there—in fact, I remember many times he yelled, "Get in the box!" And those guys *better*, or they might eat a baseball. He wanted to pitch fast. And I can see these guys today, that have two batting gloves on and they take them off and reset them. Well I can see him pitching in today's game, and those guys doing that? He liked to pitch fast, and he let them know if they weren't getting in the box. He was a mean guy, I'll tell you that.

Tim McCarver:

He had what I've called *methodic rapidity*. And that carried over to all the rest of the pitching staff, too. He affected the rest of the pitchers on the team more than just working fast. Throwing strikes, using the outside part of the plate to right-handed batters, things like that.

And catching Bob, or anyone on that team… you know, catching has a lot to do with imagination. Be flamboyant enough to get away from the scouting report, you know. Or be imaginative enough to get away. You know, if you become a robot back there, robots are more easily read because they do the same things all the time. And guys aren't robots. So you're trained, and you figure it out after a while—be more imaginative. Use your intelligence, instead of going by what other people have seen, that can lend a little aid to you, I mean, you know, you have a pretty good idea, but once you get that idea and you form it—then be imaginative. Use your intelligence.

Johnny Edwards:

When I got over there in '68, Schoendienst wanted to keep his catchers strong, and he had me catch Gibson all year, and Washburn. I had a lot better arm than Tim, and Gibson and Washburn had trouble holding people on, so I think that was why I was given those two guys, all year. And Tim caught Carlton and Briles.

But I don't know why I didn't play in the World Series. I was a team ballplayer, and I was upset that I didn't catch Gibson in the World Series, because I caught him every game, including the ones in spring training. He had the 1.12 earned run average, and MVP *and* Cy Young

Award winner, and we worked together pretty good, all year. And after the Series, after I was traded, I thought about it, and that next fall somebody called me from St. Louis and asked me about it, and I told them I felt like if I'd have caught that seventh game, that we would've *won*... And then Tim got real upset with me!

I thought, "Hell if I'd have been catching, we'd have won the World Series." Well, that probably wouldn't have been the case, but... you know, why do you change catchers at the World Series? You know, like, what's the old saying that Darrell Royal said? *Dance with the one that brought ya?*

But, you know, Bob was a super pitcher—all along and all that. But one thing that I tried to make him realize, and I think it worked, was the fact that he also had a great slider. And in the past, when he'd get behind, he'd go back to his fastball, but I remember many times when I'd call a slider when he was behind in the count, he'd shake me off, and then I'd give him another slider, and he'd shake me off and he'd call me out there, and finally I'd convinced him that, you know, "You've got to throw that slider more." And I think that really helped him that year in his pitching.

There was that "Bob Purkey slider," too—that was the one that was the backup slider. And then he had the other slider, which was a sharp breaker that would go away from right handers. As a catcher, I tried to help him out, but if he *wanted* to throw that pitch, I would *let* him throw that pitch. And I would try to convince him that he had other pitches he could get people out with.

Tim McCarver:

That was the slider to the outside part of the plate against left-handed batters. It's a backdoor slider, but, what happens is—it's good if a pitcher reminds himself that—"If I miss with this pitch, I'm gonna miss *away*." Because if you miss over the fat part of the plate, you're getting away from your strength. But what happens is, a left-handed hitter would see that pitch, think it's going to be outside, and take it. There were an awful lot of guys who took that slider from Bob. It was a backdoor slider, intentionally throwing it away. And if he missed, he missed away.

Bob was obviously good enough and intelligent enough to realize that. And it served him quite well.

It didn't take him a lot of convincing. I told him, I said, "You know, we keep throwing that slider *inside, inside, inside*... And I know from a hitter's standpoint, if I see that slider outside, I'm more inclined to take it, because it's not designed to be there. So why not, with two strikes? If you miss, you miss outside—they'll take it anyway. Or it might just nip the plate." And he said, "Mmm... worth trying. But I don't wanna miss over the middle of the plate!" I said, "Well that's up to you! But we'll try it, on lesser hitters." That's where that imagination comes in.

Johnny Edwards:

Gibson didn't mind anybody swinging hard or hitting a home run, as long as they didn't take a walk around the bases. He was a hell of a competitor, and a mean son of a gun.

And he doesn't like me to tell this story, but anyway, the White Sox had traded Tommie Agee to the Mets that year, and in spring training the papers in St. Pete were writing out how Agee was going to lead them to the World Series. And so, when Agee came up to bat the first game, and Gibson was the first pitcher he faced that spring training, Gibson hit him, the *first* at-bat.

And he said, "Welcome to the National League."

The other incident that I remember so well was—he had that streak of scoreless innings in there, you know, it was up close to where Drysdale's was.[9] And what happened was, in the game that they scored a run on him, Gibson walked one, somebody hit a single to right, and the man was on third base. And Gibson threw a slider way outside, I dove out after it and it hit off my shinguards and got away, and they scored the run that way. And that's how he lost that time, because he went into San Francisco after that and pitched I think seven or eight more scoreless innings. But, in the clubhouse afterwards—you know, it was a passed ball, there wasn't any doubt about it—when the sportswriters asked him what his thoughts were, he said: "Hell, don't ask *me*—go and talk to Edwards, he's the one that blew it." But that was Bob Gibson, I understood that.

It was just a nice ride I had. To be behind the plate when those few of runs are scored, is pretty nice.

Willie Horton:

I remember when I was a kid, my second year with the Tigers, I played in Winter Haven. And I had a day off, and the main team was going to St. Pete to play the Cardinals. And I knew Bob was pitching. So I decided, I'm gonna go on the trip—I wanted to get his autograph. So we go over to St. Pete, over at Al Lang Field. And the visitors' clubhouse was up on here, and you kind of had to walk across. I waited around, and he got through warming up, and I came through, I said, "Mr. Gibson…" And he signed my ball. Then he said, "What position do you play?" I said, "Outfield." He said, "You get your ass away from me." Just like that, man—I ran in the clubhouse! I went in the clubhouse, I told Gates Brown, he said, "You a goddamn fool for making the trip, man, you played yesterday. Hell, I never would've came on this goddamn trip, I don't give a damn *who* was pitching!"

Bob Gibson, he didn't talk to no position players, I found out later. And if you talk to Tim McCarver, he'll tell you he's about the only one he talked to on his team! Tim McCarver was the one guy he talked to on the Cardinals, he didn't talk to no position players. He said you would get traded, and then he'd have to face you someday.

But I found out he was a nice guy after he retired, he was a *real* nice guy. And I did get his autograph eventually, at the All-Star Game, in '70. He's a different man now, he's different. But that was his way.

Dick Schofield:

It's kind of funny, a lot of guys hated Bob Gibson. Now, I liked Bob Gibson! I didn't mind him, but I know he's got a side that's pretty grouchy or whatever you want to call it. Playing against him, I knew guys would give anything if they could hit a line drive and hit him. They would've been very happy!

Ray Washburn:

You mean he was a little cranky? But, as far as a teammate, he was a lot different than how he came across to other people. Gibson could be very funny. He would imitate McCarver catching… where he'd always say that all he did was knock it down, pick it up, and throw it back! And back in '64, Gibson and Uecker, they'd imitate people on the bus, all the front office people! We got on the team bus after the game, and they'd be imitating the heck out of people. Some of the front office people, the publicity guy, the others.

Orlando Cepeda:

Bob was a very funny guy—he could've been a comedian! Great team-mate, and great guy. He was a competitor, you know, he would compete.

After they traded me to Atlanta, in '69, we played St. Louis on a Friday night, and I told Bob, "Tomorrow, Saturday, I'm going to wait for you, and then we'll go to my house for dinner." But then, he was pitching Saturday afternoon, and I hadn't seen him before the game. So he got on base, he came to first base—I was going to tell him, "I'm going to meet you, at your clubhouse." Before I could say one word, he says, "Don't talk to me now. You're my enemy, OK? I'll see you after the game, but right now I can't talk to you." And the first pitch, he knocked me down—*whoa*! Knocked me down.

Dick Schofield:

He wouldn't yell at guys much or anything, on the field. There's pitch-ers like that, though. Gaylord Perry was like that. I played behind him, when he was horseshit—in '65.[10] Somebody would hit a line drive that would just undress you, and he'd turn around and look at you like you like you were supposed to catch the ball. Like, you know, "We're just trying to stay alive, Gaylord, if you're gonna throw that shit up there." I just didn't like him; I don't know why. There's not many guys, but he would qualify. I mean, and he cheated like a dog. Spitting all over the ball, or rubbing Vaseline all over it all the time.

But Bob Gibson, he could do *everything*. I mean, he could probably have played another position, if he wasn't a pitcher. Because he's a
pretty good hitter, and if he'd have hit all the time he probably would've
been a good hitter. And he could run. And another thing about Gibson
was, he liked guys that could catch the ball. Because I'm pretty sure
that year he knew nobody was gonna hit him, so he knew if he got a
couple runs, he's in pretty good shape. And I can remember he would
check the lineup, it would be posted, and he'd say, "We can't win with
this lineup! Get this guy out of there, and get that guy in." And I think
Schoendienst probably listened to him, though he might not admit it.
Gibson might say he was just kidding—but I don't think he kidded that
much, when he was going to pitch. He was dead-ass serious.

Julián Javier:

If I didn't play, Gibson wouldn't pitch. The manager would say, "Why
you not gonna pitch?" "Because Javier isn't playing." He wanted me
and Maxie to play every game he pitched. If Maxie didn't play he didn't
pitch. If I didn't play, he didn't pitch. He said, "These are my guys, I
want to win the game."

CURT GOWDY: Gibson has struck out now at least one man
in every inning...
HARRY CARAY: Strikeout number *twelve!*

Tom Matchick:

Everybody was striking out! Willie, Kaline, Cash, Northrup—The Fox.
Man, if he struck out, look out in the dugout. Look out around the
water cooler, the helmets, the light bulbs—oh my God! He'd come
back, "How the hell could he get me out!!" I mean, you don't see that
today. Our guys got *mad*. You know, if our guys took a third strike
down the middle, they were embarrassed to come back to the dugout.
They had to go down *swinging*.

I see today, where they're taking fastballs right down the middle—what are you looking for? They'd always say to us, "Look for the fast-ball, hit the breaking ball off the fastball." But I guess maybe they teach different now, you know, the hitting aspect. But man, the taking third strikes down the middle, that's just unheard of. Back then, you would swing at anything close. Although nowadays, they're being too par-ticular on that—sometimes the umpires are calling a pitch outside *that much* a strike. You've gotta foul it off, do something with it, you know. Because they're going to call it a strike anyways.

But Gibby didn't get me, that day! He got seventeen of us, or eighteen that day, but he didn't get me! I ran the count to three-and-two, and took some pitches. I saw the ball great off him. He threw hard, he threw good. He had great stuff. And he kind of stared at you.

I just went up there and tried to put the bat on the ball, and hit a line drive, somewhere. I don't know how many pitches he threw; he must've threw me ten pitches. I fouled some off, and I ran the count to three-and-two. And then I don't know if it was the changeup or he took something off it, but he might've turned it over a little bit because I saw the curveball good, the fastball good. And I got out in front of it and I made that out. Me and Gates, were the only ones he didn't strike out.

So, he didn't get me!

Tim McCarver:

It was especially impressive because the mentality there was, *Don't strike out.* If it happened today, the mentality being, a strikeout's just an out, it wouldn't be as unbelievable. That's why I'm shocked that nobody's ever broken the record, with all the great pitchers that have been avail-able to work World Series games.

Because, you know, back then the strikeout *mattered.* Today, the strikeout doesn't matter. The strikeout is just considered by players who hit today as an out. It's an out. Well, it's not *just* an out. Because if you hit a ground ball, as opposed to striking out, with runners on base, you run the risk certainly of a double-play ball, but there's more of a reward for putting the ball in play on the ground, because you move runners.

And runners are moved by outs. Runners aren't moved by strikeouts. They're moved by contact.

And we were taught that. So therefore, with two strikes, you change your approach. You make contact, you shorten your swing.

Al Kaline:

There *was* a little bit of an embarrassment to strike out, back then…

Mickey Stanley:

That's a good point, you know. To me, it was kind of embarrassing to strike out. I don't know why, but I think it was more embarrassing to everybody, back then. And maybe because we didn't hit a lot of home runs. I suppose if I hit 40 home runs a year, striking out was a little more acceptable. Striking out was embarrassing. It was.

But I didn't even know there was going to be a record set, or any of that.

And I should be ashamed of myself, because I watch a lot of baseball now—and I know I'd be a lot better hitter, after watching pitchers pitch, and seeing what they do. God, I would've taken a lot more pitches—I'd be a hell of a lot more patient—I can't believe my approach.

I had no approach. Don't strike out! So I would swing at the first pitch! You know, they'd throw me a slider, a couple inches outside, and I'd hit a ground ball to short, and say, "Oh well—that's one at-bat." And pretty soon, they'd make a mistake. It wasn't very smart. Once in a while I'd move closer to the pitcher. Not closer to the plate, because they'd see that. Closer to the pitcher. If they were a breaking-ball pitcher. But I didn't really make any changes in the box. I never moved back, I was too stupid!

Denny McLain:

As I recall, they opened up center field for the first time that game. All the seating. And I know Mayo talked about it, in the first or second inning of the ballgame, maybe sooner than that. My recollection is that's what they did. And there was a debate about it, but it was too late to do anything about it, the people were already there. But Gibson threw out of there, he really threw out of there. and I don't think he knew that in fact that was a big advantage that he had. But I threw over the top, I was above the crowd. And I'm not saying that's the reason he won or lost, but that was a pretty big moment.

In the first game, it was all sunshine. That makes a big difference.

John Hiller:

I just remember Gibson. That's all I remember.

Jim Price:

Well, he was throwing seeds.

You know, his fastball looked like *that* big—low and away, on the black. His stuff was *electric*. And just looking at him made you think twice about digging in. He had that presence about him. He was intimidating, no question.

Jon Warden:

We were all right there, we're up top of that row. And we're watching like crazy, we saw everything.

We were down there, and I'll tell you, you could hear Gibson's ball just smack in the mitt. We could hear McCarver glove *crack*. And plus, you're talking about a full house, it's sold out—and you could hear that glove just *smacking*.

Ray Washburn:

See that glove, over there? That's McCarver's! One of his old gloves— I've had it even when I was still playing. I'd take it in the wintertime and see if somebody could catch me. See his name there? It's kind of faded now. But can you imagine him catching Gibson in something like that?

Tim McCarver:

I've told Bob, I think about him every day of my life. Because when I get up, my hand hurts. It's hurt for twenty years. It's everything he threw. But, I mean, other pitchers, too. I have this vein running through the palm of my hand. See the veins there? You don't have those, and I don't have them on my right hand. Those are—that's this burning sensation. See the mixed spots there? That's all mostly from Bob. I said, I've kidded him, I said, "This has kept us friends all these years, because I think about you every day of my life—you son of a bitch!" You know, some days are worse than others. But it's rare that I can close it.

As a catcher, the most significant guy on the team is pounding you to pieces every day. And, if he weren't doing that, he wouldn't be as effective. So while you encourage that, it takes its toll. It's a tough position. It's cruel, baseball. It's mano a mano. It's a cruel sport.

And I remember, sometime in the last two innings, I went out to the mound. And that was rare. Because it was very unusual for me to ever go out to the mound, with Gibson. He told me back in '63 one game, "Tim—what are you doing out here? The only thing you know about pitching is that it's hard to hit!"

Jon Warden:

It's not like now, these guys go five innings, they're looking like, "Are you gonna take me out now? I've got my five innings in!" And then some jackass invented this quality start stat that I hate. What a slap in the face to all the great pitchers like McLain and Drysdale and Koufax and McDowell, and Gibson. A six-inning quality start? That's garbage. I might give you seven innings, but not six—that's only two-thirds of the game.

Tony Kubek:

Guys in that era would keep pitching, and they didn't like relievers coming in and taking their place. A Gibson and a Lolich, and I think McLain too, if a manager came out and wanted to talk to them about taking them out, they would argue against him—and probably be able to win! Gibson would intimidate a manager from taking him out. Even though he was taxed, he wanted to finish the ballgame.

Tim McCarver:

Early in my career, our manager Johnny Keane wanted me to go out and slow him down. I said, "John, he doesn't wanna be slowed down." And he said, "Well, Goddammit…!" I said, "Look, you're talking to me—why don't you talk to *him*?" And I'm handling this delicately, because I'm twenty-one years old. And I'm in no business to be telling a manager what to do… But, anyway, eventually, he just didn't say anything, because Gibson became *Gibson*. And who was Johnny Keane to say, "Slow him down"? Well, that's the point I was trying to make with him.

And Red? Shit, no. Red never talked to him about that.

Julián Javier:

I always liked when Gibson would say, "What the hell you doing here, Red?"

HARRY CARAY: Isn't it a funny game, with all the suspense now… just on an inconsequential thing, like a strikeout? All over the world, people I'm sure, are tensed as they are here at the ballpark, for this pitch…

Two strikes and a ball. The pitch to Kaline…

Tim McCarver:

After the fifteenth, I walked out in front of the plate, and I said, "Bob…"

And I kind of pointed with the ball in my hand to the board out there, and it said he tied the major-league record for strikeouts. He came over to me, he said, "Tim. Give me the ball."

I never paid any attention until the fifteenth. I didn't even know it, up until fifteen. But they said it tied a major-league record, and *that's* when I went out in front of the plate and he said, "Give me the god-damn ball!" And I said, "Bob, look…" And he looked, he said, "All right, well, gimme the ball." He was a little tame, tamer in his tone. Did he smile? No. Shit, no. He did after the game, but no he never smiled during the game.

At the time, he didn't notice those strikeouts. He cared overall, but he wasn't trying to go out there and strike guys out. Pitchers don't do that; he's just trying to win. He's not trying to strike guys out, or going out there with fourteen in the bottom of the ninth and try to strike out the side. No, no—that was not his M.O.

And then, of course, when he *broke* it.

Tony Kubek:

Sandy Koufax, in the '63 World Series, had the record before Gibson broke it. And Bobby Richardson batted first, I batted second, Roger batted third, and Mickey batted fourth.[11] The last strikeout from Koufax was on a right-handed hitter we had, Harry Bright, who was kind of a substitute third baseman and pinch-hitter, and he struck out. And Koufax was still throwing very hard for the last out of the game. I know Bobby didn't strike out much. I didn't struck out much. Roger didn't strike out much. Mickey went a hundred times, but he also walked a hundred times. And Koufax got the first three or four hitters to go down.

So, I could identify with what Koufax did, and then see what Gibson did as well—how extraordinary that was. That was Gibby. He threw hard, he was intimidating.

Dick Schofield:

When I played with the Dodgers, I played third base when Koufax pitched. I didn't need a glove! And that's the way Gibson was.

See, that's something you don't even notice. When that's happening, you just kind of figure, "Well, he pitched another good game." And as soon as he pitches again, we're going to win another one for sure. So you didn't even realize how good he pitched, until you got older and you started looking at the whole deal—just like with how many shut-outs he had… and everything.

Orlando Cepeda:

It was *amazing*. I was saying to myself, "This game is going to be *forever*." One of those that people remember. I said that to the first-base coach, from Detroit, in the eighth inning.

I knew he was amazing, but he amazed me that he was so *quick*. Boom—strike two. Strike three. Out of there. And I didn't have the mind to think about the strikeouts, at first. Because he didn't talk too much, you know. He goes to the bench, and he concentrates there. He didn't say too much when he was pitching.

Jon Warden:

Gibby was *on*. We're sitting there in the bullpen like, "Well, we're gonna be down one game, 'cause we're not gonna hit this guy." I mean, we knew. We're just sitting there watching the game, and it was entertaining for *us* to watch him set that record. It's like, "Damn, hate to be on the wrong end of that, but that was a hell of a ballgame he just pitched." Have to give him credit.

Orlando Cepeda:

I told Julián, "That record is going to be hard to break." But then, he got it.

Sherry Gaston-Caldwell:[12]

When Gibson had his strikeout record that day, I was in the stands then, working as an usherette. You know, they call them all ushers now, but back then in the '60s, it was an "usherette," and the ushers were the men. And so when that record happened, the crowd just went nuts. Because that was quite a feat. The roar of the crowd, and everybody up on their feet, that's what I remember. That's the biggest memory… because that was a really big thing that happened at those games.

My section was right at the first-base line, that's where my section was. So, I was looking right at Gibson when he made those strikeouts. And in my section, we had a lot of celebrities… I remember Frank Sinatra, because he came down to sit in Gussie Busch's seats, at the end of the aisle there.

But most of the crowd was just regular fans, and the regular fans wore their suits and ties and dresses to the game back then. At that time, you did not see very many in blue jeans and, you know, shorts or anything like that. It was like, when you used to fly on airplanes, you always had to dress up, you know.

Orlando Cepeda:

Frank Sinatra was there? Well, I met Frank before, one time. When we played the playoff game in Dodger Stadium, in '62. Before the game, you know, we just said hello, and that's it. And then he came to the World Series in '67, too. One of the games in St. Louis.

Tim McCarver:

The year before, we'd started the World Series in Boston. But in '68, because we were starting at Busch, you had Frank Sinatra there, Cary Grant was there, and there was a famous female actress… It wasn't Doris Day, but it was kind of a Doris Day kind of actress that was there.

Oh! And as a matter of fact, I saw Bob Hope at a restaurant where we went every night—I can't think of the name of it right now, but it was a great steakhouse, as you might imagine, great seafood, great restaurant, and we ran into Bob Hope there. I'd forgotten about that.

Mickey Stanley:

They were there? I didn't know that. Would've really taken a dump at short if I'd known that. Seriously? Bob Hope was at one of the games? I had no idea.

The only thing I ever remember is playing out in Anaheim during the year, and Ed Sullivan was in the clubhouse. God, he was… he had makeup all over, or it looked like he had makeup all over his face—and he wasn't even on TV, just visiting. But no, I didn't know those guys were there. Wow.

Orlando Cepeda:

After Bob got the record, on the last batter, the last pitch, I hoped that he would hit a ground ball—so I could catch the ball, and save the ball. But he struck out the last one.

Willie Horton:

I was up as the last batter, and had the last strikeout.

John Hiller:

I remember the last out of the game was *not* a strike—I think it was on Willie.

Willie Horton:

The one that he gets me on, it stayed right in on me. You'll see, it stayed right in, inside—it might not even have gotten the plate, but the umpire's gonna give it to him, because he lost it. But *that's* the ball I should've hit. See, I let that ball get out of his hand—I should've gotten ready before it got out of his hand, I was too late. And when you miss the one you should've hit, you *know* that. If that ball had been down, I would've swung on that. Because that's his strikeout pitch. If it had been lower, the umpire would've gave it to him, too. But I checked my swing there.

Then I found out later, he said he had two sliders—he had one that stayed in on right-handed hitters, too. But to me, I only knew his strikeout pitch, he'd go for the corner just that much outside. But the pitch he got me with, it was supposed to break better than that. The ball just stayed *in.*

But as I said, I found out later that he throws the slider like that, to stay in—but that was new to me. I just found that out at some function about ten years ago, hearing Bob speak about how he had some other slider that would stay in, too, for right-handed hitters. So that's a credit to him. Because the slider's supposed to be more out *here,* but he made it stay in *here*—it would do its spin, but it would just stay right there, it didn't break. If it broke, I would've went through with my swing, but it stayed in on me. So there ain't no thinking, I couldn't do nothing! Ain't nothing you can do. I thought it was almost gonna hit me! It caught me off guard—it *froze* me. And once you make that commitment, ain't nothing else you can do.

You just go sit down on the bench!

	1	2	3	4	5	6	7	8	9	R	H	E
Tigers	0	0	0	0	0	0	0	0	0	0	5	3
Cardinals	0	0	0	3	0	0	1	0	0	4	6	0

Hal Naragon:

In the locker room afterwards, when Gibson had struck out seventeen of us, Norm Cash said, "He'll never do *that* again." He said, "But maybe eighteen, maybe nineteen, maybe *twenty…* just wait till he finds out our weaknesses!"

Al Kaline:

Norm was my best buddy on the team, and we were sitting next to each other in the locker room. Everybody was really down after the game, and Norm said, "Hey, Al—I'm gonna get five hundred dollars, because one of the stations called me and they wanted me to do an interview. Because you *tied* the record, striking out… and I *broke* it." He said, "Oh man, I'm getting five hundred dollars!"

Mike Shannon:

That was a really fine-hitting Detroit team. These were really great big-league ballplayers and really good hitters. Norm Cash, and the Hall of Famer, and their catcher… And so to strike out seventeen like he did was phenomenal.

It was all over but the shouting, that day. With Gibson.

HOW RUNS WERE SCORED

Cardinals fourth:	Shannon singled, Maris scored	Cardinals 1, Tigers 0
	Javier singled, McCarver and Shannon scored	Cardinals 3, Tigers 0
Cardinals seventh:	Brock homered	Cardinals 4, Tigers 0

GAME TWO

Busch Stadium | October 3, 1968

Mickey Stanley:

I remember listening to it as a kid—and kind of like being in paradise. You know, back in the day listening to the World Series on the radio, that was *huge* entertainment. We didn't have all this other stuff. That was *huge*.

And at some point, I'm sure we had a TV, unless I saw reruns or something. When did TVs come out!? Shit, I don't remember… But I can still see Duke Snider, and Pee Wee Reese, Yogi Berra, some of those guys. It was a thrill to be able to watch. It was a big deal for me, as a kid. Because I think we barely could afford a small black-and-white TV, and getting to watch that big Willie Mays catch on Vic Wertz, and watching Pee Wee Reese play—that was my first experience of watching the World Series.

Ray Washburn:

We didn't have TV, but we listened to everything on the radio back then. So we were very familiar…

I know the Yankees were on a lot during that time. And one of the World Series of course was the Braves and Yankees, when Burdette had the great Series.[13] And then, I'm trying to think who was playing... of course, a lot of times back in those days, we'd be able to have a radio in the classroom and we'd be listening to the World Series. Because everything then was during the day.

John Hiller:

I grew up in Toronto, and I'll bet you honestly I never watched a World Series game, as a kid. I can't think about when I would've. We didn't have a TV until... probably '57. We didn't have a television set in the house. So I don't think I ever watched a World Series game, until I actually started playing minor-league ball.

Julián Javier:

In the Dominican Republic, we didn't have a TV, but we listened by the radio. I liked to listen to the Dodgers, the Brooklyn Dodgers, New York Yankees. And I used to listen to old games from Cuba, too, they had good baseball over there. But sometimes we couldn't listen, because Trujillo, the dictator, was there, and we had to go someplace and listen to the game. And if they find you, they probably put you in jail. We'd go to some friend's house—you had to be careful.

At home they used to say, "Go home Yankee—and take me with you!"

Orlando Cepeda:

Well, in Puerto Rico, not too many people had TV. Radio, yeah, but people didn't have TV. They would have a TV in the square there, in the plaza, and people used to go there and watch.

By the time I was playing with the Giants, my brother would get a special radio—shortwave, you know what I'm talking about? Because the American Forces Network, they used to broadcast all the games, the day games from San Francisco. Otherwise, he had to wait until the next morning to get the result for the game. Before that, sometimes he'd try to call me, for me to tell him that night.

Then by '68, they started to televise the World Series in Puerto Rico. So in '68 they saw it back home, that was a big deal.

Dick Schofield:

I can remember the '46 World Series real good, because I was a Boston Red Sox fan, and they played the Cardinals. I had to be like ten years old, or something like that. I was a Ted Williams fan—I don't even know why I was, but I was just for Ted Williams. I remember just being a kid, my folks would take me to St. Louis when Boston played the Browns—that's when I'd go to a ballgame. But that was a big deal, getting to go to St. Louis for a ballgame, you know. But that was a *long* time ago... back when St. Louis was the farthest team west.

And I remember back to '45, when the Cubs played the Tigers in the World Series. And I can remember '44, when the Browns played the Cardinals—I remember that World Series.[14] So I can remember back quite a ways, you know. And I can remember that my grandma used to have a sheet of paper, and she'd have it all lined out, she'd put the starting lineups in, and she'd keep score of the games. Stuff like that. But back then, you'd never *seen* the players, because you didn't have TV.

We listened to it on the on the radio.

Jim Price:

Well, I happened to be a Yankee fan, because my Little League coach was a big Yankee fan, and he'd always play the Yankee games. So I really became a Yankee fan. Mel Allen was a great broadcaster, I loved to hear him. And I remember the great catch by Willie Mays, against Cleveland.

That's what I remember of the World Series.

And I remember being back in Little League, I said, "You know what? I can play in the World Series." Because all of us, we all played ahead our age. I was on a mission, you know. I never, in my doubt, thought I wasn't going to be a pro player, or be a champion. No question in my mind. *World Series.*

Fred Lasher:

Giants, and Cleveland—I think it was '54. Because I would've been thirteen at the time. But I was a Dodger fan, that's when Sandy Koufax was pitching. Drysdale. They were my favorites.

So, to pitch in a World Series? God… you think of that when you're a youngster.

You dream of that. You go home, you listen to it, or take the radio to school. Of course, when I was real young, we'd use the radio at school, and listen to the game. To think you'd be playing in it someday is—unbelievable. You're reaching the pinnacle of your success, playing in a World Series. That's what everybody dreams about.

Al Kaline:

It was the Yankees, but I don't remember what year—the lady that took care of the school building, her son was my baseball coach. So she would take me out of class all the time to watch the World Series, in the library or some room. Because I didn't have a television or anything like that, where I was born and raised.

It was in the cafeteria, I think—they closed it down and they invited the athletes, from high school, if they were able to get out of class, to come and watch the game. And that's the first time I ever watched a World Series. I can't remember exactly who it was, but I know it was the Yankees.

John Hiller:

Back then, I think a lot of things were different…

When I broke in, and a lot in that era, the rookies, we just didn't say a word. I won't say they abused us but—if you were in a bar having a drink after a game, and a couple veterans walked in? You left. You finished your drink and left. But about 1979 or '78, that whole thing sort of changed.

Checking the rookies, it was just—it was expected, you know? We just knew our limits, and it was expected of us. But there wasn't anybody that would—before '68, Hank Aguirre would've done it, he would've checked the rookie, but humorously, you know. He could've said anything to you and you couldn't get mad at Hank, you just couldn't. But he did take me out to get me drunk, in '65—he tried to *kill* me! It was almost one of those things where, "OK, you're here to take my job? Well, you better watch yourself."

There was a place in Chicago we went to, called The Inkwell. It was down underneath the downtown there. Well, we went in there, second road trip I think it was. And it's way past curfew, I don't know where I'm at, and I said, "I gotta get back—come on, help me get back!" And he just shook his head. I couldn't even walk when I got back to the hotel that night. So his job was to get me drunk and sick and pitch bad, and hell, he wouldn't lose his job! But again, he would do that sort of humorously; you wouldn't get mad at the guy. But it was just different. It was *different* back then.

I get so many people saying, "You guys played for the love of the game." No. Shit, we played for the paycheck *more* than these guys today are! Because these guys don't even *need* the paycheck—they're going to be well. Sure, we didn't make much money, so it makes it look that way, but we *needed* that paycheck. Hell, I worked in a department store every winter, I had to work. So we kept thinking, "We need that World Series share!"

I think I was making $7,000 a year, the league minimum. I was living with my in-laws then, and I needed a check to buy a house so I could get out of there!

And after the World Series, I get a contract in the mail, and they *doubled* my salary. Somewhere around $14,000. So I told my wife, and it was good enough money back then. We were happy. Then about two weeks later I read in the newspaper, there's a big headline—*Minimum salary goes from seven to twelve thousand.* So I call Jim Campbell, I says, "Jim—you didn't do me well!" He says, "What do you mean, I doubled your salary!" I said, "Yeah but it's up to twelve now, I only got a two-thousand-dollar raise." He says, "No, you got double your salary, though." He wouldn't change that. I was upset, but I couldn't do anything, we had no leverage. Nothing, no arbitration, no free agency, nothing. And if you were a scrubini, you *really* had nothing.

We had a bunch of guys called the scrubinis. That's who we were— we were the extra guys. Jim Price, the catcher, and Jon Warden—he played one year! Daryl Patterson, and Wayne Comer, Fred Lasher, and then Pat Dobson and I were spot starters. McLain and Lolich, they completed every game they were in. And so the rest of us, we called ourselves scrubinis!

Mickey Stanley:

Eleven thousand bucks we got for winning the World Series.

That was a lot of money, eleven thousand bucks, back then, holy shit. In 1961, I bought a brand-new Chevrolet Impala Super Sport. Twenty-three hundred dollars. For a brand-new car.

I was making fifteen five that year. Jim Campbell, the general manager, a few years later, I said, "You know when we won the Series, that year, I was only making fifteen five?" He said, "You were overpaid." Laughed his ass off! "You were overpaid!"

Al Kaline:

Back then, we all had jobs. Representing, and calling on people and going out and speaking at banquets, fifty dollars for a speaking engagement. But Detroit was a great town for a ballplayer in the wintertime, because you could find a job to make a little bit of money.

So, we all had jobs. And going even further back, you'd work on a farm or factory—because most of the guys when I played in the '50s weren't college graduates, they had to find jobs. Six thousand dollars was the minimum salary. The only bad part about that was, you didn't have a lot of time to work out and stay in shape—but fortunately, I had a body that didn't put on very much weight!

Mickey Stanley:

We had to work. Well not all the guys did—but I had to work. During the season. We didn't make any money! We made enough to live during the baseball season, and a few bucks over. And I didn't go to college, went one semester. So I worked. And, by the time I got through playing ball, I had enough roots in the ground where, you know, I couldn't go back to Grand Rapids.

I had a company I was working with, called Beech Electric, just a small little company. And during the season, you know, I'd see a customer or two during the summer—but they had main sales guys, and then I'd go with them in the wintertime. Make calls on Chrysler, General Motors, and the Ford plants. They rebuilt electric motors for Ford trucks. I'd make sales calls with them during the winter, and then the summer, they'd keep paying me—I'd see some customers at the park once in a while, I'd say hello.

I worked my butt off, I did.

Dick Schofield:

So many things were different. Gee whiz, *everything's* different. From equipment, to your uniform, your gloves, the bats, everything's different.

See, we didn't become friendly with the other team, back then. That's different. You didn't talk to the other team. I mean, you know, you see these days when sometimes the catcher's mask comes off? I heard McCarver say the other night on TV, "Let him pick it up himself, the hell with him! It's *his* mask, let him pick it up—I don't have to hand it to him." I think that was kind of the mind-set, it wasn't buddy-buddy. You might've known somebody on one of the other teams, but I mean, hell, guys now are out there on the field giving each other hugs. Like in the All-Star Game this year, taking a picture with the umpire?

That's bullshit, as far as I'm concerned. That's not baseball—that's a *joke*. Man, when you're getting paid a whole bunch of money, you don't *need* a friend!

And you know, a lot of the guys are bigger now, that's one of the biggest things. When I started playing with the Cardinals, I was 5-9, and I betcha we had nine or ten guys that were the same size. I mean, we had Stu Miller, Joe Presko, Enos Slaughter, Peanuts Lowrey, myself, Solly Hemus—everybody was like 5-9, 5-10 at the most. I betcha now you'd have trouble finding one guy! Maybe Altuve.

But, back then... I always remember how you used to throw your glove on the field, when you left your position. You'd just leave it there—the shortstop would take his glove and kind of throw it behind third base over by the foul line. The left fielder would drop his coming in from left field, their gloves would be right on the field. Which makes no sense, either! But I think that changed in about '57 or something like that.

And as for equipment, we didn't have helmets at first—you just had your cap. But Pittsburgh wore them all the time one year, they wore them in the field and everything. We told them they ought to get a light for their coal-miner helmet!

But, you know, nobody had a beard back then, not that I can remember. Some guys had a mustache, but things are so much different now. I don't remember anybody having a beard. Now, hell, *everybody's* got one. My grandson plays with Washington, Jayson Werth. He forgot how to get a haircut! He looks like a *caveman*, for Chrissake. I tell him, "Get a haircut," but I think his wife even thinks that's neat. But I'm thinking, no it's not neat—it's a *joke*!

Tony Kubek:

Back then—and I hate to say "in those days..." But, once I went out to the airport with George Kell, and we had a long delay so we were sitting there having a beer, and we got to talking, because we had about three hours before each of our planes left. And George goes, "I'm sick of this." He said, "I'm sick of these guys today—that are saying there weren't any good relief pitchers when we played." He said, "Lemme tell you a story. I was battling Ted Williams for the batting championship, on the last day of the season. And I had to get one hit, I think it was. Three times at bat. What happened my third time at bat was—we were playing the Cleveland Indians, and they brought in Bob Feller in relief, to pitch against me!"[15]

But guys did that then. I saw one time Whitey Ford came in, we were out in Boston, and they walked Ted Williams. And Vic Wertz, a left-handed hitter, was the next guy up. They brought Whitey Ford in to pitch to Vic Wertz. And Vic Wertz hit a grand slam! That was unlike Whitey—but he had just pitched a day or two before that. He was warming up, and they called down, and said, "Hey Whitey, get one or a couple hitters, you could get us out of an inning!" He said, "OK." So, that was not the norm, but it was not unusual either.

And you know, right after that year, they lowered the pitching mound. I mean, the mound used to be, what, 15 inches high? They lowered it because of the "Year of the Pitcher." And they started checking a little bit more. When we would go into Cleveland, or into Chicago, and they had pretty good pitching staffs generally—I mean, the mound looked like it was about two feet tall! Because, you know, the groundskeepers could doctor them how they wanted. They also, when we went to play in Chicago, they used to keep baseballs in the freezer—so the ball wouldn't travel very far! You'd pick up a ground ball, you'd say, "Man, it's not raining out, but it seems kind of… *soggy*." So, a lot more controls happened after that year, 1968.[16]

Denny McLain:

That "Year of the Pitcher"… they started talking about that that year.

Baseball was upset. They didn't think there were enough touchdowns being scored! And I still believe the fans—when you're in your own hometown park, you wanna see your team score runs. But on the other hand, I believe that the majority of people would love to see the pitchers on your team win 1–0 and 2–1. Those are the best games. Those are also two-hour games. 2:15, 2:20. Now today, they could take a two-hour game and make it three and half so fuckin' fast, it's unbelievable.

And see, when they reduced the mounds from 15 to 10 inches, in '69, that's what killed it. That's what killed *us*. Someone should do some research one day, and find out—take the top 25 pitchers, and find out: over the next five years, how many guys were still in the game, and/ or still effective, five years later. After they had reduced the mound six inches. It was dramatic. It was dramatic. I mean… and I'll give you the greatest stat in the world. In 1968, I struck out 280 guys. In 1969, after they reduced the mound six inches, I only struck out 181. What does that tell you? The leverage—the velocity that we picked up from our leverage on the 16-inch mound was now not sufficient to maintain that. Although, I set a Tiger record in '69 for the most shutouts anyone's ever thrown in Detroit history. But, it was different.

Al Kaline:

I get in trouble when I say this—but the strike zone is so much different now than what it was. And the thing I'll say is, that baseball is disrespecting the great players of yesteryear. The Mayses, the Aarons, the Mantles, and I could go on and on, back in those days. Because we had to hit the ball from up here shoulder high—to the knees. Now it's belt-high. So I have more respect for pitchers today than I do hitters, although there are a lot of great hitters. But everybody's hitting 20 home runs a year. Because they only have one place to look, that's belt-high! And striking out doesn't make a difference anymore to them, so they just swing. And, obviously, a lot of them are having great years, they're hitting a lot of home runs. But—and when I say "disrespecting the great players," I'm not talking about myself. I was a good player, but I'm not the Mantles, the Mayses, the Aarons, the Musials, the Williamses. Those guys are being disrespected, as far as I'm concerned, by Major League Baseball. By not letting people know that the strike zone has changed. And that's why I respect the pitchers today, because they have such a small area to pitch to. I always told Verlander, I said, "Verlander—if you pitched back in my era, you'd win 20 games a year easy!" Because you couldn't hit his fastball up there.

Julián Javier:

Now, when you play in the major leagues, you don't have to do *anything*. They pick your suitcase, they pick your uniform—the only thing you have to do is pack. In the minor leagues, when I played, you had to move around too much. To go on those little planes, I was scared of those little planes... Central Airline, Ozark Airline. Those would go around Illinois. I used to go to those little towns close to St. Louis— Springfield, and all around.

Dick Schofield:

Travel's different, your conditions and where you stay is different. Like now, everything's at the top. When I first broke in, we traveled by train. And that was—actually, it was nice. Traveling by train was more fun than flying, as a ballplayer. And from '53 all the way up into '58, there was no team past the Mississippi back then, so you're talking about some pretty short trips.

When you're traveling by train, you'd get on after a day game and go from St. Louis to Milwaukee or someplace. They used to have good food on the dining car, you'd relax—because you didn't have to go too far! It's not like you play in New York one day and LA the next, like now. I'm sure it's easier by plane, but I didn't know anything about planes when I started. But once the Giants and Dodgers moved to California, I think we started flying all the time then. And when we started flying to California, you had some *long* trips. Because you didn't have jets, not that I ever remember—we used to go on those big four-engine prop planes.

And in the cities, back when we played, if you got in a cab, you got four guys in a cab. Now, you just get in a cab and go! Stuff like that. So I think we were a little closer as friends, because you didn't have the money to just go on your own.

And speaking of that, in 1953 I was eighteen, when I'd never been on a plane before, and then I flew to New York to join the Cardinals, in the hotel... I'd worked out with them, so I knew some of the guys. They didn't know me, you know, but I knew them. And they were kind of hanging around in the lobby, so I checked in, went to my room, and I come down because they told me the bus was leaving for the park at like five o'clock or something. Most guys took the subway or the bus out to Ebbets Field. Then, Schoendienst and Musial were standing there—and of course, they were making a lot of money then, compared to everyone else. And Schoendienst and Musial said, "Come on, go to the park with us—we'll take a cab."

Taking a cab then didn't cost much money, I'm sure, but I got in the cab, I sat between them in the backseat of the cab, and—Musial didn't know my name, he had no clue who I was. So, he called me "Lefty" the whole way. "Lefty how's this?" and "Lefty how's that?" And it was kind of—it was so different because a month before, I was driving down the road listening to a tune, playing the radio, and all of a sudden you're sitting between these two guys, and they're asking you all these questions, and… I just always remember him calling me "Lefty." Then of course, I got to know him through the years, and he was just one of the nicest guys ever.

So that was my introduction to my first big-league game.

Dick Tracewski:

Today, I see things that would never go when I was a player. For instance, I see some of the players go out there and some of them will have white shoes on and some will have black shoes. Some have these kind of socks, this kind. That didn't go, then. You dressed the way you're supposed to dress. You wore socks, and the manager would say, "This is the way it's gonna be." You'd dress a certain way.

Al Kaline:

Back particularly when I first joined the ballclub, men in the crowd showed up in shirt and ties, and seemed like everybody wore a hat. And the women were dressed up in a lot of ways. So, I don't know, but, everything changes, and it's probably for the best, but…

Dick Tracewski:

That's the way it was, when my father used to come to see me play at Yankee Stadium, he'd come in a suit with a shirt and a tie.

John Hiller:

Well the kids in the stands get balls now all the time, everybody throws them baseballs. You know, Denny McLain, he used sit with a fungo bat and hit balls in the stands—and Jim Campbell would go *nuts*. If you threw a baseball in the stands, and they saw it, they'd call you on the carpet. Nowadays, gee, I can't imagine how many balls they go through in a game. Just giving them away, it's crazy!

Dick Schofield:

Overall, I'd say that nine out of ten things are much better now than they were in 1953. Especially for the player, they've changed for the better.

But so many things have changed—it's just unbelievable.

Hal Naragon:

I often wondered, if the players from the generations before we came along, Rube Waddell and those guys, if they looked upon the times that I played, and what their thinking was, towards us.

I wonder, you know.

HARRY CARAY: Here's Willie Horton. A *big* man in the Tiger lineup. He hit 36 homers during the regular season. Drove in 85 runs.

And there she *goes!* Way back! It might be outta here!

	1	2	3	4	5	6	7	8	9	R	H	E
Tigers	0	1								1	1	0
Cardinals	0									0	1	0

Willie Horton:

You see in the swing, I didn't move. See, when Briles is getting ready to throw, you're "throwing" with him at the same time—see how I'm getting ready? You're throwing *with* him, the timing of how my hands move. You're locking yourself in, and then you plant your foot. That brings your hands, and then you have your hands come through.

Nelson Briles, he was a good pitcher. But when I'm hitting, I don't like to think about who's easier and who's not—I just always respected all pitchers. But his ball didn't get where he wanted it, at the time, it stayed where I could hit it. His ball broke, and he was a middle-of-the-plate out pitcher. If it had gotten where *he* wanted it, I probably would've fouled it off or popped it up.

Jon Warden:

Willie led the league that year with 36 home runs. Because I've got his 36th home-run ball, he gave it to me, they got it back from the stands. He goes, "Hey you keep that, rookie."

Willie Horton:

I knew how to hit a ball since I was seven years old. I'd had people who I respected, and put in time with me, but ever since I was six, seven years old, I knew how to hit a ball a *long* way—it was just something natural. You know, they program guys too much now. "Oh—you bat *here*." Ain't no such way!

But I respected having coaches who'd give me their experience, helped me be more consistent, make contact. We had some good coaches, to help you bring out the best in yourself. One of the coaches I think that helped me was Wayne Blackburn, he was an old country guy! And he helped us in so many different ways. He helped us be happy, have fun. You've got to keep that fun in, that little boy in you, son. If you don't, you stop—you're in trouble. You're an adult, but it's a kid's game. And you've got to keep it that way.

I remember one time down there in Florida, the first time I went down there—Phil Cavarretta, he was a great ballplayer for the Cubs, and he was coaching for us that year. His son Corky and I were shagging for Gates Brown taking batting practice, all I did was shag back then, and practice outfield. I was just turning eighteen that year, I'd just signed.

And one day Gates was hitting, and he wasn't hitting no balls over the fence. So I get the ball, take it back up there, and I said, "Mr. Brown, whatchu trying to do?" He said, "Hell, I'm trying to hit that damn ball over that damn fence, that's what *I'm* trying to do!" I said, "Sir, I ain't trying to disrespect you, but see that school? I can *hit* that school." This was down in Dunedin, Florida. I'll tell ya, the school's still there— where the Toronto team has their camp. So he said, "Oh *no*—you can't hit that school!" I said, "Oh yeah, I can hit it." He said, "I'mma go get somebody to throw to yo' ass." I said, "Oh no, I can pick it up, sir."

So then I did it, and I don't think I quite hit that school, but it went over the fence.

And so he said, "Lemme see you do that *again*." I did it again. He said, "Well, I want to see you take batting practice with us." So I started taking batting practice those first two days, but I stopped after that, because I didn't want them to think I was embarrassing them or shaming them—because I don't think I was better than them or anything. But I could hit that ball well over that fence.

But you know, I don't remember too much from back then, or that game, just that you're trying to win. But I remember that Lolich hit one, too. *That's* what I remember.

Lolich hit a home run and he *never* hit a home run.

Tom Matchick:

I remember Lolich's home run… He ran right by first base, didn't even know he hit it out! Wally says, "Mickey! It's a home run!" so he goes back and tags first base, and does his trot around the bases like this here. The way he ran…

John Hiller:

One home run in major-league baseball, and that was *it*. That's crazy.

HARRY CARAY: There's a *long* fly ball… way back…

How about *that one!?* Mickey Lolich, one of the lowest life-time batting averages in major-league history, has just hit one out of the ballpark!

	1	2	3	4	5	6	7	8	9	R	H	E
Tigers	0	1	1							2	2	0
Cardinals	0	0								0	1	0

John Hiller:

We'd call him "Condor"… he'd run like a condor would run!

And "Buddha." I liked "Buddha" because he had a big boiler, and *ooh* he'd get mad. We were afraid of him—he didn't like his two nicknames, and if I yelled at him, he'd chase me around the field.[17]

But Mickey was a good guy, he was a blue-collar guy, you know. He was just that type. Him and I would chum with the ground crew, talk with them, maybe have a beer with them after the game, stuff like that.

And Mickey always was strong.

Jon Warden:

He had an iron arm. He would go in the shower—you know, everybody says "ice ice ice ice," and all that shit—Lolich would go in the shower, get it as *hot* as he could, and stand underneath it after he pitched. His shoulder and front here by the tricep would be beet red. "Aaah, I feel great, ready to go." Different strokes for different folks, you know. No ice wraps, none, they'd call you a pussy—"Ah, what's with *that* bullshit, man? Let's *go!*"

Denny McLain:

I've said this about Mickey a million times: greatest arm I ever saw in my life. The greatest. And I've always said that, if Mickey had listened to the Charlie Dressens and the Johnny Sains sooner, I think he would've won 300 ballgames, easy. He had a $100 million-dollar arm, I'm telling you. In today's game, he would've had a two- or three-hundred-million-dollar career, easy.

Al Kaline:

Well, he had a rubber arm, and the Cardinals, from what I understood, all said that Mickey Lolich was going to be the toughest pitcher. Roger Maris said, "Hey, Denny McLain is great, but Mickey Lolich is the pitcher that's gonna give us the most trouble." Because he had that hard slider down and in, and a sinking fastball, and, well, it certainly worked out that way.

Tim McCarver:

Roger had told us. We'd faced McLain in spring training, and I know he had a big overhand curveball, threw high fastballs...

But the better pitcher was Lolich. Lolich was the guy. He was different—he was *tough*. He was a tough pitcher. I mean, all you have to do it face him once. The ball moved all over the place. Just all over the place. And he had a rubber arm, he could pitch all day.

Mike Shannon:

That was the year when McLain was winning those 30 games. But Maris told me in July, he said, "Don't worry about McLain—the guy that we're gonna have trouble with is Lolich."

Bobby Tolan:

I just know that McLain was supposed to be their big gun, after winning 30 or 31 games. But, you know, playing against Gibson, you've got your work cut out for you… I don't think staying out that late had anything to do with it… it's just that it turned out that their star pitcher turned out to be the lefty.

Dick Tracewski:

Their third-base coach, Joe Schultz, he came to Detroit as a coach later on. We got to be good friends. And he said they were afraid of Lolich. Because their scouting reports and the guys that knew him said one thing about him: *He's got great stuff.* And he could pitch and pitch and pitch. He was special. And Joe Schultz said, "We were really afraid of him because we were afraid that he would control Lou Brock." And he actually didn't control him that well. But he did pick him off twice.[18] But the point is, we knew that he had a great arm—and he did.

Tom Matchick:

You know, Mickey could've won thirty ballgames that year, too. We just didn't score any runs for him. What'd he win, 220 games in his career? I bet you he lost 60, 65 games by one run if you ever check his records. He lost a *lot* of games by one run.

We averaged about six-something runs a game for Denny that year. So Mickey would come in the clubhouse the next day and say, "I guess I gotta pitch a shutout, again—you scored seven for McLain yesterday." I think we averaged about three runs a game for him![19] We just couldn't score a lot of runs for Mickey, but we told him, "You didn't need as many runs as Denny needed."

But they were both two great pitchers.

Jon Warden:

Mickey couldn't catch a break that year.

When the season started, Boston was in town, Earl Wilson pitched the first day and he lost. And so, the second day, Denny pitched and he went seven, and they pinch-hit for him. So they brought me in. I get through the inning, ended up bases loaded, get out of a jam. Horton caught a fly ball to end the inning.

And that's when Gates Brown started his great year as a pinch-hitter. He hits a home run the next inning, upper deck, we win the game, man, I'm like, "Oh shit, this is awesome, we won!" And then I'm going, "Oh shit, and I got the win!"

So anyway, Lolich lockered right beside me, and then on this side was like the batting practice pitcher, and the shovels and rakes for the ground crew—I had a really plush spot. So the papers came over to me and they were sort of bumping into Mickey, and Mickey sort of had that personality like, *I'm just one of the guys*, even though he's a great pitcher, 217 wins. And they're like, "Excuse me, Mick—Hey Jon, what's it like, first game, you end up with a win?" I said, "Aw I'm excited, and thank God Gater hit one out for me."

And so, about a couple days later… Cleveland comes in to town. I come in for the ninth, game was tied. And Horton hit a single and knocked in the winning run.

Now I'm 2–0.

Well now, there's more writers over there, you know, and "Holy cow! Two games!" And Lolich was like, swear to God, "Aw you lucky bastard, your bubble will break, rookie."

So then, first road trip, we go to Chicago. It was a Saturday, the *Game of the Week*. Us and the White Sox. Back then one game a week, man, that was it. One game a week is all that's on. So I said, "We got the *Game of the Week*, maybe I'll get in the game, who knows." So they were all excited, and we're in the ninth inning, again, old Comiskey, bases loaded, one out. And Wayne Causey's up. We're up one, bottom of the ninth. So I walk Causey on four pitches, and it ties the game. And I'm like, "Shit." Bases loaded, still one out.

See, that year, we won 40 games after the seventh inning when we were either tied or behind. A lot. And this was one of them, early in the year. It was tied. We were up one, now it's tied. And I'm waiting for Mayo to come out and get me—I figure he's gotta bring in Patterson, or Dobson, or somebody. Because Ken Boyer was coming up. All he's gotta do is hit a fly ball, and the game's over.

So I'm looking in the dugout, and Mayo's—*sleeping*. I said, "Well, I guess I'm pitching to Ken Boyer!" Throw him a slider, hung it, he hits a line drive right at Don Wert. Catches it, steps on third, double play. And in the top of the tenth, Horton hits a two-run double, we score two or three that inning. Ribant comes in for the bottom, gets the save, I get my third win.

And so Lolich is going *crazy*...

I'm 3–0, we played nine games and I'd won *three*. McLain and Lolich, neither one had a decision after nine games, and we'd won nine in a row. And I won *three* of them. And Lolich was like, "Geeeee... I can't believe how lucky you are—oh my God, when's your bubble gonna break?"

And that was the start of our season.

Hal Naragon:

Mickey Lolich had good stuff, he had *good* stuff. And he had a good breaking ball. I think he liked the way that John [Sain, the Tigers' pitching coach][20] and I showed interest in him, that he could do the job.

One time Mickey was getting taken out in about the third inning or so, and he goes in the clubhouse. This would be in 1967, 'cause they didn't know us very well then. It was our first year over there. And Mickey was up, taking his uniform off, and he looks up and here comes John. And he thought, "Oh... he's really gonna lay in to me." And John said, "Mickey, do you remember that pitch you threw to that hitter, in that inning, that curveball?" And Mickey said, "Yeah." And John says, "*That's* what we want. *That's* how you get to the pitch." And Mickey said to me later, "You know, he talked to me, and I thought, *Gee, I didn't do as bad a job out there as I thought I did!*"

Well that makes a pitcher saying, he wants you getting back out there the next *day*. And that's what would happen. They may at first kind of go, "Ahh, I don't wanna do it"—but they do it and they find out, hey, it's helping me, and they're interested in me. And it gets you confidence.

And, you know, another thing we did was—when you're on the train or plane, baseball was never brought up. You didn't want that guy that you're trying to help to think you're talking too much to him, you know. We knew that Mickey Lolich had been riding motorcycles at twelve, thirteen, even younger. And Jim Campbell wanted us to see if we could get him to not ride a motorcycle. Well, I told that to Mickey, and he laughed about it and says, "Hey, I've been riding since I was twelve years old."

So we would talk to him about that—and why wouldn't I talk to him about his motorcycles, you know? How far you drive, and why you drive, and what do you do, you know, I kinda got interested. And so when he sees you coming, he doesn't know what you're going to talk to him about! You know what I mean? You get interested in something else that the player is interested in. He's not all baseball. Same way with Denny, he was into airplanes. Well, John happened to be an airplane pilot, and had an airplane. So they talked airplanes.

You just get to talking. I didn't know anything about motorcycles, you know, about the motor or anything—but it would be kind of interesting to talk to those guys. And not about baseball!

About something that goes on in the world other than baseball…

John Hiller:

Mickey used to love motorcycles, he was on those all the time.

And I'm not sure what year it was, but I went with him once on his motorcycle, and scared the *heck* out of me—I never was on a motorcycle in my life. But he had a 500 Kawasaki, and he said, "Well why don't you get a motorbike?" I didn't have much money, so I ended up buying a 170 Honda. And I was in Washington, Michigan, near Romeo, I'd say it was a good forty-five minutes to the stadium. So here I am on a Honda, on the freeway, top speed 70 miles an hour—I mean that's just floored as fast as it can go. And I'd tuck in behind him, I probably did that once a homestand. After a while, I said to myself, "What are you doing, John, that was stupid!" I mean, the bike shook. So I had my little round with that.

And then Gates Brown… now Gates, on a motorcycle, was *funny*. And he had a Kawasaki, too. He just looked funny—big guy, and then he always wore a cowboy hat sort of. I don't know how he kept it on, but… he was funny. I think it was just the two of them back then, I gave it up pretty quick.

Mickey Stanley:

I remember going to Lolich's house, he had a bunch of these little Kawasaki minibikes. And Mickey was a good rider. One time he had us put studs on our tires, and we were going 70 miles an hour, on *ice*.

Another time, there was this fellow from Grand Rapids that owned the Kawasaki distributorship for the Midwest, he gave Mickey and me bikes all the time. He gave McAuliffe a bike, for a year or two, and Gates Brown. I think he gave Gates a road bike. But, every fall, Mickey and I would go on a little excursion with the Kawasaki dealers. They had a little outing, and we'd ride with them. We thought we were good riders, but when you rode with guys that knew what they were doing, we were in the minor leagues for sure.

And this one time, we were riding in the fall, after baseball season. We were with all these Japanese people, Kawasaki people, you know, and they came out with cameras and shit. We're riding with them, and all of a sudden, I come up to this little bridge going across a little creek, that's fifteen feet wide. And Lolich is standing on the bridge. I said, "Mickey, where's your bike!?" "It's underwater!" So we dragged the damn thing out, and those Japanese are there, and they've got mechanics with them, and we turn the bike upside down, take the sparkplug out, crank the kick starter, water spits out of the engine, put the plug back in—*vrrrrrrrrmmm!* I couldn't believe it, it ran!

CURT GOWDY: Norm Cash—they're playing him *way* over to right field…

And *there's* a drive! Deep to right…

Get a new ball out, Mr. Umpire! That one is *gone!*

	1	2	3	4	5	6	7	8	9	R	H	E
Tigers	0	1	1	0	0	1				3	6	1
Cardinals	0	0	0	0	0					0	2	0

Denny McLain:

Norman was the leader. I mean, I'm not old enough at twenty-two, twenty-three years old, you're not going to be recognized as a leader on a team until much later if you stay. But the guy that was really recognized as the spirit of the team was Cash. He really was the guy.[21]

Tom Matchick:

Him and Al were really good friends, and Al misses him to this day. Them two were like brothers, wherever you saw Kaline, you saw Cash. They were really close. Like I say, Al still misses him to this day.

Hal Naragon:

He was great for the club, he really was.

Willie Horton:

Norm Cash, one of the greatest hitters I played with. First baseman. Well, I'd bet Norm never even used *his* bat—hell, he used a different bat every day! He'd come by your locker and pick up a bat. "Boy, it feels good today, can I use it?" He didn't give a shit! Whatever would feel good, he would pick up a different bat. He was funny—I'll bet you Norm used 75 percent of other people's bats every day.

And sometimes, man, I'd see Norm come to the game, and the way you'd see him, I don't know how he got to the clubhouse sometimes! He'd say he had a "headache," I'd say, "He ain't gon' play *today.*"

But he'd go sit there in the whirlpool, that hot water sometimes. Most guys would get about 100, 103, 102—he'd get it *115*. He'd be red as fire when he got out of that water! And he'd put on a sweatshirt, jockstrap, no shorts. He'd go sit there in that hot water, and then that man would go out there and play. He was a hell of a man. And he'd never wear shorts, even in street clothes. I'd ask him, "Where are your shorts?" "I don't wear them damn things—too much time putting 'em on." He'd go take a shower, put his socks on, his pants, and he's *gone*. Ol' Tex. The John Wayne of baseball.

Jim Price:

Norm was a great guy, one of the best. One time on a road trip, we'd gotten into Kansas City early, and I had roomed with Norm at different times—and I was in the room, he'd been out, he came in late and he called his fiancée, at that time, arguing with each other, threw the phone down, got so mad he ripped his watch off and tried to throw it against the wall—but it went out the window.

So, I'm thinking, "We're about on the fifth floor… maybe it's OK." So I went down, and I'm looking for it, I'm on my hands and knees trying to find it, and I get a tap on my shoulder. It was a policeman that was like a guard, you know, at the hotel. He said, "Sir, can we help you with something?" So I told him the story, he tried to help me find it, but we never did find it.

Tom Matchick:

Aw, Stormin', he was crazy, man, are you kidding me? He was funny. He was real funny. He did tricks against the rookies coming up. You know like in Chicago, he told us we had to be at Pier 6 at five o'clock in the morning to go on a fishing trip. We were only going to be out three hours, and the one that gets the biggest fish is gonna get a hundred bucks each from him and Kaline. Well, we went down there, had to take a cab down there—guess what was there? *Nothin'.* We saw him at breakfast, "How was your fishing trip, guys?"

They kept everybody loose, you know, everybody kept loose. We played cards, watched movies during the year. It went by pretty quick.

Willie Horton:

That's what makes a winner. All them guys having fun like that. That's what makes the team, the makeup, putting a great team together.

We had a hell of a team, we had a bunch of guys where every day it was *something*.

Jon Warden:

Well there are some stories I could tell, about that team…

One time that year we go to California, we're going to Anaheim. Before we flew out there we were in DC, and Mayo had a team meeting after the game. His exact words, quote Mayo Smith: "Aaallright now, we're going out to Pussyville, USA—and we're having a bed check. I want you guys in by midnight." We're like, "Yeah yeah, OK Mayo, all right." So, we go to LA, we're at the Grand Hotel, right across the street from Disneyland. And so, everybody's in—of course, Horton and Gater, they were *never* in, they were always out running around going to see their buddies and family and shit.

So, every room was checked, except for Lasher. And I forget who he was rooming with. But he got all pissed off. So the next day, we were talking about the bed check. "Bed check—everybody get checked, anybody get in trouble?" And Lasher's going, "Whaddaya mean, bed check?" And he goes into Mayo's office, "What the fuck, Mayo? I'm not part of the team?" And Mayo's going, "Waaal waaall waall what?" He said, "Well you never checked *my* room!" "Waaalll waaal …" And Lasher goes off, anybody else would've been tickled to death. And most of the other guys—like, Willie opened the door, and Willie said, "Yeah Mayo, me and Gater here." Gates is under the covers, he's all dressed, full clothed. Soon as Mayo left, everybody got out, got up and left, and went back out.

Fred Lasher:

We were playing cards, had a card game going. And as midnight started getting closer, everybody's watching the clock, figuring you better get back to your room, when Mayo called. And so everybody's watching the clock, and everybody left for their room, and I didn't bother to go to mine. Or then I went, got there, and never called. Never called. So the guys asked, "Did Mayo call ya?" I said, "No, he didn't!" Started laughing like hell—because he called everybody else's. Not that he'd fine me anyway.

Willie Horton:

Yeah, when Lasher knocked Mayo Smith's door in? We were playing cards, and Wally Moses told us they're going to have a bed check. He said, "You all go on back to your rooms, we'll check, then come on back and resume playing cards." So, we did all of that, come back, and I think Lasher starts asking questions—they didn't check his room. And he went up and kicked Mayo's door, told him he's on the team! We called him Mr. Ed... I remember one time he challenged me and Kaline, we were at the airport—he done got to drinking, "Go and get the ball, I'll strike *both* of y'all out!" At the airport!

Jon Warden:

The other thing that happened in Anaheim, they had this old World War I or II fighter jet, you know those planes with the two wings, pro-peller job and everything. And it was sitting, as you walked in the hotel, it was sitting back here just outside. And so we got tanked up that night, we said, "Why don't we just push that thing in? The swimming pool's right there." We pushed it in the swimming pool. Now, it's like four in the morning, three or four in the morning, and they called Mayo's room. "Yeah your ball team's out there, they just pushed the damn air-plane in the pool." Here comes Mayo, he's got them long johns on, like pajamas with a flap in the back and shit—and he's down there, "Whaat the hell's going on down here?" And we'd all scattered. "Who was it!?" And they went, "We don't know who it was, but we're pretty sure it was your team." "Waall I don't see any of the guys down here." And we just scattered.

It was a small fighter jet, from the '50s or '40s. But the pool was huge, and we just pushed that thing, wheeled it out, took the block, pushed her right into the pool. Oh my God, I wish we had a picture of that. Today, that would've been national news, we would've gotten fined, suspended. *SportsCenter*, MLB [Network], shit that would've been everywhere.

Mickey Stanley:

It was a real airplane. Yeah, we got in, like three in the morning. That's back when Hank Aguirre was still on the team—I must've just gotten to the big leagues. And we all go out to the swimming pool, and, I wasn't in on it, I think. I was scared to death, thinking to push this plane in the swimming pool. It was on display, but it was out by the pool. I can't remember if I did any pushing, but I probably didn't.

I'd believe Hank might've been a big part of that. I would never— even now, I wouldn't do shit like that!

John Hiller:

It was in the lobby of the hotel in Anaheim, it was like one of these models. And good old Hank Aguirre was instrumental in that. Took it apart, and then we took it out and put it in the pool, put it together in the pool. We had to take it apart, because it was too big! There was about five of us. And, of course, we'd had too much to drink. And then we all went to bed. And then Mayo Smith called Hank, I think, and he says, "If you or the guys were involved, get that damn plane back in the lobby of the hotel!"

CURT GOWDY: …that brings up the top of the Tiger batting order, and Dick McAuliffe.

The 1-2 pitch… there's a smash to center, coming on is Flood, and… he can't handle the ball! Two runs are in!

	1	2	3	4	5	6	7	8	9	R	H	E
Tigers	0	1	1	0	0	3				5	9	1
Cardinals	0	0	0	0	0					0	2	0

Dick Tracewski:

He was a hell of a player, Dick McAuliffe.

Hal Naragon:

He was a hard-nosed player... Ohh boy.

Dick Tracewski:

What he did is, he got all his weight on his back foot, and he held his bat in kind of a funny way. And he opened his stance a little bit, it was a stance that you would probably see when Ty Cobb played.

He always did that. I played against him in the American Association, he played at Denver. And he did that then. That was something that came natural, and he looked right at the pitcher. I mean, a lot of times, you'll hit, and you'll be looking like *this*. He didn't do that. This is the way he faced—he looked right at you, with both eyes.[22]

Tom Matchick:

Oh, he was *tough*.

McAuliffe was a great second baseman. Mad Dog. He stood in there on a double play, to turn a double play—you could try to knock him over and he'd still stand up there, you know.

I mean, Mac was hitting 20 home runs a year. And he's the one that extended Tommy John's pitching career for a while. We were getting tired of being knocked down, he threw one at McAuliffe, and McAuliffe said something to him going down to first base. He said something to McAuliffe, Mac charged the mound and threw him to the ground! Then after that, next thing we knew, "Tommy John surgery." So I think that's how Tommy John surgery got started![23] But after that, he came back and had a few good years.

Don Wert:

We were playing in Chicago, and McAuliffe was the next guy up and Tommy John hit him. He took a couple steps and then—*smack*—right out for the pitcher's mound, and started slugging it out.

John Hiller:

We always had fights with Oakland. Willie would intimidate, he would intimidate people. And you had to pitch him inside—but if you came inside, he'd take a step and look at you. But Frank Tanana hit him one time… Willie charged him, and Frank kept saying, "Willie, come on now, I wouldn't throw at you!" But it was funny because that whole team came out, and it was just like the Red Sea parting—wherever Willie walked, he could *walk*, you know?

And then we did have a great one against Washington—Mike Epstein came up, charged the pitcher, and I don't know who was pitching. But Willie got in there somehow, one hit—one pop, and he was out cold, on the mound. Willie straddled him, and his eyes were… see, Willie had some Golden Gloves background when he was younger, in Detroit, competing younger than what he was supposed to be. And anyways, Mike Epstein, he was *out*. And then he starts waking up and his teammates are going, "Stay down, stay *down!*" 'Cause Willie was just waiting for him.

Tom Matchick:

Willie was *strong*. Whenever we'd have fights with Oakland, everybody'd be behind Willie and Gates going out there, you know. Nobody would mess with Willie. I thought that he was a Golden Gloves boxer, but he lied about his age, I think when he was sixteen years old. Yeah, he was a boxer.

Jim Price:

Willie Horton said, which I love to hear, he used to say, "You wanna play a one-run game, we'll beat ya. If you want a slugfest, we'll beat ya. If you want a fight, you're in *big* trouble." And that's true. There were a lot of fights—and we won them all.

Willie Horton:

On the road, we went to a lot of bars—and we'd always get in a fight.

I remember in Cleveland, Don Wert—"Coyote," we called him Coyote—he had some kind of navy grog or some kind of drink he had, and you can't drink but *one* of those things. And man, he's up there just smiling! Coyote, he never talked anyway, just smiled. All of a sudden, it looked like he went to sleep, just one eye open—he was *gone.* I said, "That navy grog knocked him on out!"

And Wayne Comer, he couldn't drink. Every time he had a beer, he'd mess with people. We got in a fight one night up in Minnesota, with a lot of army guys. In Minnesota, at the Brass Rail or something like that, not too far from the hotel. A whole army unit—you know, army guys, they all hang out together.

So Wayne, for some reason, he couldn't handle his drink. He'd drink about two beers, and he'd go around to that bar—and he asked this soldier, "Where you from? Ah that's a horseshit state." And then, something happened, and I said, "Ohh, we gotta rock and roll now." Me, Wayne Comer, Don Wert, and Jim Northrup. Coyote tried to go out the back door, he couldn't—it was locked! I said, "You gotta fight, Coyote!" I said, "Coyote, there ain't but one way out—you gotta fight tonight!" And man, we had to fight for our life to get out of there. Man, we'd come out of there, shirts torn off us and everything! The next day I had a big knot on my head, Mayo called us into his office… and so Mayo Smith told me, "Get your roommate in here, Wayne Comer, old Shank."

He comes in there, and Mayo says, "From now on, you've got to stay ninety feet away from Horton." And Wayne said, "Well goddamn, Mayo, how the hell I'mma do that—the *room* ain't that big!" "Ahh waalll goddamn… Well just wait till you get out of the room. When you leave that room, ninety feet!" Comer said, "Hell, how 'bout the bus? You want me on the damn bumper?"

Wayne Comer… he'd have three beers, that's all—he wouldn't be drinking any of that hard stuff. Three beers, and wherever we were at, he'd go messing with people. We fought in just about every town we went to!

Fred Lasher:

I was always in the bullpen—I had one start in the big leagues and ended up in a fight with Tony Conigliaro, in Boston. So one start, one fight. Yastrzemski was on first base, I think he'd singled off me, first inning. Tony comes up, and I didn't try to hit him, but I grazed his shirt inside. And he charged the mound. Then Yastrzemski ran over from first base, he had my arms pinned down. So I couldn't do anything. Tony drop-kicked me, in the thigh… and I don't think I got Yastrzemski at all—Yaz kind of hit me pretty good.

And then after it was all over and said and done, I decided I could still pitch. But, we ended up getting beat, 11–2, or something… That was in '70, the year I got traded over to Cleveland.

Johnny Edwards:

One of the best fights I was in in baseball was when I was with Cincinnati, against St. Louis. That was a real thing. And then I come over there and play *with* them! What happened was that St. Louis scored I think six or seven runs in the first inning on us. And Brock, the second time up that inning, hit a double and tried to steal third. In fact, did steal third. And our bullpen told him, when he ran out to left field, that he better put his hat on *real* tight. To put his hat on *reeeeal* tight. Because, you know, that was showing us up, to steal third base in the first inning with that big a lead.

Well, the next time Brock came up, Don Nottebart was pitching, he hit him. Didn't say anything, ran on to first base. Well, Gibson's pitching that game, and our first hitter is Perez. And Gibson doesn't hit him, but he threw over his head. And when Perez then popped up to first base, and when he circled, he came back by the mound, and he and Gibson started shuffling a little bit, and then it got broke up. And we had a big relief pitcher by the name of Bob Lee, and Cepeda was going, "Turn me loose, turn me loose!" and all that stuff. And Bob Lee said, "Turn that son of a bitch loose!" And boy, that started.

And I mean, there was… I remember Cosman and Rose ended up fighting all the way to the dugout. I got in a fight with Hoerner, who later was a good friend in St. Louis. There was fights all over the place. And I remember our manager at that time was Dave Bristol, and somebody toward the end of the fight grabbed ahold of the back of his shoulder, and he turned around and he broke a cop's jaw. And then we had to be escorted out of the ballpark. In St. Louis, 1967. Never did come up after I joined the Cardinals in '68, though. But it was a *real, real* battle. There were people fighting all over the field. But the police finally broke it up.

Dick Schofield:

There were some great agitators on that Cardinals team, you know. There were some *funny* guys, I mean, gee whiz!

When I was with the Cardinals in '68, we used to have pillow fights on the airplane. If those gals would come by, you know, the guys would take those small pillows and just *whack!* It wasn't one guy; it was everybody just about. And she'd pick that pillow back up, and just drill you with it! She was OK. Most of them went along with the program—they'd get a pillow and just *drill* you with it.

And Joe Hoerner did some shit on those airplanes… you can't print what he did!

Also that season, Dick Sisler was one of our coaches. He used to give out a rubber knife. If you screwed up in the game, he'd stick it in your locker—so you could, well, kill yourself, you know! You know, say you just got thrown out for no reason, or you would round second base and fall down or something. Anything that would be really obvious that you just messed up completely, you drop a pop fly or something. He didn't do it if you lost. But when you'd win the game, if you did something stupid, he'd always find something and give it to somebody.

Julián Javier:

Let me tell you something. One day, Schoendienst was in the hole, in the dugout—where it goes down to the clubhouse—and he was sleeping or something. And Gibson got one of those little cherry bombs— like they use for some parade, or the Fourth of July, those things. And he put one down under the chair. Everybody knew that, you know— and so it goes *BOOM*! You can hear it—and Red almost hit the ceiling on top of the dugout. We all said "Hey, what happened, Red!?" And nobody said anything. And nobody found out who did it! So when that thing blew up, wow—everybody started laughing.

"Wake up! Wake up, Red!" And they were saying, "Goddamn— who did that??"

Dick Schofield:

Some of the other stories I could tell, from all those teams I was on—my God. Did you know I played with more Hall of Famers than anybody ever played with?[24]

Later on in my career, I played with Sparky Lyle, and John Kennedy—my God, those guys are *nuts!* I mean, I don't know if they planned the stuff they did, or what, but Sparky Lyle with the Red Sox, if it was your birthday, there would be all these girls and they'd bake you these big cakes, and they'd knock on the door to the clubhouse, they'd give the cakes to the guard and say, "Give these cakes to—" whoever's birthday it was. So the guard would knock, and he'd come in with this big-ass cake, and he'd set it down on the table, and he'd say, "It's your birthday…" First thing Sparky Lyle would do is take down his pants, and sit in the cake. I don't know how many cakes he sat in when I was with the Red Sox. He was just crazy! He'd do shit you wouldn't believe!

And of course, when I played, I don't think there were ever any women in the clubhouse. I don't remember ever having a woman in the clubhouse, a sportswriter or anyone. Because when Sparky Lyle was still playing, one of his favorite tricks was, when these gals would come in to interview him, he would be stark-ass naked—and you know how in those days you'd have that big ol' thing on your hotel key? Well he'd stick the key up his ass, he'd get down on the floor, he'd be crawling through the clubhouse, going, "I can't find my hotel key!"

He was the first guy I ever heard say anything about pot. That was in 1970. I didn't even know what he was talking about. I think Sparky must've been smoking it before '70, though, I'm pretty sure he was! But he could pitch. *Damn,* he could pitch.

But out of all of those teams, the '60 Pirates and the '68 Cardinals were definitely the two best teams I ever played on. We had really good guys on both teams. The '68 Cardinals were a fun bunch of guys, and I don't know anybody that didn't like pretty much everybody on the team. I can remember, with the Cardinals, Tim McCarver came back from the barber one day, and he had sideburns. Ohh, we agitated him so bad! We all just laughed at him, like, "What a jerk you are!" And then before the season was over, we all had sideburns! And then the next year, that was big, sideburns.

Tim McCarver:

I remember I had more nicknames than anybody. Joe Schultz, our third-base coach, he gave me the nickname "Doggie," in the minor leagues. And then Buckethead, Melonhead, because of the size of my head. I was like Bruce Bochy, but not quite as known for my head size, I wore seven and three-quarters. But, it was a sign of affection.

Julián Javier:

You know, I remember Cepeda called Washburn "Deadbody." "Come on, Deadbody!" And then he started imitating him, throwing like him.

John Hiller:

Pat Dobson, he made nicknames for everybody on the Tigers. Actually, he named everybody in baseball. He'd spend a half hour with you and he'd have a name, and that was it. He named the whole team. He went to the Yankees and named everybody, went to Baltimore and named everybody.

Don Wert, they called him "Coyote"—Dobson named him. McAuliffe was "Mad Dog." Cash, "Stormin' Norman"—I think he had that before. Ray Oyler was "Oil Can Harry."

And Don McMahon was a little different, he was a veteran. He was funny—we called him "Nanook of the North." He wore gloves! He got cold all the time, maybe he was a California kid or something, I don't know. But he was the old-timer in the bullpen, and the rest of us were very young.

Wayne Comer was "Snaggletooth." "Bushhog." Those were his nicknames, two of them. Dobson nicknamed him Bushhog because he was always scrubby-looking. He looked like he'd come from the hills of Virginia—which is where he comes from! Shenandoah. He was my locker mate in Duluth, and we both got voted "Dirtiest Lockers in Baseball."

And Dobson, him and Price came up with "Ratso" for me. Before that, it was just silly old "Canuck." We were watching *Midnight Cowboy* in New York, in… it had to be '68, I guess. And as soon as Dustin Hoffman came limping across the screen… I'd twisted my ankle, and I had a reputation for maybe being a little… colorful, or a little different. So right away, both of them said, "There's Ratso—there's Hiller!" So that stuck, all the way from then. I was hoping that the limp had more to do with it, but it probably was my lifestyle had more to do with it than anything else. Not a whole lot of scruples back then…

Fred Lasher:

They called me "Mr. Ed"—Gates Brown came up with that one, I think. I think he thought I looked like Mr. Ed, the horse. It was probably '68, because I came up in '67, but it was late in the season. It was August ninth I think. Baltimore, that was the first team I pitched against. Quite a bit different than the minor leagues—fifty thousand people in the stands, yelling.

Dobson was the one who used to give out the nicknames. Kind of gave everybody a nickname.

Jim Price:

We had nicknames for everybody, you know. I was "Big Guy." Larry Sherry gave me that name in '67. Seeing the national anthem, we're down in the bullpen—it gets boring down there at times. So I said, "Guys, let's have a glee club, let's sing the national anthem." So we got them all together, and I'm directing them! And so Larry said, "You know what, you *are* the Big Guy."

John Hiller:

And then Denny McLain, we called the "Dolphin"—that was his nickname. That's what I called him, even when he called the other day.

You know, he wasn't really a good card player. Sorry Denny, but you weren't!

Jon Warden:

Denny, they called him "Dolphin," he was such a fish for cards. We played the hell out of cards, we played poker all the time. Gates and Willie and I, Matchick, we always played. Hiller, Dobson. We were always into card games. Cash'd play once in a while, we'd get Denny in there once in a while. And we played big money, we'd have a couple hundred bucks in the pot.

Fred Lasher:

Pat Dobson liked to play gin, he was a big gin player. They probably played chess, too. We never played in the clubhouse, but we played a lot of poker on the road. Get our meal money and go meet in Gates's room and Gates would be ordering up some ribs! Greasy fingers, dealing cards. Oh, shit, it's funny.

John Hiller:

We played a lot of poker. I remember one night, Jim Northrup got so mad, he had a big piece of cherry pie in Baltimore, and he threw it at somebody and it hit the wall. The next day we get up, and they're in there painting the wall. I mean, they fixed it up that quickly. Jim, you didn't want to beat him, because he'd put his chair up against the door and not let you leave, until he won his money back. So you didn't really want to stay and play poker with him, because if you won, he wasn't gonna pay. I mean, he'd pay, but he wasn't gonna let you leave!

Jon Warden:

We're playing poker one night in DC, we got rained out. Willie orders food—we got ribs, chicken, lot of beer. And so we're playing cards, we're going to play through the night. And McLain comes down to play. He's got a pocket full of money, and he's got on this Japanese smoking jacket, it's got like black and white stuff on the inside, with red, this sort of velour type thing, you know. He's sitting there, and we'd come around to him and he was going to call the bet. And he wouldn't put his money out in front of him, he'd just reach in and pull out another twenty. But, it got to be where he was light, which meant he couldn't match the pot, so he would pull money out to his light, from the pot. He'd said, "I don't have any money, I'm twenty dollars light. Then it was sixty, then forty, and so on." And then, we played High/Low. Split the pot: high hand, low hand.

So let's say it was you and me, and we split the pot. Well, you get whatever I was light—that's your money, because I was pulling that out of the pot. So, Northrup and McLain end up splitting the pot. Well, we played on the bed—we'd have chairs, and other guys might be on their knees. And so when they declared, and Denny won high and

Northrup won low, Denny took his arm and pulled his lights back in front of him. And Northrup goes, "Hey, Dolphin, don't you be taking my money, I get your lights." He goes, "I wasn't light!" He said, "The hell you weren't, you asshole!" He jumps up, takes that jacket, and rips it off McLain's back. And all shit broke out. I mean, there comes a fight. Here I am, a freakin' rookie. Matchick and me, Gates, Willie…

John Hiller:

All I know is that somebody accused somebody of not playing fairly, and then Gates Brown jumped in and says, "You can do what you want to that man when the season's over, but *no*—he's gonna win us a pennant, so lay off." And then the n-word came out, and then Gates stood up, and I put my arms around Gates, and you know, pick the biggest pine tree here in the yard, and that was like me with my arms around him! And he turned around, he was all teeth, and he looked at me, and he says, "Johnny, what are you doing?" And I says, "I don't know what I'm doing!"

Jon Warden:

Willie and Gates broke the fight up, they said, "Man, leave that man alone," talking about McLain. "That man's gonna win the World Series for us—we're gonna win the pennant, the World Series. Don't touch that guy!" And the money's all over the floor, hell, nobody knew how much was in the pot. That was a big night. Midseason, we were in Washington, DC. That jacket was out of the picture, that jacket was history. Northrup tore that thing right off of him. Northrup was a mean son of a bitch, he was tough. He was moody, very moody. And a *great* player. As a player, great player, but very streaky. You know, he could carry you for a month, and then couldn't hit that lamp if I threw it at him.

Willie Horton:

Northrup told Denny, "You've been hiding behind Jim Campbell all these years—I'm about to come and getcha." I remember McLain had that smoking jacket on… he said, "Well, do what you got to do, boy." Northrup hit him and money went everywhere—I picked some money off the floor! And then even Ray Oyler got up, he was up there, looking at Gates—Gates had his hand on his head, and Ray's swinging and swinging! He saw all the scrapping going on, got up to throw a swing and Gates is just holding his hand on his head.

And Gates, he became a bodyguard—Denny hired him. Gates said, "Hell, I made more money being a bodyguard than making a salary!" Because Northrup told Denny, "Anywhere I catch you, down in the lobby, in the elevator, in the lobby, I'm gonna deck you—I don't care where it's gonna be." So McLain told Gates he's got to sign a contract, become his bodyguard. And so he paid him! One day, McLain was getting ready to leave his room, Gates said, "I told you I'd be there in a minute—now just keep your ass there!"

John Hiller:

I'll tell you what, though, we didn't have hardly any of those instances at all. And I didn't go to bed—we'd be playing poker, or in a bar drinking someplace. We played a lot of cards, it was always the same—Warden, Dobson, myself, Willie played sometimes, Gates liked to play, Denny sometimes, Northrup most of the time. And we just played a little poker, and no fights in the clubhouse.

You don't fight when you're winning.

When you're winning everybody's happy, and everybody gets along, you know—everybody that wins a pennant has the greatest bunch of guys there ever is, right?

Willie Horton:

We had a special bond of guys. We were all fortunate, we all came up within one or two or three years apart, playing together down in Tiger

Town. The city loves us because we all came up together, almost. We all came from Tiger Town. And many of us from Detroit and Michigan. Freehan, myself, Stanley, Northrup. And Dennis Ribant, Lenny Green, they were from Michigan, too.[25]

Don Wert:

We always had a close-knit ballclub, wives, everybody. The children grew up together.

Dick Tracewski:

Primarily, that was a homegrown team. Gates, Willie, Mickey, Northrup, Kaline. McAuliffe, Oyler, Werty, Freehan. Cash came from the White Sox. Price came from Pittsburgh. I came from Los Angeles. Lasher came up through the organization. McMahon came from the Braves. Dobson came up, Hiller came up. Earl Wilson came from Boston. But primarily, it was a homegrown team, which is probably the case in most good teams.

Denny McLain:

I'll tell you one other thing we had. We had a much bigger personality than anybody else did in baseball. I mean, no matter how many card shows I do, people know our starting lineup. They don't the Cardinals. They don't know the Cubs. They don't know the White Sox. The bottom line is, you knew the personality, and you knew the guys on our team. There was a story with every one of them. The quietest story on the team was Don Wert, and Mickey Stanley. Neither one ever opened up their mouth. All the other guys, you ask them a question they'll go on for thirty minutes! It was just a great club to be with.

And, of course, the timing has to be right for you to get the opportunity at that age, to get to the big leagues. And with the Detroit organization, they hired a new manager, Charlie Dressen, who'd been really upset with the older guys that he had not listening to him. So Charlie went the way the Dodgers went, got all the new kids coming up out of the minor leagues, put them up there, all of a sudden you had a team! Just a shame he wasn't there to see it.

Al Kaline:

Most of the players were young, that came up together in the minor leagues—except me and a few other ones, Norm Cash. But most of the players, like Northrup, Stanley, Horton, they all played in the minor leagues, they progressed and came up together.

Jim Price:

Well Kaline skipped the minors, he went right to the show.[26] I rub it in all the time—"You didn't have the pleasure of riding buses like I did!" But the rest of the guys… they were all down there a while together. I played in the real minor leagues, no question. And I played against all them other guys. I was with Grand Forks, and they were with Duluth. By the water. I remember, it was frigid—I think it snowed in *June* up there. I'm not sure, I'm just kidding, but it was *cold*. You grew up fast.

Mickey Stanley:

You know that saying Price has, on the radio? The *"Buggy whip"*? He got that from Wayne Blackburn. Blackie. He was a hitting instructor we had in the minor leagues, just the nicest guy. Didn't have a pot to piss in, probably made ten grand a year, in the Tigers farm system. He was probably in his sixties, then, and he worked his ass off, trying to help all of us. So back in 1961, I remember, we went down to Decatur. And Blackburn had Jim and me and everybody up for batting practice early in the morning—he says, "Hey Northrup… y'know, stay back on that back foot… and *buggywhipit*!!" Northrup would be standing there, and he'd grab his belt, to hold him back, so he'd stay on his back foot, you know what I mean? And he'd go, "Take a rip… *BOOM!*" He'd bonk him on the head and knock him colder than hell! *"Buggywhipit*!!"

Jim Price:

Mickey Stanley said something to you about *"buggy whip"*? I heard that from Willie Horton! Mickey acts like I steal all that stuff, I don't steal anything, I'm disappointed in that, actually. He should listen to the games, because, well—"buggy whip," I've always said, "That's Willie's."

And the guy he said that said it, well I didn't go through the same minor leagues. I came from Pittsburgh—I didn't know Wayne Blackburn.

And then "yellowhammer" is my other one. I got that from Pat Dobson. McLain's would've been a yellowhammer. If he had it down, when it had a lot of bite, and went *down*. Yeah, his would've been a yellowhammer.

Mickey Stanley:

Yellowhammer, that's Pat Dobson. The ol' yellowhammer, curveball. That's a straight over-the-top curveball. Dobson said it, then everybody kind of picked it up. I mean, Price might not admit it, but that came up through our minor-league system. "Got yer ol' *yellahammer!*" That's a straight over-the-top curveball, it broke straight down. I mean there's sliders, and, you know, curveballs, then there's yellowhammers. That's straight over the top.

But, anyway—when we were down in the minors, I was at Duluth. Willie and I were there together. And Northrup was there also, the first year. He got sent down to Decatur, the two of us got sent down. We didn't room together there, but we roomed together in the big leagues.

And it was pretty special, because most of us were from Michigan. Freehan was from Michigan, Northrup, Horton, myself. And, they all made it ahead of me, by a year or two. My bat wouldn't let me get there at the same time that they got there! So it was pretty cool, and everybody pulled for each other. There was no animosity, and yeah we had a nice chemistry with that group of guys.

We played winter ball in Florida, instructional league together, and Northrup and I and Willie went to Puerto Rico for three winters, played winter ball—so we knew kids, wives, and families pretty darn well.

John Hiller:

I played ball in Puerto Rico, and every inning I drank a beer, as one of our sponsors. It was Corona, but it was not—it wasn't the same. They had a Corona, but it was a Puerto Rico Corona. In a can. Or I think it was Indios, that was our sponsor. Because I've still got the damn uniform downstairs. "Indios" was the name of our team. Mayaguez Indios. And it was Indios Cerveza.

And speaking of that, Willie Horton and I used to have—you know, and you do these things because of no reason. They don't help anything, they don't hurt anything. Well he had a bottle, a milk jug, like that—and it was half brandy and half honey. Now, what did it do to help? *Nothing!* But, we'd take it and put tape on it, so nobody would know what was in it. Well they knew—it was all sticky on the outside and… he goes, "You keep it in your locker, John."

So Willie might come back in, between innings, and take a slug, or I'd take a slug if I was pitching. You'd get a good sweat going, and you'd come in between innings, you'd shake it up, and take a mouthful. But why did we do it? I don't know why we did it. Habit? Maybe thought it would help—but what did it help? It didn't help anything… Did it hurt? No, it didn't hurt anything.

We just did it, that's all.

Mickey Stanley:

We got in a little scrape one time down there, in Puerto Rico… One of the other guys threw at us or something. So, everybody comes off the field, it was just a short little thing, and we went back out on the field. And on our way out to the field, the pitcher from the other team that started the thing yelled something at Willie. And here comes Willie. Charging back, and he meant business. So I was about to second base, on the way back to center field, and I saw him coming back, and I got in front of him and grabbed him by the chest—grabbed his shirt with both hands, and kind of got my weight underneath him so I could keep him from going forward. Well, he took his hands, underneath *my* hands, about waist-high, lifted me right off of the ground and started walking me across the infield. I said, "Willie—put me down!" I thought, *This is a strong man.*

And another time, he broke that finger right there, of mine—this broken finger. We were fooling around, and we were in the minor leagues, I think we were in Duluth. And we were just wrestling around, and I got my hand caught up in his shirt, and he yanked away, and my finger was in his shirt, and somehow it broke my finger! It was not a mean thing on his part. But I used to have to try him out for size once in a while—didn't work out very well! Oh, he was *tough*. But, really, he didn't have a mean bone in his body. Don't mess with him, don't make him angry—but, he kept his nose clean. If you didn't bother him, he would not bother you, ever.

Willie Horton:

Broke his finger, he had that little knot on his finger? Yeah, I carried him 'cross the field! That was over in Arecibo, Puerto Rico.

Mickey Stanley:

I *still* remember that. It was in San Juan; we weren't at home. I don't know if he broke it, or I broke it. We were screwing around, somehow we got to wrestling, and he went, you know, and it snapped.

So, that was the end of the season. I mean, that ended my season. There was only about a week left in the minor leagues. I played golf the next week, with a splint on it. And I'll tell you what, I can remember playing really hurt, like that. Because I felt lucky to be in the lineup. Even after several years. I went to spring training not knowing if I had a job. That's just insecurity a lot, on my part, but that was our job. You couldn't play one year and retire like they can now. We had my wife and the kids—and, you know, we were trying to make a living.

I think there was a DL, but, it didn't get used very often. And I think the DL might've been for longer periods of time than the 10-day thing. But, you hate to say it, just like old-timers going, "When we were kids, I walked to school ten miles!" It's not like we were tougher or braver, I think we were—maybe not as *smart*.

I know I had four wisdom teeth taken out one morning, before a game. It must've been 1969, because I was playing shortstop. And, they put me in at shortstop—you know, they ask you how you feel, you didn't say "I'm really hurtin'." I said, "I'm OK." I was sicker than a horse. End up hitting a home run off Blue Moon Odom, and I couldn't hit him normally—I couldn't get a single off him! So it was kind of a goofy deal, but, those kind of things… I can remember playing hurt, not only me, everybody did. And I'm sure the guys do today, but I think it was a little different back then, in that regard.

Dick Tracewski:

I know Stanley liked to ride motorcycles—and he turned it over one time and almost killed himself. He got beat up, and everything was all bruised up and everything. But he never missed a game. He came to the ballpark barely walking. And we all knew that had happened, but we didn't know how bad it was. Guys played. And there was no such thing as the DL, the disabled list. What!? Unless a bone was sticking out of the skin, you played.

Al Kaline:

That's another phase of the game that a lot of people don't realize—that you didn't want anyone taking your job. Injuries, you wouldn't go to the trainer's room, you didn't want anybody to get the opportunity to take your job away. So you played when you were hurt, and it's a little different now. I'm not taking anything away from the players today, there are a lot of great players, but back in those days, you didn't want anybody taking your job away. And it wasn't as friendly as it is, either. Because I remember as an eighteen year old, there were very few guys that were friendly to me—because here I was, eighteen coming out of high school, and I'm taking a guy who's thirty-one, thirty-two years old's job away from him. And he gets sent back to the minor leagues, or released.

Willie Horton:

Shit, when you're young, you don't go in the trainer's room. You don't go in the training room until about the fifth, sixth year. They'd tell you, the trainer would say, "Get on outta here."

Johnny Edwards:

You know, at that time, ballplayers often had one-year contracts—and you didn't want to come out of the lineup, or somebody might fill in for you. Like Lou Gehrig or somebody, and you never get back in the lineup. So you wanted to play. So yeah, we played with more injuries. We got a team down here in Houston now, that's got a really nice club, but they jumped off to a lead, and now if you've got a hang toenail they put you on the ten-day disabled list.

Dick Schofield:

I can remember one time when I was with Pittsburgh... Roberto Clemente. We're playing the Mets, second game of a doubleheader. He said, "Ahh I'm sick. I can't play, I can't play." A couple guys went over to him and said, "You understand you're *playing*. I don't give a shit if you're sick or not—you're *playing*." Because we were trying to win a pennant! So, he played.

Mickey Stanley:

We got days off if we were in a slump, or hurt—bad enough where you couldn't play. But I don't remember ever saying anything about a day off. And Freehan, jeez, he just caught every frickin' game, just about.

But there was a flagpole out there in center field, which I punched once and broke my hand. That was fun coming to the park, they never knew it! I thought I should've been starting a game, and I wasn't. It was a drizzly evening, we weren't taking batting practice, so went out to the warning track to run, and I come by the flagpole and—*bonng!*—broke my left hand.

Never said anything to anybody. Later in that game, I had to go in for defense, and my hand was just *killing* me. So I go out there, and then, frickin' last out of the game, fly ball hit to me. And so I kind of opened my glove up with this hand, because, I mean, I couldn't move shit, and then caught the ball. And the next day I came to the ballpark and said, "I fell down the steps today." "What steps?" "Laying on my hand."

Nobody ever knew… Bill Behm, the trainer, later, I told him. Later, I mean, after I was out of ball. I don't think I even told my wife until a long time afterwards. "Hey Ellen!" "Yeah?" "'Member when I broke my hand when I hit that flagpole?" "Yeah—you told me a year later…" "OK—if you'd have been nicer to me I would've told you sooner!"

Willie Horton:

You know, we all came up with that old Wally Pipp story—"You get out of the lineup, you might not get back in!" Remember Wally Pipp, with the Yankees? Took a rest, and never got back in there! We thought that the guys on the bench could play just as good as you could—I think that's why Norm kept having good years. Like, "Those guys can play just as well as I can, I can't get out of the lineup."[27]

So that year, it was *everybody*. It wasn't no particular guy. I hit a lot of home runs, but, you know, you had every night somebody different. See, the chemistry of your team is very important. You don't have to be a leader, to be a star. We had guys on the bench that didn't play every day, but we were all close guys. I mean, it's—*whew!*—that's a brother-hood that we had…

Dick Tracewski:

You know, every team during the summer will have at least two crises that you have to get over. And if you get over them, if you have good enough talent, you'll win. And we had a couple in '68. In fact, we had one bad one, in June or July. And I hit a home run. I hit a home run to beat the Cleveland club, and then we went on to have a winning streak. And Mayo Smith always said, "That was the big home run." It was a big homer, and it won a game. But, it didn't turn our season around, let's face it. It was one home run.

And obviously Kaline's injury was a crisis, because you can't lose a guy like that. But the guys stepped in and they did OK, you know?

Tom Matchick:

You gotta remember, the important thing was: all them wins we had to get to the World Series. I mean, how do you get to a World Series? To get to the World Series, that year, we all contributed. You know, Price hit a home run one game to win a ballgame. Dick Tracewski—I remember Dick, we were losing ninth inning against Cleveland, and wild man Sam McDowell's up pitching. He could *throw*; 6-foot-6, looking down on you. He threw two fastballs by Tracewski, I don't even think he's seen them to this day. Then he come back and he threw a changeup, and Trixie hit it in the stands! We won the game. And then Price had one, he won a game too in the ninth. And I had a couple big hits, beat Baltimore that night with a two-run homer...

Jon Warden:

Tom Matchick, in one of the biggest plays of the season, was when he came up against Moe Drabowsky in the bottom of the ninth when we're down one with a guy on base. And Tommy wasn't a home-run-hit guy, he was steady, a journeyman middle-infielder. He hits a fly ball to right field, and the Tigers had about a six-foot overhang on the upper deck. So Frank Robinson's just standing there, man, he's just patting his glove, to end the game, you know, two outs. And *boop*! Right in the overhang. Two-run homer, we win. Front row, boom. And the place went *ballistic*. I think it was 2–1, we won 3–2. And that was a *huge* win.

And then the next day, McLain's pitching. He's got the bases loaded, Boog Powell's up, nobody out. Powell hits a *pea* right back at

McLain. Catches it, throws to Matchick at second, and he throws back to first—*triple play*. And that just took the wind out of their sails.

Tom Matchick:

Oh I wish I could see that homer right on the TV now, if we could find the thing. I ran the count to 3-2, bottom of the ninth. Freehan on first. We were down, I thought it was 2–1. And Moe Drabowsky threw me a 3-2 slider. He tried to backdoor me, and I just hit it.

Jon Warden:

It's funny, I went to a golf outing up in Marion, Ohio. And this guy's real excited, he had Earl Weaver there, for this golf outing. He'd bring in one big name every year: he had Killebrew, John Havlicek one time, Jerry Lucas. Different sports, football, basketball. He said, "Hey I got Earl Weaver!"—this guy was a real nervous guy—"We got Earl Weaver coming!"

So this guy, all excited to introduce me, he goes, "Hey Earl, Jon Warden—he pitched for the '68 Tigers." And Weaver goes, "That fuckin' Matchick! That son of a bitch hit that fuckin' home run right in that overhang off of Moe Drabowsky—and I'll never forget it, that turned the whole season around." And it did, it knocked them out of the season, it knocked the wind out of their sails. Here's these two games that they could've won, and we took them *both* right away from them.

Jim Price:

The one I hit… if I remember right, it was very hot that day. I remember Bill saying in the dugout, something about how hot it is, and, "We've gotta win this—we gotta win this game." And in those days, when you were called on to pinch-hit, a guy would be in the bullpen, he'd call me down. I'd get two bat swings, and have to go up. Not like now, where they take batting practice before they go up, you know, inside. So I went up, and Wilbur Wood was pitching. I'd caught Wilbur at Triple-A, and he threw knuckleballs. And I knew catching him, you would wait for the ball—you wouldn't try to go get it. So I thought hitting-wise, I've got to do the same thing. Wait for it to break, and then hit it.

And that's what I did.

Dick Tracewski:

Of course, off the bench we always had the ace in the hole—Gates Brown. I remember one doubleheader we played, and Gates Brown got the base hit in the ninth inning in both games![28]

Willie Horton:

Gates Brown, man, this guy was one of the best pinch-hitters I'd ever seen. And he didn't believe in taking batting practice. But he could hit that ball, man. I'd be sitting there, we'd be out there all day, having struck out two times—and he'd get up, eat a bucket of chicken, and hit a home run!

Dick Tracewski:

Gates was an outstanding hitter. And people don't realize, he could really fly. We got two guys that you couldn't double up. You couldn't double Dick McAuliffe. He could hit the hardest ground ball at somebody with men on base, and he'd be safe at first. And Gates was the same way. You have a man at first and third, and you put up Gates or Dick is up there—you're gonna get that run! If they're gonna hit that ball on the ground, you can't double them, because the kind of speed they had. Gates Brown was in the middle of a lot of those comebacks. Because Mayo would never use him unless the game was on the line. When the game was on the line, you didn't want to face him. And a lot of the managers knew that he was on the bench, and it kind of shaded the way they played.

Tom Matchick:

Gates won us some games. He could wake up out of his sleep and hit line drives. He was *some* kind of hitter, line drives. They were *big* men, they weren't small. And Gates had to be 235, 240, but he could move. He could *move*.

Jon Warden:

You know, he was a stout, stocky guy, and everybody thought they could just blow it by him inside. But the guy was quick as a cat with his hands, and he'd just *turn* on that thing, and, I think he hit .467 or .487, it was something crazy. He's got the American League record.[29]

You know, in Detroit, you just say "Gates"—everybody around knows who that is.

Jim Price:

In '63 I was with Pittsburgh, they sent me down to Ponce—and I played against the Tiger team, which had Gates Brown. Poor Gates, I wish he was here to tell the story. But, he said, "I kept reading the English newspaper, and there's this *big bad Jimmie Price, best player in the minor leagues* coming down…" I was minor-league Player of the Year, of all of baseball, in '63.

He goes, "I hated you before I met you!" So lo and behold, playing down there in Puerto Rico, Gater came up to pinch-hit. Didn't say anything to me—just looked at me, gave me the bad peeps. Hit a triple. Sacrifice fly, I'm blocking the plate, he bowls me over. You know, in those days, you could block the plate. And he knocked the *heck* out of me. And I'm kind of dazed, and I woke up, and he goes, "Gater." Says that he's a fan of me. He says, "You know what, Jim Price, you're a good man." He cut my chest protector and everything. But he was out. I held on to the ball, which was pretty good. And we became best friends after that.

Big, big guy. I was probably 200 pounds. But he was *built*.

Jon Warden:

Gates would always come down to the bullpen—and see back then, you could dial nine on the bullpen phone and dial anywhere you wanted to, straight out. He's calling gals, and you know, he always had something on the line, ordering *food*. So it's like a smorgasbord. And we had binoculars, checking out the chicks in the stands. Lolich would come down sometimes with his telescope, we'd go, "OK, oh man—Section 330, upper deck, row 25!" and scope in on some gal.

So, we're down there and Gates just got two hot dogs. And he never pinch-hit before the seventh, eighth inning. Never. So, and he would come down, he'd always tease Hal Naragon—he'd go, "Hey Hal, come down and help me warm up the pitchers," in case they got two guys up at once. And Hal said, "You know Jon, he always came down but he never brought a glove, he just came down to eat and talk on the phone!"

So anyway, Gates just got these two hot dogs, they're wrapped, the phone rang—and Hal says, "Gater, they want you up, you're hitting." He said, "Man, it's the damn fifth inning—Gates don't hit before the fifth inning!" He said, "Well, Mayo called down here to get you up." So he took a hot dog, wolfed it down, and they're in the white wrapping paper, you know. He opened up his jersey and puts the other one *inside* his jersey, says, "Well I'll eat that after I hit."

So he goes up to bat, typical Gater hits a double, slides in headfirst to second, and that shit's all over him. And I forget who the umpire was, but he's going, "Stay there, Gates, stay there! You're hurt, you're bleeding!" He said, "Nah I ain't bleeding, that shit that's ketchup! But don't you say anything because Mayo'll fine me a hundred dollars if he sees that!"

So he's in safe, and he's got his arm like this, and I think they pinch-ran for him, because then he's coming off the field, and he's running like this with his hand. And back then, Ernie Harwell—everybody had transistor radios, they'd just sort of come in the middle of the '60s—and you could hear the feed, you could hear Ernie. And Ernie's like, "Looks like Gates might've hurt himself, he's sort of holding his arm up against his side." Well he's trying to cover up that ketchup! So, he gets in the dugout, and Mayo come over—"Hey, nice hit," and he looks down,

"What the hell is—?" "Uh… hot dog." And he fined Gates a hundred dollars, for having that hot dog!

Tom Matchick:

Well, they said that he stuck it in *here*. And when we were in the club-house, he had two hot dogs and he put mustard on them, he's gonna take them down the bullpen. And he put them in his back pocket. I think it was two, he just put them in a light wrapper. And they called him from the dugout: "Gates, Mayo wanted ya!" Mayo said you're pinch-hitting now, but he didn't pinch-hit until the late innings, and I think it was the seventh inning. Then he just got his helmet, forgot about that, and he hit that triple and slid into third base—and Cuccinello come over and help dust him off, and he said, "Gater… you shit yer pants!!"

Jim Price:

The reason he did was because, well he's in the locker room eating these hot dogs, and one of the coaches came back to get him. And you would've been fined if you were caught eating during the game, you know, I think even Mayo was pretty loose about that. But, he had the hot dogs, he didn't want to turn around and have the coach see him, so he put them in his jersey. The coach followed him out, he had no choice, you know? And he hit the double, and hot dogs were *everywhere*.

Mickey Stanley:

I can't see a situation where he had to walk to the plate with hot dogs in his shirt—can *you*? How can you *not* take a hot dog out of your shirt, before you walk up to the plate? In case he had to stay on base too long!? There must be *some* truth to it, but… it sounds pretty effed up, to me.

Willie Horton:

Guys like Gates made us all better. He helped me more with mental preparation than anybody in my life. Let me tell you a story about him. When we started out, he started asking me questions. And we're traveling, we might be playing the Yankees, and he'd be talking about *Chicago*. So-and-so is pitching, they're taking him out, bringing in guys. When we were playing in New York! I'd be up to bat, ground out or something, come back to the dugout, and he's talking about this or that. And he kept doing that—and I said, "Damn, what are you talking about?" And then we'd play the play the White Sox, he'd be talking about *Cleveland.* "Two outs, man on second, they change the pitcher, and you go up to bat." He kept going back and forth for about a week with this, so I told the trainer, I said, "Man, they better check the old man out, he's losing his mind!" So I found out later, he'd been getting in that mental preparation—he taught me, you don't wait until you get to the ballpark to get ready. You should know when you leave that hotel, or when you're at home, you should know everything in that bullpen, the starter, who they're gonna use when they've got three runs, two runs. You don't come the day you play the Yankees and worry about playing the *Yankees*—you should have *this* game out of the way. So you'd go out there and enjoy the fans much better, because I'd be in batting practice thinking about facing the *next* guys. Everything ahead. And it helps you get better preparation, get your mind set. He taught me that mental preparation.

And every night, he had 80 percent of the guys in his room. He was a smart man; he was very smart—he was always talking the *game*. Him and Frank Howard were about the two smartest people in this game that I've been around. Twenty-four hours a day they're talking the game. We'd stay up all night, talking—everybody used to go to Gates's room, play cards. Talk baseball, and play cards. We didn't *ever* get baseball off our minds. We had fun, but we always talked the *game*. We didn't ever just take our enjoyment time and just stay away from the game. If we'd go out to dinner, we'd be talking about something.

John Hiller:

Gates didn't like to leave the hotel, might've been a throwback to the minor leagues, you know, they had it pretty rough back then. So he'd call me some nights, two in the morning, he'd call me "Johnny." "Johnny—what are ya doin'?" I said, "Well, Gates, I'm… sorta sleeping." "Come on down, I wanna talk to you." I'd put my clothes on, went down. He roomed with Willie. And so I spent a lot of time with Gates—he was a pretty intelligent man, I call him the Old Philosopher.

Jon Warden:

Unfortunately we lost him, two years ago. I went up and spoke at the eulogy, at his funeral.

It was Willie and me, and then Jack Harbaugh—went to high school with Gates.[30] His two sons are the football coaches. So I get up there to talk, and Gates used to come up to me—we'd be on the road, because we always played cards on the road. Soon as we got in town, we'd get a poker game started. And Gates would usually lose his ass. And he'd come up and he'd go, "Hey Warden, hey hey, lemme hold a twenty." I said, "What? Hold a what—hold a twenty?" That was his term, and then Willie Horton goes, "Hey, he wants twenty dollars, he wants you to give him twenty bucks." I'm like, "Hell, I don't have—I'm a damn rookie, I'm the lowest-paid guy on the team!" But so, I gave him a twenty dollar bill. "I'll get it back to you man, I'll get it back to you." Never, *never* got it back.

So, we're at the funeral, and I told that story about Gates. I get up there and I'm talking, and I said, "Well, Gater…" told him what a great guy he was, what a great teammate, and I said, "I got something for ya—you always asked me to hold a twenty." I had a twenty-dollar bill, and so I walked around the podium, and went and stuck that twenty-dollar bill in his hand. And people were laughing and crying, it was really pretty neat.

So Jack Harbaugh gets up, he's one of the speakers, and they'd gone to school and all that. And see, Gates got in trouble after his junior year in high school. Summer of junior year, he got caught breaking and entering. So he goes to Mansfield Correctional Institution.

But Harbaugh was saying, one of their games at Crestline, Woody Hayes from Ohio State was there, Bear Bryant from Alabama, they were all coming up to watch Gates. And during the game, they've got the ball back on their own one-yard line. And Harbaugh's telling the story, he said, "See, I ran Gates like *sixteen* times in a row. And we got to their one-yard line." And so, Harbaugh goes, "At that point I just thought, I'd just take it in myself!" So he calls a snap, and he runs it in for a quarterback sneak. And Gates went off on him: "Man, I get that damn ball all the way down there, and you take it in for the touchdown... what is that!?" And I'll tell you, the people died laughing, it was funny, when he told that story. He said, "Gates, you ran it sixteen times, you take it easy, I'm gonna bring it in from here."

Oh, we died laughing...

Willie Horton:

I played, and been in baseball fifty-something years, and I wouldn't take no team over our team. The closeness we had, knowing each other, from the roots and Tiger Town up, that's something we had an advantage over most all teams.

We were there to help each other, support each other. Just like Bill Freehan told me, Gates Brown was in Denver, Colorado—they played ball in Denver together, in the minors. And I guess he messed up his money. Everybody had gone on home, and Bill goes by the neighborhood, and he sees Gates sitting there on the porch, in Denver. "How come you ain't going home?" "I messed up my money." I'll tell you the type of man he is—Bill drove him all the way to Crestline, Ohio. *Then* drove home to Florida.

That's the kind of relationship we had. And the fans can feel things like that—they're part of the whole thing.

You're more than a ballplayer, you're *part of* something.

CURT GOWDY: One more out, and Lolich and the Tigers are all even.

Cepeda's on first, two down. A pop up down the right-field line... Cash... has room—that's it! And the Tigers, have evened the Series. Lolich waiting on the mound for Cash to bring him the ball.

	1	2	3	4	5	6	7	8	9	R	H	E
Tigers	0	1	1	0	0	3	1	0	2	**8**	13	1
Cardinals	0	0	0	0	0	1	0	0	0	**1**	6	1

HOW RUNS WERE SCORED

Tigers second:	Horton homered	Tigers 1, Cardinals 0
Tigers third:	Lolich homered	Tigers 2, Cardinals 0
Tigers sixth:	Cash homered	Tigers 3, Cardinals 0
	McAuliffe singled, Horton and Northrup scored	Tigers 5, Cardinals 0
Cardinals sixth:	Cepeda homered	Tigers 5, Cardinals 1
Tigers seventh:	Northrup grounded into double play, Kaline scored	Tigers 6, Cardinals 1
Tigers ninth:	Wert walked, Kaline scored	Tigers 7, Cardinals 1
	Lolich walked, Wert scored	Tigers 8, Cardinals 1

GAME THREE

Tiger Stadium | October 5, 1968

Jim Price:

Tiger Stadium was *rocking*. I mean, let me tell you. Fifty thousand people, that's a lot of people. The fans of Detroit were great—they were outstanding.

Oh man—it was crazy. The whole Series… it was, how can I put it—there's a word—it was just… it was crazy. It was great.

Don Wert:

Just having that many people there, you know. Although we had big crowds before, but when it's filled up like that, it's a different feeling.

Jon Warden:

There were a lot of celebrities there that afternoon. Romney, the governor, was there. Bob Hope was there. The Supremes, Diana Ross was there—because Willie had that connection with the Motown group, a lot of them had tickets. We didn't see a lot of them while we were getting ready, because you just weren't out there checking everybody out, but you knew they were there. But we did see the guys throwing out the first pitch—it was Charlie Gehringer in that first game at home, throwing the first pitch.

Tim McCarver:

They were proud to have you in Detroit, they were proud that the Series was there. They were happy. When was the last time Detroit was in it? Cardinals beat them in '34, when Dean pitched an 11–0 shutout or something, removed Ducky Medwick from left field and throwing garbage on him.

But, for the most part, the Detroit fans were great to us, and go out to eat and they were happy to have us. It was very harmonious. And I think we played an exhibition game there, in '66. I don't know why we played an exhibition game, but we did. We'd been to Tiger Stadium before. It was *during* the season, it was a weird deal. May have been from spring training, but I don't think so. It was like '65 or '66, somewhere in there.

Al Kaline:

I'll never forget, as an eighteen-year-old kid, trotting into the ballpark and they wouldn't let me in. I said, "I'm the new player!" They said, "Nope." So they had to call upstairs to get me in to the stadium.

And actually, that very first time I came to Detroit—I was coming on a train from, of all places, St. Louis. Into the old train station, that was the first building I came into in Detroit.[31]

And, you know, we got our luggage—and of course, you had to get your own luggage back in those days, they wouldn't pick it for you. And then we get on the bus, and they're taking us down, dropping us off, and I said—"I don't know where I'm supposed to stay!" The secretaries didn't take care of you back in those days, you had to find your own stuff. And so Harvey Kuenn told me, "You're staying with me—one night. And then go find your own place." So that's what I did. It was about 2:30 in the morning. We came right past old Tiger Stadium, and I was sitting next to Johnny Pesky, who was my mentor. He was the guy I had to sit next to on the bench. Freddie Hutchinson, our manager, said, "You sit next to him, and he'll explain what's going on, what you're supposed to do, and so on." And so we're going past old Briggs Stadium, at the time, and he says, "That's gonna be your home, the next couple years." "God," I said, "that looks like a battleship." It hung out over the street, and you had all those enclosed ramps going up the outside...

Willie Horton:

My freshman year, in high school, I played at Tiger Stadium in the all-city game—I hit the same light tower that Reggie Jackson hit in that All-Star Game. The ball hit that light tower. And the umpire had to tell me to run, because it *scared* me. So the umpire had to tell me, I was like, "*Wow*!!" He said, "You've gotta go around the bases—you hit a home run!"

See, I was raised up about six blocks from there, in Detroit, and we used to play strikeout on the wall down around there when I was a kid. Me and my two buddies, Jake P and Johnny Mack—we were raised up in the projects. So we'd hang around and make blocks on the wall, play strikeout, and then when a delivery truck would come by, we'd get behind them and get in a dumpster, and sneak in to watch a game. But one day, we got caught. And that particular day, Cleveland was coming to play the Tigers that evening. Colavito was with Cleveland then, and Don Mossi—he had big ears, we were scared of him. I ain't *never* seen nobody with big ears like that! And he was a pitcher.

And I guess they were coming to the ballpark, getting ready for the game. So, they saw that the security guy had us, and they said to the guard, "Let us have these kids." We thought these guys were detectives, or policemen! But they said, "Let's have these kids"—and then they took us around the park, the visitors' clubhouse, they took us in there. And after that happened, we actually started working down there part-time. And then later, Colavito came over to the Tigers, that's who passed down left field to me. And we talked about that, we talk about that now. He's still living, in Pennsylvania.

And so I always tell people, I'm the only one to go to that ballgame and never paid! Slipped in as a kid, and then always as a player.

And back then, before I started with the Tigers, I used to go watch Jake Wood play, at Tiger Stadium. He was the first black player that came through the Tiger organization, twelve years after Jackie Robinson. And he's the reason I'm with the Tigers. My dad let me skip school to see him play, and made me sign with the Tigers after that.

But that one summer, I thought I was going to be signed by the Yankees, Boston, or Baltimore—because I'd been working out with them. I thought I'd maybe be leaving to sign with the Yankees, because I just received a catcher's glove a week before from Mr. Patterson, their chief scout. And I'd known Yogi Berra for a long time, he'd been helping me catch. Ever since I was about thirteen, fourteen years old, I'd go work with the Yankees—in New York! They used to fly me there, and I went and worked out with them.

But one day my dad and I were driving down Trumbull, and I asked Papa, I said, "Where are we going? Why are we going toward Tiger Stadium?" He said, "Well, that young man that you see who skipped school to see Jake Wood play? I think he's gonna stay home, to play with the Tigers." And just like that...

You never asked your dad why, you just do what you're told. So, you know, I was very fortunate that my dad put me in a position to sign with the Tigers. I've been blessed.

Dick Tracewski:

When I got to Detroit, it was a big city. I mean a *big* city. I think it was the third of fourth largest city in the country. New York, Chicago, maybe Philadelphia... and then Detroit! It was a beautiful city, and it was—employment and everything, it was all just sky high in Detroit.

But at the ballpark the clubhouses were not good, the bathrooms were not good, facilities—everything was just poor. It was the oldest ballpark, that and Fenway Park. But, in its own way, it was prettier than

Fenway Park. It had double decks, and triple decks, all the way around. Beautiful ballpark.

Tiger Stadium had pillars over, but the fans were *close*. Even when Ernie Harwell used to do play-by-play, when I would look around, I'm at home plate hitting, and Ernie Harwell is about from here to that picture away. He's up, you know, but he's close! I could almost hear him, and at times you *could* hear him. The broadcast booth was so close, it was hanging off the second deck. Right there! And that's the way it was at Tiger Stadium. It was a gorgeous place.

Mel Butsicaris:[32]

Ernie Harwell was the big voice of the Tigers, and he was quite a man. He was unbelievable. He was also a songwriter, and he wrote a lot of jingles for different companies around Detroit—and if you whistled that tune, people would still remember, "Oh that's that car company, 'Nine Mile & Mack', he wrote that song." Because they were so popular, but people didn't know he was the one that wrote them. And he was quite a character.

He would study the attendance of a game, and look to see when different organizations would buy blocks of tickets for a group outing—different churches or clubs and things like that. And he would know where these groups were sitting, so when somebody hit a foul ball into the stands, he goes, "Oh! Somebody from South End Detroit Club there!" Or, "There's a woman from Flint, Michigan, that just caught that baseball!" And so people would regularly listen to those, and he became real popular in doing that—and most of the time he was right!

Tom Matchick:

In old Tiger Stadium, you could hear your *mother* yell at you from the seats. And Ernie, he was just right up above you. Great announcer, Ernie was a great Tiger announcer. You wanna talk about a baseball mind? You could ask him a question from thirty years ago, and he just pops up an answer, just like that. He had a great baseball mind.

Tim McCarver:

We all knew, going there, that all you had to do was walk out to Tiger Stadium and look. You didn't need a reminder that it was a great hitter's park. Of course, there were the dimensions. Especially in right field, with the overhang. All you had to do was get on it, and get a fly ball to go just deep enough.

The other thing about Tiger Stadium was, the ball looked twice as big. And the reason for that is all that dark paint, that dark green paint. It was a lot darker than Busch, a lot darker than any stadium in the National League that I can remember. The backdrop was just, I mean, you picked up the ball so well. There was nothing anybody wore that could've interfered with the sight of the ball at Tiger Stadium. We even mentioned, "Man, if we we'd have hit there all our careers, we'd have been much more damaging as hitters." Because it was a ballpark *made* to hit.

Orlando Cepeda:

The background was great—the background there was all *green*.

Denny McLain:

Everything was green. *Dark* green. Dark, dark green. It was always called one of the great hitter parks of all time.

Dick Tracewski:

It was a crackerbox as far as home runs were concerned. The balls to right field would *fly* outta there. And on certain days, they'd really fly out of there.

Ray Washburn:

Well, what I remember about Game Three, of course, the first game in Tiger Stadium after opening in Busch Stadium, was that Kaline hit a two-run homer off me. I had two strikes on him, and then I left a pitch up…

CURT GOWDY: Al Kaline the batter… one of the finest ball-players in the history of this organization.

Two-and-two…. *there's* a long drive to left, that one is *gone!* A home run for Kaline!

	1	2	3	4	5	6	7	8	9	R	H	E
Cardinals	0	0	0							0	1	0
Tigers	0	0	2							2	2	0

Al Kaline:

I remember that. He hung me a breaking ball, and I hit it out. I don't remember a lot, but I remember *that* one. He obviously made a mistake, and I took advantage of it. It was a hanging breaking ball. Upper deck, left field. In fact, McCarver said later that they should've been pitching me *inside*. Whenever I see him at the Hall of Fame. "Because," he says, "you could tell with your approach to the plate that you were looking for a ball out over the plate." And they still kept pitching me out over the plate. They should've been coming inside, with fastballs. Not with breaking balls, unless it was a left-hander maybe.

Tom Matchick:

You know, Al Kaline said: "Always keep your hands back—look for the fastball all the time, and hit the breaking ball off the fastball. As long as your hands are back, you can hit it." That's how Al, that's the way he hit.

Mickey Stanley:

Kaline was a smart hitter, I should've listened to him. Every once in a while, he'd say something. I should've pulled more information out of him. I know Kaline guessed a lot. Which was smart, what the hitters do now. I was… not very smart.

I didn't guess very much. I always looked at the fastball and tried to adjust. Well, you're always looking for the spin… and good hitters will guess. But I'd look for the fastball, and they'd throw me a breaking ball and I'd be out in front and hit a ground ball to short.

Al Kaline:

Oh, I would anticipate *a lot*. In fact, Ted Williams—I used to talk to Ted Williams a lot, and one time I asked Ted, "Do you ever guess?" "I never *guess*, I *anticipate*!" So you can say, is that guessing or not? But in his words, it's anticipating.

So yeah, I would do that. And of course, every pitcher's different. The good pitchers are going to hit their spots a lot better than the not-so-good pitchers, the young guys. So that was always my way of thinking, that especially if there were men in scoring position, they were definitely going to pitch to my weakness. So yeah, I anticipated. A lot. And I guess you could say that's guessing, too. I'd guess, and anticipate, and of course with two strikes you just look for the ball.

Tim McCarver:

Every hitter guesses, to some degree, depending on particular styles. Some guys look definitely inside, or definitely away, or something like that—that's why it's a very difficult skill. *Toughest job in sports*, Ted Williams said. I don't know—there are a lot of tough jobs in a lot of different sports, but hitting is certainly among them. Top three or four.

But, when Ray Washburn threw that curveball to Al Kaline, and he hit a home run, Bob Gibson and I had an argument, as a matter of fact. I came in to the dugout, and he said, "Tim, you've read the scouting report…" And I said, "Yeah, I have. No shit!" And he said,

"Well, throwing Kaline a curveball?" I said, "Bob…" He says, "You know better than *that.*" I said, "You know, because the guy's an off-speed hitter, does that mean you *never* throw him an off-speed pitch? That's nonsense! You know that. You never have to worry about that, because all your stuff's *hard.*"

We had an argument, in the dugout. And that was common for that team, we had arguments all the time. But we got along. We got along beautifully, we loved each other. But doesn't mean you can't—a lot of guys who love one another have arguments.

Ray Washburn:

I shouldn't have thrown a breaking ball! I know I've heard that before, that he was a breaking-ball hitter. And probably the reason I had, well my success was the breaking ball all year, but I thought I could've gotten the call on the pitch before, and didn't. It was a borderline call. But with two strikes, I came back with that curveball. Maybe hindsight is always easier, right, you don't ever make any mistakes.

But I did, and that's what happened. It's easy to second-guess, and of course you read about it all the time in the paper. And plus, Kaline did hit pitches other than curveballs. He wasn't a lifetime .300 hitter for nothing. The good hitters, you can't just pitch them one way and get him out get him out get him out. You had to make good pitches, and you couldn't pitch them one way all the time—they were too good. You've got to try to stay ahead of him, get him out one time, and maybe they're looking for that and you give them something else.

The secret to pitching is all location and it's all movement on the ball. Being able to throw three different pitches at any point in the pitch count. But with Kaline, the location maybe wasn't so bad, but it was that he was more of an off-speed hitter, and I gave him that curveball.

Willie Horton:

There's certain people that are *leaders*. And Al Kaline was a quiet leader. He was just quiet! You know, that's just the way it is! I think me and Al talk more now than we ever talked then, and we played all them years together! I think he came up being shy—just think about it, he came up out of high school, to the big leagues. By the law, he couldn't hang with the guys till he was twenty-one. Well, you learn to be in that shadow by himself all the time, so I think it just became part of him. You know, quiet, shy! He was more of a loner. Just think about it, all them years he couldn't hang out with them, he couldn't go out! And so, I guess that's why they called him the "Line"… because he could walk past you too—with his *cleats* on, he walked so soft!

Al Kaline:

You know, I've been here since—God, I've been with the ballclub since 1953…

And back then, before I signed with the Tigers, there were three teams after me to be a bonus player. And two of them offered me a lot more money than Detroit. But my dad had gotten really friendly with Ed Katalinas, who was a scout in Baltimore and Pennsylvania. He got very close, and my dad promised him that he would get the last chance to talk to me, when I graduated. So anyhow, the other teams offered me money, and my dad said, "You're going to Detroit." And I said, "Dad—they offered me a lot more money, and *you're* gonna get it, you and Mom are gonna get it." He says, "Don't worry about us—you take care of yourself. You don't want to sit on the bench for two years. You want to *play*. Detroit's in last place, and you might get a chance to play." And he says, "Don't worry about us, we're fine—all you want is the opportunity to play." So that's why I signed with Detroit. I got a $15,000 bonus, which was *a lot* of money back in those days.

When we sat with the scout in our kitchen, before I signed, my dad asked Ed Katalinas, that scout, "Who was your best minor-league player, and what did he hit?" And back in that day, Bill Tuttle was the minor-league player in Buffalo, our Triple-A ballclub. And my dad asked, "Well what did he hit?" And I don't remember, he said .280 something. And he said, "My son could hit *that!*" I said, "Dad, wait a minute, you're talking about the big leagues now!" So he wanted to know, which outfielder he thought the Tigers were going to bring up. And, again, he was wiser than any man I ever knew. As far as me, anyhow.

A lot of people in Baltimore always said, "How come you didn't sign with the Orioles?" I said, "Well, they were the St. Louis Browns!" And it was one year later that they made that move, to Baltimore.

I was a guy that put all my efforts into being a baseball player—and I wasn't a good student. But back at that time, nobody went to college, you had to get a job. My dad worked in a factory, and I'd rather have been a baseball player than work in a factory, and that's why I put all my efforts into playing baseball. All summer long. And where I really learned how to play baseball at a high level was semi-pro. I played three years of semi-pro, and I was fifteen years old playing against former guys that had been away—got signed, then got released, but at least they were good enough to get signed. And that's where I really learned how to play. And so I always tried to play above my age. I wanted the competition to see how I would fare against older, bigger, stronger, more experienced players. That was my background. And of course, I was born right in downtown Baltimore, less than a mile from the stadium, and we didn't have any baseball fields close by, so it was my father and three or four uncles that had to drive me every place I had to go to play. And had it not been for them, there's no way I could've gone and played on teams, because I couldn't get there. So they took their time and effort to get me out of school, or during the summer, after their work, to take me the ballpark.

But it worked out great for me, because it worked out exactly as my father had predicted, that I got a chance to play at a very early age, and fortunately I was able to hold my head up a little bit and get the experience I needed. And, of course, when I was twenty, I led the league.[33]

Had I not had the opportunity, would I have ever been here? And thank God to my father, for pushing me to Detroit—it all worked out.

Ray Washburn:

For the Series, the Tigers of course had a great lineup: Norm Cash, and Freehan, Kaline, McAuliffe, Willie Horton. They had a balance of left-handers and right-handers. I knew Kaline was good, and Cash, and of course McAuliffe wasn't an easy strikeout—he'd put the ball in play somewhere.

And like we did at the start of every Series, on the Cardinals we'd go over all the hitters. How you're going to pitch them, and how you're going to play defensively. And if I was pitching, I almost always wanted the shortstop towards second. Flood shaded toward right-center, Brock off the line. But I don't understand all the overshifting today... if you do that, you've got to pitch a hitter a certain way. They're overshifted sometimes so much, there ought to be another .400 hitter. All that he's got to do is drop the ball the opposite way, and it's a hit every time. But they seem to keep trying to hit it through their shift. If you're a left-handed hitter, you could *walk* to first base—you wouldn't have to run hard!

Julián Javier:

We got the shifts before the game—to move to the left, or move to the right. Then, we go by the catcher's signs, too. If they throw a breaking pitch, we move a little bit. Fastball, we move a little bit. Sometimes Maxvill would take the sign, and give it to me at second base.

That's why we move, for a right-hander, you know. Some guys, like a Dick Groat, he hit more balls to right field, so you had to move a little bit to the right. And with Clemente, too. I played Clemente like a left-handed hitter. Clemente would hit a ball so hard he could hit it between you, like a left-handed hitter. So that's why we'd have the meeting before a series, and the World Series, of course. For guys like Kaline, we'd go by the book—if he hits it a little that way or this way.

If it's a fastball, you move a little bit to the left.

Johnny Edwards:

We had received a book on all their hitters, from our scouts that were watching them before the Series started. So we had an idea whether they liked the ball up or liked the ball away or down, and so we had a pretty good idea of how we wanted to pitch them. But then, we had to see during the game whether our pitchers had that control, and what pitches they had working for them.

Tim McCarver:

We went over all the reports, before the Series. But, you know, as Gene Mauch used to say, "You can't have paralysis through analysis." You've got to, you know, let it sink in, have an idea, and then let your feel for the game work. You can't get locked into scouting reports.

And plus, guy's changed over the years, too. I mean, guys become different hitters. So we'd go over the teams, and you cemented it in your head—but you didn't need to keep going back. That's overrated.

Tony Kubek:

My first year, when I played behind Whitey Ford, in '57, Whitey said, "Listen to the scouting reports on the off-day, but—*I'll* tell you where to play the guy." He used to turn around to me, and just with his eyes move me right or left. And one example would be Al Kaline. Early in the ballgame, Whitey might pitch inside to Kaline, maybe let him pull the ball. But late in the ballgame, he pitched him away. Made him hit into the big part of the ballpark. Detroit was 440 in center field, Yankee Stadium was 461 back then, and deep in the alleys. So I could be playing in the hole for a Kaline the first time he came up, and then playing him up the middle. And Whitey would do that, he would do it with his eyes. You can do that one or two games, but what's going to happen? Al Kaline's going to figure that out. And Whitey's going to say, "Yeah I'm not gonna do the same thing *this* time." That's what makes a great hitter and a great pitcher, the ability to adjust to the situation. That's part of understanding how to play the game.

Ray Washburn:

We'd have the team meeting with the coaches, the pitching coach, and the staff would go over hitters with the pitchers—but we didn't spend hours on it. No film. Of course you knew who the hitters were, and we'd played them in spring training.

McAuliffe, we saw he had a short little open stance, high quick chop-type swing, contact hitter, not going to strike out a whole lot. Hard to double him off on a double play.

Stanley, as a hitter, I don't remember many significant differences than the other hitters. Like McAuliffe had kind of his own style. Where Stanley was more, as I recall, a standard right-handed hitter that you would see. But they said he liked to hit the first pitch—not many hitters *do*. There's always a certain amount of first-ball hitters, but most hitters, they swing at the first pitch and they're out, then they're kicking themselves till they come up again, "Why'd I swing at that first pitch?"

Well, the first play of the game, I was pitching and McAuliffe hit one back at the mound. It hit off my leg or ankle or something—I can't remember exactly, but then I remember Cepeda and myself, and then McAuliffe and then all crossing over the bag together. Those kinds of breaks come and go. They'll go against you, but we happened to get that one.

You always try to get the leadoff hitter out in the first inning. It's not always successful, but it's always important for me, keeping that leadoff hitter from getting on. But then you have games like that, I'm sure I had some too, where almost every inning the leadoff hitter's on, and then you're pitching the whole game from the stretch.

And then Cash, he had a bigger swing, he had good power. I don't know how many home runs he hit that year, but must've been close to 40.[34]

Kaline—oh, he was a *great* hitter. Won the batting title at twenty! He didn't have that kind of a weakness you could just get him out on. Fastball, curve, change, I mean... I don't know if he preferred one over the other, but he was the kind of hitter who you would just try to keep off balance if you could.

Horton, he was a free swinger, he'd take his cuts up there.

Northrup hit with some power, left-handed hitter. I don't recall much, other than was pretty much a free swinger, trying to hit with power. Other than that, I don't know if he was a specific type of hitter, trying to slap the ball the other way or anything.

Freehan would have some big hits for them. He was a big right-handed hitter, but I don't recall him being a big dead pull hitter or not, he probably more could hit the ball to right-center, left-center.

Wert—defense mostly, great glove, and remember that third base was the feature of the '64 Series, Boyer against Boyer.[35]

CURT GOWDY: Washburn really hung in there—he could've been through, a few years ago, with a bad shoulder. But he never gave up on himself, and the Cardinals never gave up on him.

Throws a lot of breaking stuff. Throws a lot of sinking fastballs to left-handers, sliders to right-handers.

Ray Washburn:

I always threw to try to extend myself in the bullpen, especially about the last five or six minutes, at game speed. I always felt I wanted to go out there ready, right from the first pitch. And I could always tell what I had.

But once the game actually starts, you're just playing another game. You get past the hype, and all those things are going on around you with the media and all the festivities that go with it. Once you're on the field and playing, you're trying to do the same things you did all season. You don't try to do anything different, or beyond anything you did before.

So I was always pretty much throwing strikes, no matter what. I would very seldom struggle with the control early in the game. But later on, I would, because the arm wasn't as strong. The ball sometimes will straighten out, or wouldn't quite have the movement on it, or the velocity, in the later innings. But we always went out with the idea that we'd throw a complete game.

Dick Schofield:

Washburn was a good pitcher. He's probably one of those kind of guys that wasn't given as much credit as he should've gotten—because he was more of a contact pitcher, you know. He wasn't like Steve Carlton or Gibson, but he was a good pitcher. He was one of our better pitchers.

Johnny Edwards:

Pitching wins pennants. You could say all you want about hitting and all that, but pitching is what comes to the forefront when you get to the end of the season. And we had *four* good starters—Gibson, Carlton, Briles, and Washburn.

Dick Tracewski:

Their choices of pitching, in my mind, were kind of questionable. The way they used their pitchers.

Here's what happened. We were—if you controlled our left-handed hitters on our club, you had a good chance at beating us. But they didn't pitch Steve Carlton. And I knew about Carlton. Carlton was this: when he was with the Cardinals, he pitched out of the bullpen. And this is what he was. He had a good fastball, and he had a twelve-to-six curveball, I mean a good one. But he never got it over that much. So he was basically a one-pitch pitcher when he was with the Cardinals. And I could visualize Schoendienst being a little bit afraid of him, you know? So, he had other guys, he had Joe Hoerner who was a sinkerballer, and so that's who he went with, that left-hander. And I always knew, I say jeez, this guy, keep him out of the game, because of his stuff.

Aside from that, their choices of pitching were kind of questionable. Washburn was a good pitcher, sliderball-sinkerball pitcher. Winner, but wasn't a shutout pitcher. Nelson Briles was a curveball-fastball pitcher. Good competitor, et cetera et cetera. But he wasn't gonna shut you out.

Ray Washburn:

In '67 and '68, with our pitching staffs... in '68 I think the whole team ERA was 2.45 or so—and so the writers had that "Year of the Pitcher" thing going. I don't remember it being called that as it was going on, but... You know, teams in the National League would roadtrip to St. Louis, go to LA and then to San Francisco, and hitters were struggling. Dodgers had the great pitching, the Giants, a lot of teams, even the Cubs.

So in '68, I had an opportunity that season and was successful early on. I got in the rotation and stayed there, 220 innings or something, and an earned run average of 2.26. Pitching late in the game, deep into the games all the time, and I remember we had a lot of games 2–1, 1–0, 3–2. It'd help to check the record, but I had quite a number of no-decisions, where I gave up two runs or less. That was kind of how we put together that whole season. And with good defense, too.

And back in '67, that's when I had the bad arm, so I was still recovering basically. I pitched some in '67, in relief in that year's Series, but I didn't start.

So in 1968, that was my first start in the World Series.

Johnny Edwards:

After we won the pennant in '68, Gaylord Perry threw a no-hitter against us the *very* next night. And I don't know where Timmy was, he was supposed to catch, but I had to catch that game. And then Washburn threw another no-hitter the *next night*. I caught that game, too, and so I was in both those no-hitters.

It was a nice bounce-back because, here we were, we win the pennant in Houston and we fly to San Francisco and then we have a party afterwards. And so, you know, we're a little bit under the weather the next night. And then Perry throws that no-hitter, and so, "Dammit—if we didn't come back and throw another one just to show 'em."

We always wanted to win, but to come back and throw a no-hitter after we'd been no-hit was icing on the cake.

But I've slept too many nights since then, you'll have to ask Ray about that...

Ray Washburn:

We were playing out at Candlestick Park, and oh it was cold! It would be cold at night... the wind would come up at night sometimes.

And so that game, I just took every hitter that came up there. And I had a good curveball that day. Of course, I walked five but I struck out eight. And I mean, you don't *think* about it—you know you haven't given up a hit, because all you have to do is look up at the scoreboard between innings. But you don't think about it much in the seventh, and then you get to the eighth and you realize you're only six outs away. And by the ninth, nobody says anything to you in the dugout or anything, between innings. And so I got Ron Hunt to ground out. But the last two hitters were Mays and McCovey! I got Mays to ground out, to Shannon, on a curveball. And McCovey, I got a ball in on him, that he pulled way out there towards the bay, but it was quite a ways foul. Then the next pitch on a breaking ball, he hit a high fly ball to center field. That was the last out.

And Perry was tough the next night. He had the sinker, and you probably never got a chance to go to Candlestick and see what it was like. But if you're a sinkerball pitcher, it's the place to pitch. The grass is about this long, thick all the time; the infield was super slow if you hit the ball on the ground. And I think in some of those games, there were only about two balls hit out of the infield. So, hitters would come back to the dugout all the time moaning and complaining, going, "Oh I hit that ball on the *nose!*"

But, I don't know if we celebrated any more than we normally do, after winning that pennant—it just happened to be the timing of it made it look more like that was happening than maybe it was. If we would've gotten no-hit earlier, I don't think anyone would've noticed!

Orlando Cepeda:

We got the pennant in Houston, on a Sunday afternoon. Then Tuesday night was Gaylord's no-hitter. It was my birthday that night. And then Wednesday afternoon was Ray's no-hitter. I played in that game, and quite a few other no-hitters. Warren Spahn, 1961? Marichal, in '63. Then Gaylord and Washburn. Four no-hitters that I was involved in, during my career.

	1	2	3	4	5	6	7	8	9	R	H	E
Cardinals	0	0	0	0						0	2	0
Tigers	0	0	2							2	2	0

CURT GOWDY: It's one out. Runners on first and second. And the runner's going! The throw to third… and they *got him* at third base!

And now Joe Schultz is arguing, so is McCarver! The Cardinals thought he had third base stolen.

Tim McCarver:

I remember that play—in the third game, early. I was thrown out at third base by Freehan, and I was *safe*. I remember that play vividly; I slid in under the tag. It was a quick tag by Don Wert, but I slid in—the throw was high. And we had been told we could run on Freehan, and I'm sure they were told they could run on me, too.

Guys didn't run that much in those days. But we were an aggressive team, on the bases. And were down 2–0 already in that game, after Kaline hit that home run off Ray Washburn.

Shannon was on at first, and I was at second, so trying to steal was important—because if Shannon gets to second, then you get two men in scoring position. A base hit scores both, that's what we were thinking.

But there are a lot of writers who continue to think that third-base coaches give baserunners the signal to steal third. Unless it's a 3-2 pitch, you're always on your own—to this day. You don't get a sign to steal, because it's all feel. And we were an aggressive baserunning team. And so you're stealing on your own, if you can get a jump, go! And Red allowed us to do that, all the time. Before the Series, he would tell us to be aggressive. He didn't have to remind us about anything like that. I knew, you know, we were versed on these guys. I mean, the scouting reports were all manual in those days.

Mickey Stanley:

I find that hard to believe, but, if he said it. I mean, I could see Schoendienst saying that to Brock and Flood, and whoever else could run on that team. Those are the only two guys that I can think of. Oh and Javier, he could run.

So, they weren't running on their own, a double steal. Because it's hard to believe that Tim McCarver—but he ran pretty good, I think, for a catcher. I think he did. But it's hard to believe everybody had the "go" sign on their own.

Tim McCarver:

That play was bang-bang, you know, but the throw was high and I thought the tag was made when I was on the bag. I slid *under* the tag. And we were always trying to go in directly, not any of these fadeaway slides or any of that stuff. It takes time, it takes longer for you to get to the bag, so going in straight was the way we were taught.

Bill Haller was the umpire, at third. Tom Haller's brother. Tom was a catcher for the Giants, and then the Dodgers, and eventually was the general manager of the White Sox.[36]

Joe Schultz and I were arguing with him—and I was fired up. But how can you *not* be fired up, in the World Series? We were both very vocal, no question about it. But we didn't touch him. And in the World Series, you'd be given a longer leash by the umpires. All the World Series, the three I played in, were like that. You're allowed to argue your case—they realize the emotions are running high, and Bill certainly realized that then.

Bill Haller:[37]

That's McCarver at second? *There he goes.* Was that argument that bad? I guess it was! Why didn't I run his ass out? In a regular season game, you know, he's gone. But this is something way bigger. You don't run him. Maybe in the regular season you say, "Hey! Shut the *fuck* up." But in the World Series…

Here you play 162 games and, for example, I call you out on strikes. I liked you as a person, I liked you as a player. And you'd said something to me, that, in the regular season I would've knocked you out of there. I would say to you, "I'm gonna tell you one time: I respect you too much, you're a great ballplayer. And if this was the regular season, I'd knock your ass out of here so fast you wouldn't know where you're at. But I'm not gonna do it, because it's not right. It hurts the team too much. But if you go crazy, now that's a different story. You will get run." The thing is, you don't wanna hurt the team, especially on that level.

My reputation was—you wouldn't fuck with me! "Don't fool with that asshole, he'll knock your ass outta there quick!" Because I grew up in an era when you were an *umpire.* Your job was to *umpire.* And if they give you too much… I'll tell you what, if you're an umpire and I'm Hubbard,[38] and I see you have a play—and in my mind, you should've run the player out there, and you *didn't?* You're in trouble. What, don't you have any *guts?*

Depending on who the player was. If you liked him, you tried to act civil. If you didn't like him, just knock his ass out of the game.

Hal Naragon:

The umpires really back in those days, they really liked the players it seemed like. Now that doesn't mean that they wouldn't throw you out of the game, but they would give you a chance to explain your side of the story, and then that's it. They were very understanding about the players, especially a young player coming up. Like today, it seems like the umpires throw the player out just like that. And I think they ought to be careful, because people pay a good price to come in and watch the players, and naturally you want to see the player if he's on the ballclub. You wouldn't want to see an Al Kaline thrown out of the game in the first or second inning, or *any* inning. A great player that you really paid to see play, just because they question a decision. They called it as they saw it, you know.

Julián Javier:

I remember that play. McCarver—looked like it was a hit-and-run there. And Schoendienst was a little slow out of the dugout, you know. He'd go out like that all the time. He's too late—Red, come back!

I was watching from home during that, what else can you do? When something happens like that, they're going to argue, nobody can go over there. Everybody stays where they are. And Schoendienst was a little late!

Jim Price:

See, that's the easiest play for a catcher. Left-handed hitter up; a throw to third base. That's the easiest throw. The hitter's over there, you don't have to worry about the hitter. Pitchout, good throw, got him. They guessed right. Good pitchout. The pitcher's the key with the pitchout. You've got to give it a chest-high throw, off the plate.

And they knew he was gonna be going. Once he got on base, he was going to try to steal, there's no question about it. We guessed right. I don't know if the sign came from the bench, but probably Bill did it on his own, because he was very smart. And we knew coming in, we had meetings coming in, that this team could run. Mayo said, "Be alert—be alert like you did all season." But we didn't need much coaching or managing, we really didn't. Great athletes, all good athletes, could play, no question. You were on your own, you knew when to take a pitch, you know, knew when to throw to the right side, we knew all those things.

And the pitchout was performed the right way—it was high, about shoulder-high. And he got a good jump, but the throw was perfect. The pitcher's throw to the catcher is the key thing. And then it was an easy throw for Bill. Got him easily.

That's what you try to do, to neutralize them—keep them off the bases. And Lou Brock... I don't know *how* many bases he stole that Series... He caused us some real trouble.

But—we did get him a few times, too.

So we took away some of the things they could do, no question.

Tony Kubek:

I think you saw the difference in the style of play, between those two teams. What you saw in the Tigers was from the Yankee tradition—the big inning kind of team, that was the style of play they played in the American League. And the National League was pretty much still kind of a stolen base league—you saw what Brock did, he stole seven bases in that Series, as I recall.

I think Earl Weaver always said—he said, "You know, I don't like to steal—I like to hit and run." Because there are two things can go wrong with a stolen base. And it happened in that World Series with the Cardinals. They were also caught stealing like five times in that Series, the Cardinals. That doesn't seem like much, but you lose a baserunner, and you lose an out. And twenty-seven outs are precious. Weaver used to say, "I want the big three-run inning." You wonder with some of the hitters like Cepeda and those guys—what *might* have happened, hypothetically, had they not been thrown out and lost an out, and lost a baserunner. There was a difference in the style of play, and I think over a seven-game Series, that may tell a story.

Dick Tracewski:

They had speed. Julián Javier could fly. Flood could run. McCarver could run, actually. And Brock, of course.

Bill Haller:

Brock? I don't remember that stuff. I could care less who's running. As an umpire, what do I care who's running? Is that the year he broke the record for number of steals?

John Hiller:

Flood and Brock, I kept saying: "Don't walk 'em." Don't walk 'em, you know. You walk 'em, they're gonna be on second base. Maybe third base.

Denny McLain:

You don't want Lou Brock going from first to third all the time. You need to get Lou Brock out. You got to bear down on those guys to keep them off the bases. Because those are the guys that'll beat ya. It's not the guy hitting the two-run homer, it's the Lou Brocks of this world that'll fuckin' beat the shit out of you. So those are the guys you've got to keep off base.

Tom Matchick:

Oh we went over everything in the clubhouse, how we were going to play them and pitch them. And keep them close. But I don't know, there wasn't much you could do with Brock—you just had to catch him at the right moment. Change the count. Because Brock when he got on base, as soon as you brought it down here, I know Brock would be, "*One thousand one, one thousand two…*" and if you were going, next time you'd bring it right to here, and he was gone on *one thousand two*. So a lot of them just tried to change their pitch *count*. You know, hold the ball just a little longer, get rid of it a little quicker. Because he would time you. And he could *run*. I mean, you couldn't stop him. Flood, too! Flood could run, too. And he was a good ballplayer, he had a couple hits against us. Javier at second base.

Hal Naragon:

With runners like that, you're always alert to them running. You can't just say, *Well, I'm gonna forget about 'em.* You let them know that you can throw over there. But you don't want them to take your thinking away from that hitter. You can't do anything, you gotta get that hitter out.

Only once, they were stealing on us, and Bill Freehan came to me, and asked me what he thought, what would I think about. And I said, "Bill, they have stolen bases in the National League for more than one year, and they're gonna steal 'em in the World Series." And I said, "You know, if we just play our game, just play *our* game, we're gonna win." And how can you stop those guys? You don't want the pitcher to worry about them, you know. If they're gonna steal, well you do your best, but hey—get that hitter out. Get the next hitter and you don't get hurt. But that's the only thing I ever talked to Freehan about.

But I'd never met Lou Brock, really. You know, in the World Series you nod to everybody but you don't talk. But anyhow, years later, he had a thought about the Jackie Robinson story. And he wanted to know how John Sain felt.[39] What was his feeling, well John wasn't here to explain, he was passed away. And they wanted to write a book. So, Lou Brock called Mrs. Sain, and he was not married to her during his career. And she said, "If you want to know anything about John Sain, I'll give you Hal Naragon's number." So he gave me a call. I said, "Well, we've gotta get together." And I said, "Where are you now?" And he said, "Well, I'm at Firestone Country Club." I said, "Well that's fine! You're not too far from where I live now." And he said, "Well, why don't you bring your wife over, and we'll have dinner together." So that's what we did. And we had a lot of conversation about, how did John feel. Now, John didn't talk too much at all about Jackie Robinson, other than he knew how he pitched to him, and he didn't make a big deal out of it.

And he said he didn't think they made a big deal when it really happened, when it actually happened. He had said it wasn't really that big of a thing, you know. "What would do you?" Brock was saying. "What would you do if he happened to hit Jackie, on the first pitch. What would it be like?" Well, it didn't happen. And Jackie Robinson said, "If I had to hit off guys like Johnny Sain, I'll be going back to the minors!" He was really a nice guy. I really enjoyed meeting him.

Julián Javier:

Earl Wilson, he pitched a few innings in that game, no? He started the game, but we got him out in the third or fourth. I remember Hiller coming in, the left-hander.

Hal Naragon:

You always think you're gonna go nine innings. But, you don't know, so you find out what pitchers you think might—you'd say to Joe Sparma or Pat Dobson, "Can you be ready?" We always had 'em ready, always thinking ahead of time. Even though we didn't get the signal from Mayo, I knew who would be next, and maybe I'd say, "Hey, maybe you better get out and make a few tosses." So you don't have to hurry to get warmed up, see. And that was a nice way to do it, and a nice way they let me do that.

Ray Washburn:

When I was playing semi-pro ball, Earl Wilson and I went to the NBC semi-pro World Series, back in Wichita. They were with the San Diego Marines, I think, and Floyd Robinson was on that team as well. So I'm sure we talked, at the World Series. Probably just about the fact that we'd faced each other, whether he remembered or not. Because that was back almost ten years earlier.

Tom Matchick:

Earl Wilson, he could hit the ball out of the stadium, he could *mash*. He could hit.[40]

Hal Naragon:

Too bad you couldn't meet Earl, oh boy. He was a classy guy. In 1968, he hit seven home runs! That's pretty good.

And in spring training, in 1968, in Tampa I think it was, I remember this. Earl had a great year in '67, and so in spring training, you know, the pitchers they're just loosening their arms, but they don't want to be knocked around too much. So Earl goes out the first inning and they get about three runs off of him and he didn't like it. Earl was a very cool guy, you know, but he came in and he didn't like it—and he let everybody know that. They got three runs, and he didn't like it. And John is sitting there and never says a word, see, never says a word to Earl. So they go back out the second inning, and they get about *five* runs off of him. And Earl comes in and sits down beside John, and he's very, very quiet. And John—he's from Arkansas, you know—he says, "Earl... you know... that first inning wasn't so bad after all!" And Earl busts out laughing.

John wasn't much of a talker that way, you know. John was more on the quiet side, and he wouldn't rush at a pitcher or criticize him—he wanted always something that was positive. And he, to this day, Earl called me years later, and wanted to know that story again, you know. And so we of course had a good laugh. And he wrote us a note and thanked us for helping him in the major leagues.

CURT GOWDY: Here comes McCarver now... Tigers ahead two to one.

There's a drive, deep to right... and *that* one is sailing into the seats...

	1	2	3	4	5	6	7	8	9	R	H	E
Cardinals	0	0	0	0	4					4	5	0
Tigers	0	0	2	0						2	2	0

Tim McCarver:

That home run I hit was in the upper deck. I'm not too sure how deep, but it was certainly deep *enough*. And I hit it pretty well—I was so exuberant. But I didn't have any kind of home-run trot. I figured if I ran fast enough around the bases, they wouldn't know who hit it.

It was a breaking ball, a curveball, from Pat Dobson. About *that* high off the ground, but I was a good breaking-ball hitter. I could handle breaking balls. They didn't throw me many breaking balls, in the National League. And I think catchers have a slight advantage in reading pitches, because he sees so many. And when you see that many, you are certainly ready to adapt. You know, the curveball is not a strange pitch to me—I've seen it. I've seen it come from the likes of Gibson, Washburn, Carlton from the left side. So I wouldn't say it's *easy,* but it's a slight edge to a catcher, because of seeing that many pitches. You know, you see one hundred or more thrown from *your* pitcher, and then you see upwards of twenty-five to thirty from the opposing pitchers, depending on how many balls you foul off. So that's a lot of pitches. And you see the development of breaking balls, fastballs, balls in tight and stuff like that.

The thing about hitting is waiting, and quick hands. Because you don't want to commit too early. If you don't commit too early, you get a read on the pitches. So if you wait, a curveball has a tendency, because it's a slower pitch, to get you out in front. If you're out in front, you're hitting off your front foot. Unless you're Musial, who was arguably the greatest low-ball hitter in the history of the game. You can't be any better than him. And he would commit, but his hands were back. So if you commit with the stride, and your hands are still back, you still have your power. If, on the other hand, the curveball comes, and your body's out in front, and your hands go forward, you have nothing left with which to hit. Your power is gone. The pitcher, in effect, has robbed you of your power. So, that's the technical explanation of how to hit a curveball. The hands have to be back. You can be fooled on the stride, but I wasn't on that particular pitch. I just reacted. So, you leave yourself with the confidence of knowing your hands will react. And that's what extra hitting takes, extra, extra, and you see the ball, you see the ball. And I was prepared to hit in that Series.

But, you know, when I first came up, they could knock the bat out of my hands, I was not a strong hitter. And George Crowe[41] changed my style of hitting around, he made me instead of an open stance, where I would swing my leg around and close, he closed it up. He said, "That's too much movement, it's too much wasted movement. If you're closed anyway, you can hit against that front side, and hit against that stiff right leg." For a left-hander. In other words, when you're swinging, your leg is stiff. If you're like *this,* your leg is bent—you don't have a chance to hit again, there's too much to do. And that was his point. He said, "Why not be prepared, and close your stance to begin with, instead of having it open like that?" And it made all the sense in the world to me.

So, you know, he may have saved my career at a very young age. Because they were knocking the bat out of my hand. I mean, I couldn't handle that inside pitch. Then, I became an inside hitter, I worked on it so much. And I remember Chuck Hiller—I didn't get along with him—but he was Whitey Herzog's guy, ultimately. As a player with the Giants, he said, "You've really worked on that inside pitch, huh?" And I said, "I don't know…" I didn't want to tell him anything, you know. "Think whatever you want to, and you're a student of the game and all that, but don't be asking me any questions." Guys didn't talk to one another in those days anyway. I didn't like Hiller. I didn't like him because of that. You know, he was trying to get too much information out of me.

But anyway, I became a predominantly pull hitter. Particularly from the middle to the latter part of my career. And for the most part, I didn't strike out a lot, and made contact—I walked more than I struck out. You don't see that today. Almost *nobody* does that.[42]

I was a contact hitter, I didn't strike out very often, 340 times maybe in my career. So, the curse for me was I made *too much* contact. Meaning, that I put the ball in play too frequently. I would foul out on a ball like that, I'd put it in play. I didn't swing through many pitches. But how do you correct that, come out and try to swing through balls? You can't do that—it's just a nuance of your hitting style.

But with two strikes like I had there, I wouldn't choke up.

I don't believe in that. Because, you lose your place on the bat. Everybody has a place on the bat. They say Joey Votto chokes up, but Joey Votto chokes up on the *first pitch*. He doesn't wait until two strikes—he has the same approach with that much bat showing. He does that from the beginning. Because otherwise you lose your place on the bat.

Why would you choke up on the *bat?* It's not necessary. To choke up on your *approach* is what you're looking for. It's a misnomer, really. It's the feel of the bat, in the crook of the hands. It's not the palm. Most laymen would pick up a bat, and the first thing they'd do is they'd grab it right *here,* and that's inappropriate. It's right *here.* The fingers are the directors of the swing, if you will, the Toscanini, if you're a good hitter. And some dog musician, if you're a bad hitter. Get it?

So that home run was a big deal. That ball was down and in, and I used to kid Dobber about it, all the time. Not ruthlessly or anything, we were real close friends. He was a good pitcher. And in '71, he was one of the four who won twenty for Baltimore.

But I knew it was a big hit.

Ray Washburn:

In the sixth or seventh inning of that game, I came out and Joe Hoerner came in for me from the bullpen. And he really did the job at shutting down the Tigers the rest of the way. He was *tough*. He'd come in, and with that low sidearm delivery from the left side, and with a good sinker—and he'd just challenge hitter after hitter. But mainly his thing was getting guys to hit the ball on the ground a lot.

I probably wasn't totally happy with myself, coming out, but knowing we had the lead, and watching Hoerner the rest of the game… he *really* came through. So I don't know that I was beating myself up, but just knew that I didn't have the kind of control that I sometimes did at other times. Then we got a nice cushion and all that, but you never know until the last out. Things happen.

But Hoerner shut them down, and we went on to win. We could've lost that game, and if we did, the Series might've been over much earlier.

Jim Price

Hoerner was a crafty left-hander; he'd been around a long time. He came in and held us.

Dick Tracewski:

Joe Hoerner was a sinkerballer, and so that's who he went with, that left-hander. And I always knew, I say jeez, this guy, keep him out of the game, because of his stuff.

GEORGE KELL: Cepeda's the batter, with runners at second and third.

And there's a *long* belt to left field, this one is well hit… And *another* three-run homer, for the Cardinals.

	1	2	3	4	5	6	7	8	9	R	H	E
Cardinals	0	0	0	0	4	0	3			7	9	0
Tigers	0	0	2	0	1	0				3	3	0

Orlando Cepeda:

I hit it well. High fastball, you know—I hit it so hard. Line drive. We felt like maybe we had the Series won at that point. In the dugout, we were happy, you know, because we thought we had it. "We got it, we got it." Because then were up, 7–3.

Julián Javier:

Cepeda, we called him "Bolillo"—*bolillo* is like the knee, you know? Comes from *la rodilla*, the knee. Sometimes when I called him like that, he got a little mad. I said, "You're my friend—I can call you anything I want!" Real good friend. We're supposed to get together in Puerto Rico sometime. Someplace on the island.

Orlando Cepeda:

They called me "Perucho." And then "Peruchin" came later, now they call me Peruchin. And "Charlie"—they called me Charlie. You know who Charlie was? Charlie was a guy, in '58, we went to Portland, Oregon, to play an exhibition game against the Portland Triple-A team. And so when we got to the hotel, there was a black guy with a straw hat named Charlie. Looking for *me*! He liked my name. And so he came with me to the ballpark, and I stayed around with him, and then I left. So the trainer for the Giants, Frank Bowman, was there with me and Charlie. So he called me "Charlie." So then I went to St. Louis, and Charlie was my nickname there, too. They called me Charlie. They still call me Charlie today! "Hey Charlie—where's Charlie?" Bob called me Charlie, Lou Brock called me Charlie. Tim McCarver called me Charlie, Roger Maris called me Charlie. The whole team called me that—they still do today! McCarver said, "Hey Charlie, how ya doing?" He called me today.

And "Bolillo," too. They called me in Puerto Rico, "Bolillo"—nickname. Hard to explain, hard to translate. But they called me Bolillo, friends called me that.

And with the Giants, they called me "Cha-Cha." It was Johnny Antonelli—remember him, the pitcher? Because I was playing Latin music, like, "Chee chee *chee...* cha cha *cha,* cha cha *cha,* cha cha *cha!*" I played drums, you know. So he called me Cha-Cha.

I always played my music—jazz music and Puerto Rican music, both. I was the only one who listened to jazz. Because I *loved* jazz, and I played the music. So I played that a little bit for the team. I knew all those guys. I have a picture with Cannonball, with Coltrane, me and Miles, Sonny Rollins. And I loved Cuban music. But Shannon, McCarver... they all liked hillbilly music! Memphis music. But, you know, Tim McCarver got me on José Feliciano—"Light My Fire" and all those hits by José Feliciano. He's a good friend of mine.

My teammates, they didn't care too much about my music, I used to go out to shows on my own. And the musicians used to come to the game—Miles Davis used to come. They used to come a lot. And Dizzy Gillespie. Modern Jazz Quartet. They're all dead now, they're all gone. I would go to the clubs, they'd see me, they'd come down to say hi, and then when they'd come to the ballgame I'd see them.

And when I got traded from the Giants, I was kind of sad because... We got there on a Friday night, in St. Louis. And it was rumored that I might be going to St. Louis. And me and Herman Franks, manager of the Giants, were having problems—because he accused me of there being nothing wrong with my knee. He said I was faking, I didn't want to play, and so that's why they wanted to trade me. And so Friday night, when we got into St. Louis, there was a rumor in the newspaper that Orlando's going to the Cardinals. So the team doctor from the Cardinals, Dr. Middleman, checked my knee. I gave him the *good* knee. My left knee. So he says, "It's perfect—get him! It's perfect, he's in great shape." So the next day, they made the trade.

And I was in *great* shape, maybe the best shape of my career. Because I worked hard during the winter, to get my knee in shape. I used a lead shoe to recover, a 40-pound shoe. I used to carry it with me, so I can build those muscles. You'd go *here,* and *here.* If you do it *here,* that would ruin your knee—keep your leg straight, and build those muscles. It was a shoe, 40 pounds. And so I was in *great* shape. But Herman Franks, he had his mind already made up—that they were going to trade me. Because they had McCovey. Which, you know, I can't blame them. But I was in great shape.

And Red Schoendienst told me when were together this year, in May, that Bing Devine, he didn't want to make the trade—he didn't want me. Bob Howsam was the GM. And Bing Devine was the assistant to him. He didn't want to get me. But Musial said, "Let's get Orlando." Musial said the last word—he told Gussie Busch. Schoendienst wanted me, and Red and Musial told the owner, "Let's get Orlando." And they made the trade. That's what Red told me, in May.

I was sad, because I didn't want to leave the Giants, you know? I came here in '58, I'd just bought a house here, and things were going good for me here. And so I was sad. I cried like a baby when they told me that. But right away, they made me feel welcome. I remember McCarver saw me crying and stuff, he said, "Forget the Giants—you're here, right now!" Right from that moment, they made me feel welcome. Gibson came down, Lou Brock, Curt Flood. They came to me, and I loved it.

I remember Franks had said I was through as a ballplayer. Over the hill. And so, every time we beat the Giants, I used to get up on top of a trunk in the Cardinals clubhouse, and shout, "Screw Herman Franks!" "Yah!!" "Herman Franks!" "Yah!!"

Ray Washburn:

When he came over from San Francisco, he was still coming off of that surgery. So he was a big part of '67 and '68. He's sitting there in that picture I have—I always liked that, you've probably seen it. It was on the cover of *Sports Illustrated*. You got Maris, McCarver, Gibson, Shannon, Brock, Cepeda, Flood. The first million-dollar lineup, with all their salaries combined.

And of course '67 was the year he kind of started that "El Birdos." He got that going.

Julián Javier:

When Cepeda went to St. Louis, everybody got so happy, the whole town. And we started jumping—the team went up. And somebody put out the "El Birdos" name, I can't remember who did it. I think it was a fan—some fan did that. So, the team was playing good ball, and Cepeda came, and in '68 same thing.

Orlando Cepeda:

That was Joe Schultz, the third-base coach. He coached in Puerto Rico, winter ball. And he didn't learn Spanish—a few words. For example— *Cerveza fría*. Cold beer. That was the sign for the squeeze play, in '67. He'd say, "Cerveza fría!" He was a funny guy. "Cerveza fría!" Nobody knew what he was talking about. And then he came up with another thing. Bird. Birdo. He'd say, "El birdo." So he started all of that—*El Birdos*. And the fans got into it because it was Amadee, the cartoonist.[43] So he drew "El Birdo," for the paper, and they pick it up. And they were selling El Birdos banners and everything, you know.

And back then, there were not too many Latinos nowhere—and in the minor leagues, none. When I first came up to the big leagues, when I first came here to play ball, my first year playing in Kokomo, Indiana, it was maybe me and somebody else in the whole league was Latino. It was so hard for me to communicate, until the guys from Cuba came there. And then my roommate was from Cuba, in Kokomo.

In '58, in the big leagues, with the Giants, the *whole* league had five Latinos. The whole league. Tony Taylor, remember him? In '58, the Cubs had Tony Taylor, second base—from Cuba. And myself. Clemente. Román Mejías. Who else? No Dominicans had come. Maybe one Venezuelan, Luis Aparicio. And then Chico Carrasquel. I think there were five altogether. So I was proud to be one of the first—because when I first came up in '58, after I started doing so well, the scouts started going to Puerto Rico more. To look for more Orlando Cepedas.

GEORGE KELL: Well here's the new Tiger pitcher in the eighth inning, the left-hander, John Hiller.

He's won nine and lost six this year… and had a 2.39 earned run average during the regular season.

John Hiller:

That's not a bad breaking ball right there, pretty sharp. Now in this day and age, guys are *swinging* at that—I've never seen so many people swing at balls that bounce. I think it's because guys throw harder now, and they've got to get the bat going earlier.

When I came into Game Three, Naragon probably would've said in the bullpen, "You know, hold 'em there, John—you never know." It's the only sport without a clock, you know. The clock's never gonna beat you—you've got to get 27 outs.

I tried to pitch to their weakness, as long as it's still my strength. But, I guess it depends on the batter. But I found out later on—don't throw him anything but fastballs! He was a good off-speed hitter, Cepeda. And… big strong hitter like Cepeda, he looks like a fastball hitter to me, you know. But I found out later from a guy named Bob Didier, in the '70s, he says to me, "Whatever you do, don't throw this guy a changeup, *ever.*"

But anyway, things like that, I didn't know. See, we'd never faced these guys before, so all we went by was the scouting reports. Normally I pitched to guys I knew. And if you face somebody a lot, you don't need a scouting report. You don't need a team meeting, you just know how to pitch 'em. You remember home runs, you just do, and you might even remember hits. You remember the pitch, you almost might remember the count.

But, I'm basically going to do what Bill Freehan says—I probably would never shake him off in the World Series there. Because he's catching all these other guys, and he's going through the scouting reports, and he's sitting down with the pitchers, so—whatever Bill calls, I'm gonna throw.

But, Cepeda was big, and he's got a closed stance—Clemente had a stance just like that. So you threw him inside, no matter what you threw him, you know, you threw him inside. He liked the ball away, he stepped into it. So, I would've known that—so I threw him a shitty little breaking ball, the second one. I don't know where he hit that thing, but he hit it pretty hard. That was a bad pitch, I got lucky there.

And you know, I almost made it to the '84 team—but I couldn't have made it quite that long, I think I could've played till maybe '82, got '82 in. But Sparky Anderson and I didn't see eye to eye too much, and he wanted to get rid of me I think, and clean house with all the new players there. He couldn't get rid of me, because I was the last guy from '68 on the team. I could've never gotten a batter out, and Campbell would've still kept me around for some reason. But I wasn't doing real well, and I saw it coming, and so I retired in about June, I think, of 1980.

But back then, Sparky came to me one day, because he got rid of everybody that had a big mustache. Jerry Morales—mustache. Aurelio Rodriguez, my good buddy—mustache. Jack Billingham—mustache. He got rid of everybody, or he at least approached them and asked. So he came to me and he said, "Would you consider shaving your mustache off?" And I knew his policy, no hair down here, and he wanted everybody the same. I understood. So I says, "If you're asking me, I'll probably do it—but don't *tell* me." And we left it like that, and I showed up the next day without a mustache. I wasn't going to cause problems, you know.

But I remember we went out to Anaheim, and Sparky lived near there—something "Oaks," I think that's where he lived. And Sparky always sat in the hotel, he'd sit by the pool, I mean *all day long*. He was just black, black, black. So, we walked out there, and we're sitting around the pool having a Coke or something—and I looked over and there's this kid with his hair way down past his waist. So I just comment, I says, "Huh—who's that guy over there talking to Sparky, is that a fan?" They said, "No, that's his son!" And I just went *nuts*. I said, "He can't control his own kids, but he's got everybody else with no hair!?"

And speaking of Sparky, when I was a kid in Toronto, I used to go down and watch the Triple-A once in a while, they were right down at the waterfront. And Sparky Anderson was the second baseman! Way before I got to know Sparky, I watched him.

And then Charlie Dressen, he was the Tiger manager when I broke in around '66 or '65, and he was the manager in Toronto. I went for like a tryout, with my coach in Toronto, and I was about sixteen—he got a couple of us to go down to Toronto and throw. And Dressen looked at us, and he looked at me afterwards, and he says, "Don't throw your skates away, kid." So when I came up in '65 from Double-A ball, I relayed that story to him—and he goes, "No, no I wouldn't have told you that." But he told me, he says, "I hope you didn't throw your skates away!"

Growing up in Canada, it was mostly Stanley Cup, you know. I had a couple of friends who happened to get into baseball one summer—and then we didn't have Little League, it was run by Kiwanis, we had a T-shirt and a hat. So I did that just to do something in the summertime. I played all the sports, but I wasn't really good at anything other than baseball, really.

So I just started off in Canada, playing baseball, no ambition, no thoughts... and a scout saw me pitching when I was sixteen—I struck out 22 guys in seven innings. The scout was traveling from Detroit to Montreal. And I struck out every batter plus one, the catcher dropped the ball. And that scout approached me, and asked me if I thought about pitching. And I laughed at him, I said, "Nah—I'm a hockey player!" But we talked a year later, and eventually I signed with him.

You know, most athletes, we're just blessed with a talent. Sure you've got to hone it a little bit, but fortunately I could throw strikes. Left-handed pitcher who threw strikes. And more or less a rubber arm. Not quite like Lolich's, but. . . I had arm trouble one year out of my whole career.

Then, a couple years after '68, I missed a year and a half with my heart attack—I didn't face a batter in a year and a half. Not one. And Billy Martin, once I got back to the team and I got all the OKs from all the doctors, he put me in the ballgame one night. We didn't have rehab back then! I'd never faced a batter coming back, and he put me in a major-league game that night. It was in Chicago, and Dick Allen hit a home run off me, my third pitch I threw. It hit—still there had to have been a dent there in Comiskey, at least when they tore it down. Almost went out in left field. I don't think I ever saw a ball go out in left field there. And I pitched three innings that night, didn't walk a batter. But the Lord works in funny ways—I'll tell you, he really does.

There was no reason for me to be as good as I was afterwards. None whatsoever.[44]

CURT GOWDY: So, there's two down in the ninth, and here's Jim Price coming on to bat. Takes a *strike* at the knee.

Jim Price:

In the ninth inning, we were down I think, 7–3, and Mayo said to me, "Get up there." And at that place, Tiger Stadium, there was no place to loosen up. Like here now at Comerica with the batting cages, guys hit all during the game. But we just had to go up, to the on-deck circle, with lead-weighted bats, swing the bats, and get up there. You didn't have time to go to the locker room—sometimes you'd go to the locker room and swing a little bit. But you'd warm up as you're going up, and the umpire's telling you, "Hurry up!" and all that stuff. You've got to swing a lead-weighted bat, get up there, and get in.

So, I went up there, and—we were four down, just trying to put a good bat on the ball. I got ahead in the count; I didn't want to strike out. And it was a little cold, you could tell—I was trying to warm my hands between pitches. And I know I just missed it—just got underneath it a little bit, hit one to the warning track.

I just missed it. *Just* missed it. Just got under it.

And Hoerner, he was a good pitcher. I mean, he had a good tailing fastball, and that's basically what he threw me. A little sinking action going away. I knew him, I'd batted against him before, but that's always been in my memory bank, how I just missed that ball. Off the bat, I thought it had a chance, then I said, "Nah—I just missed it."

Tough, no question about it.

	1	2	3	4	5	6	7	8	9	R	H	E
Cardinals	0	0	0	0	4	0	3	0	0	7	13	0
Tigers	0	0	2	0	1	0	0	0	0	3	4	0

Tim McCarver:

Well, we knew we had Gibson going the next day, and any time you've got Gibson going...

HOW RUNS WERE SCORED

Tigers third:	Kaline homered, McAuliffe scored	Tigers 2, Cardinals 0
Cardinals fifth:	Flood doubled, Brock scored	Tigers 2, Cardinals 1
	McCarver homered, Flood and Maris scored	Cardinals 4, Tigers 2
Tigers fifth:	McAuliffe homered	Cardinals 4, Tigers 3
Cardinals seventh:	Cepeda homered, Flood and Maris scored	Cardinals 7, Tigers 3

GAME FOUR

Tiger Stadium | October 6, 1968

Jon Warden:

Game Four, that's when it rained, and we shouldn't have even played.

I mean it poured, it *poured.* It was like, "What are we doing here, why are we waiting around? Just cancel the damn thing; we'll play Game Four tomorrow." The mound dirt was all caked, the pitchers couldn't get it off their shoes—they took that Diamond Dry and put it down. Well shit, it was so wet it just sucked that stuff right up. That was history.

And we got our asses kicked. I mean, they blew us out. We were *done.* I mean, Brock hit one up in the deepest part of right-center field, home run, to lead off the game. And Gibby was pitching—so we were history.

Willie Horton:

It wasn't rain, it was *snow.* Or sleet, at least.

Dick Tracewski:

That was a terrible, terrible day. It was on a Sunday. And it was just horrible. The rain, you know, and we *stunk*. And we played horrible. We didn't play well defensively, it was just bad.

Al Kaline:

I think we were getting killed that day, I believe, is that the day we got bombed by them?

Denny McLain:

The game in Detroit when we had all the damn rain… I've never been a mudder, but Gibson had to pitch in the same rain I was pitching in, so it's not much of an excuse. But I've never been a mudder. And, boy, that was—they never should've played the game. And everybody admitted it later, but that didn't do us any good.

Orlando Cepeda:

The managers, they didn't want to stop the game. They didn't want the pitcher to have to stop the game and start all over—that's bad for the arm. And they wanted to take Gibson out, but he said no.

Fred Lasher:

I know they probably wanted to play it, when you're playing before a national audience, and overseas and everything else—I don't know if a game's ever been rained out.

Jim Price:

That game, we'd hoped it *would* be rained out. You're going to get Bob Gibson…

Bob Gibson pitches to Norm Cash on his way to 17 strikeouts in Game One: "It almost looked like a pro pitcher pitching against high school guys."

Denny McLain faces the Cardinals in Game One: "If I had good stuff I knew we would win. If I didn't have good stuff, I thought we'd still win."

Goose Goslin, Hall of Fame member of the 1935 World Series Champion Tigers, throws out the first pitch to Bill Freehan.

Mickey Stanley, the Tigers' longtime center fielder, makes an out at shortstop: "I only had five games to prepare, I never played shortstop in my life."

Al Kaline's home run lands in the left field bleachers, Game Three: "He hung me a breaking ball, and I hit it out. I don't remember a lot, but I remember that one."

Tim McCarver and Joe Schultz argue with umpire Bill Haller: "I was fired up. But how can you not be fired up, in the World Series?"

McCarver hits a home run, and the Cardinals take a 4–2 lead: "I didn't have any kind of home-run trot. I figured if I ran fast enough around the bases, they wouldn't know who hit it."

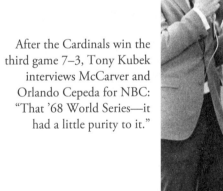

After the Cardinals win the third game 7–3, Tony Kubek interviews McCarver and Orlando Cepeda for NBC: "That '68 World Series—it had a little purity to it."

The Tigers fall behind early in Game 5, after Cepeda's home run: "In the first inning, Lolich threw me a 3-2 slider. But, well, you know— sometimes you're there." *Tony Spina Collection, Walter P. Reuther Library, Wayne State University*

With the Series on the line in Game Five, Lou Brock is called out at home: "Bill has always said: 'Willie, it was the perfect throw.'" *AP Images*

Joe Schultz and Brock argue the call at home with umpire Doug Harvey: "That was the big play of the game, you know. Before that, the Tigers were dead." *Tony Spina Collection, Walter P. Reuther Library, Wayne State University*

Lolich and McAuliffe score on a single by Kaline, and the Tigers lead 4–3: "We knew we were coming back. We knew it." *Tony Spina Collection, Walter P. Reuther Library, Wayne State University*

The crowd in Detroit, for Game Five: "In old Tiger Stadium, you could hear your mother yell at you from the seats." *Tony Spina Collection, Walter P. Reuther Library, Wayne State University*

The bottom of the third, Game Six, after Detroit scored ten runs: "They were a cocky bunch, the Cardinals. And then when we put up that ten-run inning, all of a sudden they weren't as happy anymore." *AP Images*

Gibson and Lolich match each other in Game Seven, with a scoreless tie lasting until the seventh: "Lolich goes out there, and he and Gibson are in a head-knocker."

In the seventh inning, Jim Northrup hits a two-run triple to center field over Curt Flood's head: "I know he hit the hell out of it."

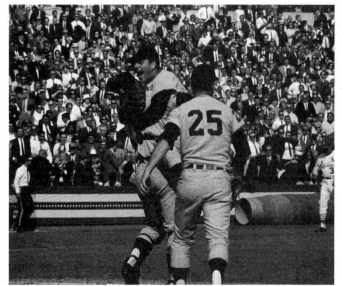

Mickey Lolich leaps into the arms of Bill Freehan, as the Tigers win Game Seven: "We did it. We *did* it."

Mickey Lolich, the last pitcher in baseball history to win three complete games in the World Series: "I've said this about Mickey a million times: greatest arm I ever saw in my life. The greatest."

Photos courtesy of AP Images

Dick McAuliffe, Jim Northrup, and Mickey Stanley hoist the Commissioner's Trophy: "It was a great moment, it was a great time in Detroit history." *AP Images*

The home of Bill and Pat Freehan, after the Series ended: "When we got home, my Lord, our street was decorated and there was a bonfire—everybody was celebrating!" *Courtesy of Pat Freehan*

Bill Haller:

The weather was horrendous, it was raining, cold… and we should've never started the game. On a regular day, you wouldn't start it. Yet, they started it. And that's because of the commissioner, I think it was Eckert or whatever his name was. He was *lost*. But they started the game, and we had Stan Landes for the National League, Harvey umpiring for the National League. Well anyway, Cronin's the league president, for the American League. And the Cardinals go up big in the third inning. But they shouldn't have started the game—the weather was *brutal*!

GEORGE KELL: Umbrellas are everywhere. The bleachers in center field *covered* with umbrellas.

And they're gonna stop the ballgame, right now! The umpires are meeting, in the center of the infield. They're gonna stop it, right now.

	1	2	3	4	5	6	7	8	9	R	H	E
Cardinals	2	0	2							4	6	0
Tigers	0	0								0	2	1

Jon Warden:

During the rain delay we went back in the locker room, sitting around. Guys are reading the paper, guys are on their cell phones—oh no, just kidding! No, just people sitting at their lockers, thinking about the game. Basically just snacking, having a candy bar, shooting the shit and stuff. We never played cards in the locker room, but everyone sort of sat at their locker.

Bill Haller:

Mr. Cronin's on the end of the dugout of the Tigers, and he's hollering at Jim Honochick, Jim's third base. Jim's our lead umpire for the American League. "*Better get this game in, you fat bastard*!!" And of course the umpires heard it, too.

So after the game we go into our clubhouse, and this little guy who was the commissioner's man in there, he was in charge of the clubhouse, so to speak, for the umpires. And no one was allowed in there, except, they would ask this fella in here, "Can we come in?" And he'd ask the commissioner yes or no. And Stan came in, Landes, and he said, "Get outta here, you no-good so-and-so…" And so the guy got scared, and left. Little tiny old guy, he was the guy in there for the commissioner. So Stan's hollering at him, calling him everything under the sun. And he leaves. And finally, nothing happened. So the next year in spring training I see Stan, he's living out in Phoenix. I said, "How's it going, Stanley?" He said, "Good!" He said, "Oh but one thing,"—this is what Stan told me—he said, "I got fined five thousand dollars, that's what we *made!*" Because of that incident. Now if that's a true story, I don't know. But that's what I was told.

See, the commissioner runs everything. I say the umpires are supposed to be in charge of rain, but you're not gonna call the game if you're an umpire, because you don't wanna lose your job. You go to the commissioner first.

But today, a five-inning game by the rules, in the Series, it's a suspended game. It's no longer a complete game. But then, it was a complete game. That's what the rules said. You had to have five innings. So if the visiting club is, say, losing one to nothing, in the top of the fifth and they don't score to tie, now it's an official game. Because the other team is ahead one to nothing, and even if they don't score they're still the winners. It's five innings. If the visiting team is either tied or losing after they bat in the fifth inning, it's a legal game.[45]

But we should've never started that game. If they asked the umpires, it was the older ones. Didn't ask me! I would've told them, "Hey, this is ridiculous!" It was *pouring* down there. And then when Gibson gets that lead, *whoooo!* Now you're gonna call the game? Umpire isn't—he's not going to lose his job for them being stupid in the office.

Jon Warden:

During that delay, McLain, he might've been wondering, I think, if he was going to go back out, since they had that gap. Wondering if he was going to go back out to the mound. But I think Mayo probably said, "Yer done, we'll see you in Game Six, if we go that far."

Fred Lasher:

McLain wasn't going back in. How many runs were we down? That's enough for Bob Gibson.

Bill Haller:

Well, McLain was the one that got whacked—he wasn't gonna come back. You don't bring guys back who gave up ten runs in three innings, I don't think, do ya?

Hal Naragon:

There's always a certain point in the game, especially when it's a big game, that you probably find the manager is more eager to take the pitcher out, or have him ready or not have him pitch as long. He thinks he's putting the best shot in there, and that's his job. And you always think that the next guy can do the job. You know, I never thought any other way—I always thought that, *Hey, he's a major-league ballplayer, you know, he can do it, he can handle it.*

Al Kaline:

As for Bob Gibson, I don't think we had any thoughts that he wasn't going to go out there and finish that game—no, no, not Bob Gibson. Maybe some other pitcher, but not him. He was a bulldog.

Jon Warden:

Well, Joe Sparma started that game we won the pennant, in September.
He came out and pitched a one-run complete game. Beat Lindy
McDaniel. McDaniel gave up the big hit, to Wert. At the end of the
game, scored Kaline.[46]

Dick Tracewski:

We won the pennant, against the Yankees, and Don Wert got the base
hit. Werty got the base hit, against Lindy McDaniel. Hit a line drive
into right-center field. He threw a split-finger, and he was tough. Werty
hit good pitching, and he got the base hit.

Don Wert:

I hit it between first and second. Lindy McDaniel was the pitcher. And
the bases were loaded, Kaline was on third. And I hit the ball between
first and second. And Lindy McDaniel, I knew what pitch was coming—he was a forkballer. It was a 2-2 count, and he threw it and I hit
it, between first and second. Scored the winning run. The thing about
it, after I hit the ball, I had to run to first, touch the bag. By that time,
there were so many people on the field, that it was unbelievable, really,
the grounds crew came out and got me back to the dugout. It was wild,
just wild. In that instance, I don't think anybody could've kept them off
the field, it was just crazy.

But we had a big lead—I think we won it by nine games, or something like that. We were pretty much ahead at that time. We were just
waiting until we got the winning game. We felt that we could do it.

Jon Warden:

And you know how Sparma got into that game?

Earl Wilson was supposed to pitch, but he got sick or something—so Sparma's in the clubhouse, he's doing his normal routine, not scheduled. They said, "Joe—you're in." "What?" "You're startin' the game."

And he went out and threw a masterpiece.

Hal Naragon:

Sparma had great stuff, he had great velocity, you know. And I don't think the manager, Mayo, he really had that much confidence in him. Why, I don't know. And Joe was a good athlete, he was a quarterback at Ohio State, and boy, he had good stuff. In fact, he pitched the game when we won the pennant. I thought a lot about Sparma, why we couldn't get him to be a little better a pitcher. I think it was lack of confidence, more than anything, from the higher-ups.

Jim Price:

I got to catch Joe Sparma, you know, at Tiger Stadium, and Dan [Dickerson], my broadcast partner now, was in the bleachers watching me play, in those days. And, you know, to catch Joe Sparma, with the shadows... He had the best stuff on our staff. But he didn't know where it was going. We always say shadows are tough for the hitter, but it's also tough for the catcher. Once the shadows got in front of home plate, it was tough. *Very* difficult. And, like I said, *catching* too. With the time of day, you knew where you were going to be in trouble, and when you were going to be able to see the ball.

Jon Warden:

Sparma, I'll tell you, he had an *arm*. I mean, he could throw. He was probably the hardest throwing on the team. He'd be the long reliever, the long man. It was a four-man rotation, and he was that fourth guy. It started off: Wilson, McLain, Lolich, Sparma—that was the four. But Sparma, I mean, he could have a no-hitter for four or five innings, I've seen him do it four, five, six times. But before you get somebody warmed up, he's walked the bases loaded, and he can't find the dish. He'd lose control.

John Hiller:

Sparma had the best stuff of anybody on our team, he just couldn't put it together. He threw it away—but Joe had the best stuff on the team. His nickname was "Square Deal"—he always had a deal for ya. He worked for a Dodge dealership, I think. And he was a good-looking Italian guy, he could talk, and he just—he looked like a car salesman, he sounded like a car salesman.

Fred Lasher:

One time during that year, we lost two or three and our lead shrunk to five or six. And there was a little talk about choking and that. And then we went on a winning streak, kind of finished off the season.

And then, we won it that night.

Al Kaline:

We didn't care who we played in the World Series, we just wanted to get in it. Although the one thing is, I think we would've stayed in better shape had we clinched maybe just two days before the season ended instead of clinching earlier. Because, you know, you sort of relax, and you're really not intense, you take it easy, and all of a sudden you may fall into some bad habits.

Dick Tracewski:

When we won, we were going to St. Louis. And we knew that, and I think there was a purity in that.

Tony Kubek:

That was maybe the last—I won't say "pure" World Series, that's maybe too strong of a word—but right after that '68 season, they were now starting the league play-in to get in the World Series, three out of five. But in 1968, if you won the American League or National League season, you played each other. The team that had the best record from the entire season was the team that got in the World Series.

So, that '68 World Series—it had a little *purity* to it.

Dick Tracewski:

After we won the pennant that night, when they all came into the clubhouse, they got Jim Campbell—and it was unique, they had a whirlpool that could seat four baseball players. It was a big, big whirlpool. And guys used to sit in there, especially on cold days in April in Michigan. After the game was over, you're freezing, you get in there. But they threw a lot of guys in there, and Campbell that night. Everybody went in a little bit, you know.

Denny McLain:

I remember the TV people were filming us in the clubhouse after, and we had the champagne going… I couldn't get that motherfucker open! It took me forty fuckin' minutes… On top of that, I was sick as a dog that night. I had the flu, and I'd been drinking that fuckin' champagne from the fourth inning on. I couldn't find my ass with both hands.

Mel Butsicaris:

When they clinched the American League pennant, for the first time in twenty-some years, the town went *crazy*. And the bar itself was a little less than a mile away, straight down Michigan Avenue, on the corner of Michigan and Cass. We were right at the edge of downtown Detroit, with all the tall buildings and we were the short building. And when the Tigers clinched the pennant, from the stadium to our place you couldn't drive down Michigan Avenue because it was so packed with people, because it was like thousands and thousands of people cheering and celebrating on the streets. And the bar itself was just *packed*. The doorman couldn't hold the people back; they were packed in there like sardines.

And all of a sudden, we hear police sirens—and the thinking was that they'd come to break up the crowd. But what it was is that they were escorting the team bus, the Tigers' team bus to our place. The whole team wanted to celebrate at our place after the game, so they made their way down the street and they pull up to the back in the alley, but there was no place to put them! We couldn't get people out of the bar, they were stuck there! So we managed to get one little pathway from the back alley where the bus was to behind the bar, that was the closest shot in—and we put them behind the bar. We had twenty-two ballplayers behind the bar, and for almost six hours, *they* were the bartenders! We sat on the steps, and we let them be the bartenders! We just locked the register and they just gave everything away! So they were like, they would just pass a full fifth of booze to somebody, going, "Take a swig and pass it around back to the crowd!" And the coolers behind the bar, they held about 175 cases of beer—and they just gave all that away.

Jim Price:

Lindell AC was the place. That's where most of us hung out most of the time.

One night, we drove over to the big Lindell AC and got behind the bar and tended bar and everything. Everybody was great. I wasn't a drinker, but I had some champagne, and I was feeling a little drunk. So Willie carried me out to the car… Willie Horton carried me out!

That showed you how *strong* Willie was.

Willie Horton:

Yeah I remember that. Down there, it was just like at home. Jimmy Butsicaris and those guys… back then, we hung out with the basketball players, football players, everybody hung out down there. I didn't never hang out at bars too much, but every now and then I'd go down there with the guys. And when we were at home, after the Series, I went by there; Jimmy had a couple things going on.

Mel Butsicaris:

Mayo Smith never did send us a check for that night, we always joked about that. But we always thought of it as a huge honor, that the team wanted to celebrate with us. It wasn't about the money that night.

And one of the biggest things about that team was—you actually have to go back a year. In '67, Detroit was on *fire*. August was the start of the Detroit riots, and it really destroyed the city and burnt out some of the neighborhoods where the scars are still felt—some areas never came back, you know? But everybody thought that in the beginning of '68, the big talk was, "Is Detroit gonna burn again this year?" But when spring training started, people started talking *baseball*, you know? White people and black people started talking again, and set their differences aside watching games together, you know? And the Tigers themselves actually were a big cause of that, because they didn't see each other as white players or black players, but they hung out together. Back then, teams associated with each other—after a game the whole team would go to a place together, or a big portion of them. Especially the out-of-town team, you know. After a game the team bus would pull up in front of our bar, and the whole team like the New York Yankees or Boston, whoever they were playing, the whole team would come in there. And a good portion of the Tigers hung together, too.

When they were out of town they all hung together, but even when they were *in* town they popped into the Lindell, said hello and talked to some of the other players and stuff... You always saw this group of young black men and white men, professional athletes that people looked up to, drinking and socializing together, going out and having fun together, pulling jokes around each other, and it made other people in the community feel the same way, that they could have that same thing. Gates Brown was black, and Earl Wilson, and Norm Cash was white, southern boy—and they were all good friends. You always saw them *together*.

I remember Norm Cash and Gates Brown standing there in the middle of the bar, and the loud voice of Norm Cash grabbing Gates Brown by the head—and Gates Brown was a *big* guy, actually rough fucking guy! Because he spent some time in prisons before playing baseball. And I remember Norm Cash grabbing him by the head, and putting his hands on both sides of his ears, pretending like he's *squeezing* hard, yelling at the top of his lungs in that southern drawl, "Gates! What am I doing!?" And Gates would say, "You're squeezin' a blackhead!" And then Gates would do the same thing to Norm, and say, "Norm, what am I doin'!?" And Norm would yell, "You're squeezin' a whitehead!" Things like that, you know?

And usually when the Tigers would come in, we'd have a table for them, but they didn't want to sit in one spot—they mingled, they walked around talking to people and stuff. People are going to talk to them anyway, so they walked around. And Cash walked around singing to the jukebox with Gates Brown... I'll never forget, Norm Cash and Gates Brown sitting on top of the jukebox—we had this one jukebox, it had a flat top on it where you could look down at the selections, when it played 45 [rpm] records, that was the entertainment we had. And they were actually sitting on *top* of the jukebox, I thought the glass was going to break on it, singing the Johnny Cash song, "A Boy Named Sue"! Sitting there, holding their arms around each other, singing to it.

Norm was the jokester, right. And he was very outgoing, in a funny way, you know. And he played the Southern aspect up a lot, the "I'm a hillbilly and proud of it!" type of thing... "This is what we do up in the hills!" And he got people going, you know? And Lolich was a funny guy, so they were all partying. Jon Warden, being a rookie, he was just like a little kid, he was just so happy to be a part of that team.

And one night they actually had a water fight—they were throwing ice cubes at each other behind the bar... And from there it went glasses of water to *pitchers* of water, and then grabbing the—they call it the "gun"—the big hose that dispensed soda and juice for mixed drinks, they started squirting it at each other... that was kind of a sloppy night! I think Norm Cash would've started that.

And on Saturdays, after the game if they would really want to come and have a beer or something like that, they'd settle in a corner—Cash, and Kaline, and Gates Brown, and Mickey Lolich, and John Hiller, Sparma, Jim Price, Earl Wilson, you know, they'd all be sitting together in the corner, and they'd all come in with bags, grocery bags filled with baseballs that they'd used for practice. Well they'd come into the bar with bags of these balls and they'd just be signing them, you know, and there'd be a line of kids, youngsters going out the door waiting to get a ball from these guys. They didn't do it because someone was paying them, or someone told them to do it, but they were just doing it because these are their fans, they love kids, and that's how they played the game. If you look at some of their salaries back then, they did it for love of the game. The people in this town just fell in love with them, not because they were a winning baseball team, but because of the kind of characters they were.

Jim Price:

After all that and we'd clinched the pennant, we were rained out the next day, so it was kind of a noon-time game, you know, not many people there. We normally packed them in, but this was a makeup game, two days after we clinched the pennant. And I think it was a noon-time start, to get the game in. Against the Yankees.

So, Mickey Mantle came up for his last time at-bat, I walked out, I grabbed the umpire, said, "Let's let him have center stage." Which we did, standing ovation. And then, Denny says, "Hey—let's let him hit one." I said, "Come on… you gotta be serious?" I looked down, I said, "You *are* serious. All right—I'll find out where he wants it." So when I went back behind the plate, I said, "Mick, we want ya to hit a home run." And he's like, "What are you talking about?" I said, "Yeah—we want you to hit a home run, it's your last time here!" Look out at Denny, Denny's shaking his head *yes.* So he says, "High and mediocre cheese."

Ernie Harwell says it was like the fourth pitch or fifth pitch. Got it, hit it in the upper deck. Well, when he was rounding second base, McLain was clapping, crossed home plate, he thanked me.

And the next hitter was Pepitone. He says, "Gimme one of those." I said, "We're gonna give you one in the *ear,* how's that?"

GEORGE KELL: Bob Gibson will be the leadoff man for the Cardinals.

One ball, two strikes.

Here she goes—a *long* belt to left… this one's well hit, and it's *gone!*

	1	2	3	4	5	6	7	8	9	R	H	E
Cardinals	2	0	2	1						5	7	0
Tigers	0	0	0							0	3	1

Don Wert:

I think in that game, Eddie Mathews started instead of me.[47] I don't know why he started that game, other than being a left-hander. But we were happy to have him on the team. If we didn't pick him up, he probably would've retired, I feel. He was ready to retire.

Jon Warden:

A lot of people forget Eddie Mathews was on that team. So that's always a good trivia question—ask: "Who are the two Hall of Famers on the '68 Tigers?" Well they get Kaline right away, and then they go, "Lolich? Cash? McLain?" I say, "Think about it. Five hundred twelve home runs. Played for the Braves a lot." "Ohh… Eddie Mathews!" "Yeah."

Well, he'd been on and off of the DL that year, his back was bothering him. So, he was activated, before the season's over, and he was playing, spot-starting, playing third. And then Mayo had him start that one World Series game.

Al Kaline:

It was special to play with a great player like Eddie Mathews—even though he didn't play a lot for us, but he was a great influence on us, mentally, physically, and how to play the game.

Tom Matchick:

Ed was a lot of fun, Mathews was a good guy. It was just like a normal guy. Didn't expect anything special from him or anything else, he just blended in with all the guys.

And, you know, he sort of knew it would be his last year. He sort of knew. We sort of knew, too. Especially when he would come to the ballpark with one blue sock, one black sock. Or one green sock, one blue sock! They'd say, "Who dressed you today, did your wife dress ya? Or did you dress in the closet?" Our guys, they were funny, they were one of a kind.

Mickey Stanley:

I wonder what the Tigers were thinking, picking him up—because he didn't play much, when he was with us. He mostly just pinch-hit, once he came over near the end of '67.

But it was comforting to have him around. And to see what a real humble human being he was. And, he'd just say—I can't remember the things he'd say—he'd just say little things, to give you confidence. Like, maybe, "Hey—you're a hell of an outfielder," or something. That he noticed you had some talent, and that he took the time to tell ya, you know. I really liked him, I *really* liked him.

Jon Warden:

He always loved talking to the pitchers, he got on great. He'd go, "How would you pitch me? How would you try to throw a right-hander that had a lot of power, would you take him in or out?" And a lot of the guys were scared to death of him, because he was such a tough guy, and a great player. They didn't know how to approach him, you know. Even Earl Wilson, and he was a real hard-ass.

Many years back, they were having a reunion, and they had everybody that played on the '68 team. Might've been the twenty-fifth or thirtieth reunion. So, we're on the bus, on the way to the card show, and I wanted to get Mathews on these baseballs. And I said, "Eddie, I got a dozen baseballs"—and I took a dozen, I put him and Kaline on the sweet spot, and I'd have it filled in everywhere else, with everyone signing it. So, I'm on my knees on the seat, and here comes Northrup: "Hey hey, have Eddie sign a couple balls." Here comes Earl Wilson, "Hey… have Eddie sign these two balls." I'm like, "Fuck, you guys— I'm the rookie, I'm the young kid!"

But Eddie liked me, and so, I'm handling the balls and he's signing. And so I got my dozen finished, and then I'm going, "Oh—can you sign these, too?" Then he goes, "How many fuckin' balls are *in* a dozen? Holy shit, Warden." I said, "Well, these assholes are afraid to ask you!" He said, "What do you mean they're afraid?" I said, "They're asking me to get you…" and he's looking at Northrup and Wilson and these other guys, going, "What's the matter with you guys? Hell, we were teammates!" And so, he must've signed twenty-five balls by the time we got to the card show. But Eddie did it—he didn't care.

Willie Horton:

You know, it helped us as young guys, to have him. I remember in the first game in St. Louis, me and Stanley and Northrup just sitting in the clubhouse, nervous, when everybody else was out on the field practicing. Like someone nailed us to the stool! We felt like you were glued to the seat.

And Eddie Mathews came in there, and he said, "What is *wrong* with you guys?" He could pick up on that, and it got us out there, and I think he helped each and every one of us.

Tony Kubek:

Of course, speaking of Eddie Mathews, the Cardinals had another great player at the end of his career—Roger Maris.

And Roger, he was a different player with the Cardinals—after he was MVP back to back in '60 and '61 and broke the Babe's record… the next year he'd hurt his wrist, he ran into a fence. Roger thought that they could seal the injury, the fracture in his wrist—and he never really had it repaired, it healed over the wintertime. Well, he wasn't a home-run hitter anymore. But the interesting thing was, at spring training in '63, I remember seeing the Cardinals with Bill White and Dick Groat, and Shannon—Mike Shannon was very upset when they traded for Roger, because Mike moved from right field and had to move to third base, where he became a pretty good third baseman. And more than one guy said, "You know, being in the National League, we thought all Roger could do was hit home runs." And they said, "But we found out—how he ran the bases, his throwing arm…" He could run, he could throw, he was a good hitter. They were so surprised how much he understood the game, and how good he was defensively, and how he'd go from first to third on base hits. They found that he was not just a home-run hitter. And I think that's the reason why maybe you play Roger—even though, you know, he was a left-handed hitter in a key time in the Series, but they put Roger in because he was a veteran, he knows how to play the game, and you hope he does something aside from just hit a home run or get a base hit—that he might cut a runner down at the plate, or save a double or a triple. So, Roger was not the same player, I mean he was still the same intensity, the same drive, the same kind of team player, but he was no longer a home-run hitter.

Johnny Edwards:

Well, I remember back in '61 he was going through heck, as far as the pressure on him. And he was *really, really* quiet, when I played against him. You know, I tried to talk to him when he came to the plate and all that stuff, but he didn't say much. And I thought, "Gosh dern, he's kind of a stuck-up guy."[48] But then I went to St. Louis, and you know, he was just a farm boy that was really a nice guy. And Schofield and I, until the wives came, had an apartment there and Roger had an apartment next to us, until his wife and kids came. And so we rode to the ballpark all the time together, and rode home.

Dick Schofield:

Well, Maris and me got to be pretty good friends. See, I played in Omaha in the minors, he played in Indianapolis for Cleveland, so I played against him—and then I went to the Yankees that year I was hurt.

And then in '68, on the Cardinals, we lived next door to each other, in a little townhouse thing. His wife and my wife got to be good friends, and our kids played together every day—they were in and out of each house, you didn't know who was who.

The kids had a ball, I mean... When I was living next door to Maris, out in the parking lot they had a game about every day. And one day Roger made me go out there with him, and we would throw balls to them, and they hit *rockets* off these buildings. And one day somebody broke a window, and I turn around and—I'm the *only* guy in the parking lot. I'm holding my glove, and people are looking out the window saying, "What's that guy doing!?"

When I played in St. Louis—we had more kids in the clubhouse than we had players. Because, see, a lot of teams won't allow kids in the clubhouse. There was Johnny Edwards's son, and Maris had three kids, and my son—they had a great big area outside the clubhouse, big square area with real high ceilings, those kids were out there hitting baseballs, playing catch... It's a wonder they didn't kill somebody! But, Dal Maxvill had a son then, who wasn't too old—but he was just a *mean* little shit! They used to take him and hang him on a hook, in the locker, he couldn't get down! Because he was just all over the place... I mean, all those kids were.

Orlando Cepeda:

I knew Roger in '58, spring training. He played with Cleveland, and I was with the Giants. And we became good friends, you know. And then, I saw him in the All-Star Games—he remembered me, I remembered him. So when we came to St. Louis, we were good friends.

GEORGE KELL: Roger Maris, the batter.

There's a bouncer to second… the ball bounced *high* in the air, and McAuliffe had no chance to get Brock. It'll be a run batted in for Roger Maris, and the Cardinals lead *six* to nothing!

	1	2	3	4	5	6	7	8	9	R	H	E
Cardinals	2	0	2	2						6	8	0
Tigers	0	0	0							0	3	2

Dick Tracewski:

We had a lot of guys that could do things, and it was a good mix of guys. We had great players in key positions, and other thing that we had—and it was very important, probably *the* most important thing, in my mind—is that we had great defense. We had great infield defense, and we had great outfield defense.

The thing that was constant, constant every day, was defense. I don't remember us booting many games away. You always boot a couple; somebody makes a mistake or misplays the ball. But we never did that.

So we had good defense, and our infield defense was outstanding, you know. Werty was as good as they came, at third base, he really was. And he was so underrated, nearly as good as Brooks Robinson, in the American League. Cash was as good as they came. You couldn't get much better. McAuliffe was as good as they came. Oyler was a good shortstop on balls hit to him. He had great hands and a good arm. And

Freehan was a great catcher. It was a good defensive team, and that was a constant. Hitting comes and goes. Defense doesn't.

Don Wert:

Third base is your base, you know, and I was always pretty good at it. So I didn't have any reservations as to playing third base. You know if they're gonna hit 'em that way, you've gotta field it. You know who pulls the ball and who doesn't pull the ball, and just allow for that. Normally they try to pitch away from that area, so that they don't pull the ball too much, but if they do, they knew they had a guy there to field it. I could field. I could field.

I never played as deep as the guys play now—*gosh,* they play deep. But I always just got a good jump on the ball. I'll tell you what I did. Every pitch that came from the pitcher, I took a little hop. Before the ball got right to the hitter. And I could move right or left very quickly, and I took that hop to get me started. So that I could get a good jump on the ball when it was hit, and I reacted to how the hitter swung at the pitch. If he pulled around, I knew it was gonna be to my right. I didn't jump—just a little hop, to get me started.

Dick Tracewski:

Al Kaline was just a great, great defensive player. He had a very, very accurate arm. Now there were stronger arms, but not as accurate. You should see him throw from the outfield during infield practice. He'll bounce two balls into third base right on the money, and two balls into home plate. Right on the money. He had a great, great throwing arm, and very accurate.

Stanley had a good arm. Northrup. And Willie Horton made the big play throwing out Lou Brock. And he was a little better an outfielder than you think.

Willie Horton:

In the outfield, me, Stanley, and Northrup, we were almost like brothers. Triplets. I remember one time in Boston, there was a fly ball, we were trying to get Northrup to move—and he told both of us where to go. And we said, "We'll see what you get in the dugout." Because Stanley was the boss! That's just the way it is, he's supposed to move. I'm hollering at Jimmy, and he's going, "Hey both of you—go *up* yourself!"

But Mickey and I, we played together a long time. In Duluth, Minnesota, Puerto Rico—that's where we grew our bond together, as brothers. Stanley also, he laced up all my gloves—he was the best glove man in all of baseball. He knew how to fix gloves, and he always kept my glove right. See that right there? That glove right there is the glove I wore in the World Series. And I used that the rest of my career.

He *really* helped me in that outfield. And he was one of the greatest center fielders I'd ever seen. I put him, Paul Blair, and Berry, the kid from the White Sox—them guys, they used to play *right* behind second base. I don't know *how* they'd catch the ball! On my team and playing every day, I would take Mickey over *anybody*. Seeing him go up them walls like its steps… I mean I'm in the outfield, I'm almost wanting to start clapping myself!

Dick Tracewski:

Mickey was a *great* center fielder. He was really one of the superb athletes. There were a few center fielders in the league then that were pretty good, Mickey was as good or better than all of them. He could track a ball, I mean, you never saw him make a mistake in the outfield, never. Mickey was a fantastic center fielder.

Mickey Stanley:

You know, when I played center field, I used to cheat a little bit. I could tell, you know, if the ball's hit on the outside of the plate, I could lean, and could cheat. I could see if it was a sloppy curveball going up there.

And I just… could cheat. Probably got a good jump on the ball because I paid attention to every pitch.

But a shift? No—never. I played the pull. I mean outfielders… it's the infielders that do the shifting. I don't think anybody ever had to tell me to shift. You know, if there's a pull hitter up there, we just knew. We just *knew!* We knew our hitters. You know, we knew. Don't ask me how we knew, we knew. I still know! I still remember those hitters! I still know, I know where to play 'em. I can still remember like, if Yaz is coming to the plate and McLain was playing, I'd play him straight-away—because he hits a lot of balls the other way. And, I mean, you just *know.* After you play it a time or two against a guy. Doesn't take long, you just remember it. It's your job! It's not like you're smart. Just like when you take a dump, you take your pants down—you don't forget! Oh that's not a very good thing to say, is it?

But, in fact, Jim Northrup—and I agree with him—he found out center field was the *easiest* position to play. And he let me know that. He goes, "Boy, this is a lot easier than right or left!" And you know what? It's true! Because, first of all, you're further from the hitter, you've got more time to react to the ball; you see the ball coming off the bat. Whereas in right field, left field, a lot of times if the ball's hit anywhere between you and the line, it's usually hooking, it's curving, and you're a lot closer to the fence. I mean, center field is pretty easy compared to the other ones!

Tony Kubek:

When you look at that Tiger infield, you know, you look at Wert, you look at McAuliffe, and you look at Stanley, and whoever came in late in the ballgames—they knew how to play the game. And as I recall, they made some decent plays defensively. They knew how to play, and they knew how to adjust. And that's an important thing in the World Series. You get a scouting report on a specific guy before the Series starts—a scout will follow a team that's going to win the pennant, and they'll watch how other teams play those hitters. Well, that doesn't work against good players—good players adjust to the pitching the next time they see it, and the pitcher has to readjust to the hitter.

And I think that's what, you know, maybe Mayo Smith did because he'd done advance scouting. He understood that.

Denny McLain:

Mayo was the best manager I'd ever played for. I don't know how many guys would say that, but I thought he knew and managed his players better than anybody I ever saw.

He had a talent that allowed him to determine who was playing the best at the time, but more importantly, who were his best players. Mayo had this talent, inside talent, that he knew who the best athletes were. And, you know, if you've got a team full of athletes, you've got a chance, you really do. And before the '68 team came together, Mayo got rid of them assholes, you know. We had some bad guys on that club—and he got rid of most of them.

Willie Horton:

You've got to pick the *right* guys—we didn't have no hell-raisers.

Like Jim Price, our backup catcher. He could've been a starter on any other team. And people don't realize, but we were fortunate, because we stole him from Pittsburgh. And you'd respect him because he accepted his responsibility, and he'd stay ready. He respected that Bill was there as the starter, and that was it.

Jon Warden:

Mayo and Wally Moses, our first-base coach, they always had a little brown bottle—he and Mayo liked to have some sauce, they drank a lot. And Mayo was pre-mature gray, almost like Sparky Anderson. And I thought Mayo was seventy, I really did. I thought, this guy is *old*! Of course, when you're twenty-one, someone forty-five looks old.

And he'd always talk like, "Waaaaalll, aaaahh, now ahh aaaah ahhh here's what we're gonna do, aaaah aaaah aaah."

Tom Matchick:

Mayo, he'd go, "Waall waaaal waaal I'll tell ya, waal waal waaal."

And you know, where the "D" is, on the uniform? Mayo had an inside pocket and he kept a little flask in there. About every third inning, sometimes he and Wally Moses would go in the tunnel and take a sip. And come back to the dugout and go in the corner and fall asleep!

One day in the dugout there, Mayo was in his corner sleeping and that, and Johnny went over to wake him up, I think Wilson was pitching that day—and he woke up Mayo and he goes, "Whaddaya want—whaddaya want, John!?" Me and Gates were on the bench, he says, "Earl's getting tired, who do you want me to bring in?" Mayo goes, "Waal, waall—bring in Timmerman!" He said, "I'd like to, Mayo, but you sent him to Toledo four days ago!"

I'll tell ya, there was never a dull moment with that team.

John Hiller:

He might've done that, with the pocket, I don't know. He might've been half in the bag anyways... I don't know if anybody mentioned that story—the pitchers used to make jokes about that, "When he'd come over you could *smell* the scotch!" Cuccinello used to go to his locker and take a little sip.

As it got down close to it, these guys weren't used ever to being in a World Series—so they got a little tight.

Bill Haller:

Mayo was very fair. Great guy. Didn't bitch and moan about every little thing. And the Cardinal manager was the same way, Red Schoendienst. Very few managers would just be constantly moaning and groaning. Weaver was one of them, and Dick Williams.

Tim McCarver:

You know, it's impossible to talk about that Series and that season without talking about the problems our nation had, from a racial standpoint, and with Vietnam going on. It was *tough*.

Jim Price:

You know, the Vietnam War was having problems, during '68, those guys were coming home a lot. So every place we went, people wanted to buy you dinner, buy you a drink or whatever. Because it meant so much. You know, I still run into guys that were in Vietnam—they thank us, and we thank them. They say, "Thank you for helping me get through Vietnam." Getting the scores and all that stuff. That's special. That's very special.

And I was very aware of the war, because my dad had been in the military. And I remember coming out of the Roosevelt Hotel, and there were a lot of protestors with Vietcong flags, and one of them put the flag in my face, and I broke his nose with a punch. And the police were so great, they said, "Come on, we'll get you away from here, no one's gotta see about anything." Roosevelt Hotel, in New York. Right outside. They threw the Vietcong flag in my face—wrong thing to do. *Wrong* thing to do.

Mickey Stanley:

I was born at the right time—I'd married and had kids by then. We were mostly all married. I could've enlisted, but, I had wife and kids, and didn't feel like killing anybody. Lolich was in the National Guard, though, and I don't think he was married by then—so I don't know why I was exempt and he wasn't. But it seemed like during the season he was gone once in a while. I don't think he ever missed a start, but I think they worked around him.

Tim McCarver:

It was a hard time in our country's history. With the problems that were in Detroit at the time, with the social strife. Taking the bus from the ballpark to downtown—like in Philadelphia, the ballpark was at 21st & Lehigh, and even taking the bus... Number one, you don't go wandering around after the game, black or white. And when you get on the bus, and you're glad that the bus is there for you. Because you're going through some real tough areas. There was social strife all over, some real tough times.

And I remember talking to Bob, I said, "Bob, you know..." Bob said, "You know, black people are having a tough time in this society." And I said, "Well, you know, when I grew up, Tennessee was six percent Catholic, and I grew up as a Catholic, and there was prejudice there, too." And he said something that'll always stick with me, he said, "Yeah, but you were *white.*" And that made an impact with me.

You had Martin Luther King killed, you had Bobby Kennedy killed, in Los Angeles. It was a real *tough* time.

Jon Warden:

In '68, once the team was set, and spring training ended, all of a sudden Martin Luther King gets assassinated... and I'm like, "Oh my God."

And they cancelled opening day for like three days. And with that delay, we stayed in spring training a few days. So here's four rookies make the team: Les Cain, Daryl Patterson, Matchick, and myself. The four of us fly into Detroit from spring training, and at this time Detroit's the fourth-largest city in the United States. But it's on shutdown, it's on curfew. *Nobody* on the streets. Can you imagine going to someplace like downtown Chicago today and not see anybody? *Nothing*—not *one* person on the street.

I don't know how long the curfew ran, it wasn't long after we got there that they dropped it. But still, man, you look around you're like, "Holy cow..." Well the Tigers, somehow, dropped the ball. They never made any provisions. Earl Wilson took Les Cain with him. Matchick goes with his wife, and all the others guys, *bah-bah-bah* they're gone, bus pulls out, there's Patterson and me standing on the corner of Michigan and Trumbull by the stadium like, "Where the hell we gonna go?"

So here comes a cop car pulls up. *Woopwoop!* And we're like, "Oh shit, here we go, just got in town…"

They said, "What are you guys doing?"

I said, "Well, they just dropped off the—we're on the Tigers, we made the team."

"What?" He said, "What's your name?"

"Jon Warden," I said.

He goes, "Get in the car."

I said, "I swear to God, we're Tigers!"

So he's radioing people or whatever… and I say, "Daryl Patterson, he's from California, I grew up outside Columbus, Ohio. We made the team. I'm a left-hand pitcher, he's a right-hander."

He says, "All right… well, get in." And he took us to this Leland Hotel, and they had like one bedroom. He said, "Well I know this place is pretty good, they got a restaurant inside and all that." So we went over and stayed there—and then we ended up living there the whole season!

Holy cow, what a way to start out your career.

Willie Horton:

You know, things could be bad back then, with race relations. But don't ever forget it was what that brought us together—Ernie Harwell's voice. The newspapers were on strike that year, there was no paper. So with Ernie Harwell's voice, you could see people coming together. I saw people black and white enjoying the games, in '68, just mixing together.

But things could still be bad, you know. People don't realize, when the team all went to the White House after the World Series, I didn't go. They said I had pneumonia. Think about that. That's how bad it was. Earl Wilson didn't go, and Gates didn't go, either. That's how tough it was then. And one time, when I first started, see, they found somebody in the organization, man. I found my wife lying on the floor one time, scared, he'd threatened my kids… And it wasn't the *fans,* son, you know—they'd found somebody in the *organization.* So for about five years, I went through some hell here. Then I understood what Ernie had told me, that they just weren't ready yet. So, you started just getting through with it.

But then, when Mr. Campbell came in, that's who changed our organization around—before then, it was tough. Jim Campbell brought Charlie Dressen over to manage, who brought the Dodgers' concept to the Tigers.

That's when ballplayers started mixing, doing things much better. There were some tears, but a lot of happiness.

CURT GOWDY: Driving rain coming down…

And Fred Lasher, who appeared in 34 games with the Tigers this year, winning five and losing one. Born in Poughkeepsie, New York.

Fred Lasher:

It's kind of fun to see that, because I've never seen myself pitch!

I'm glad you had some of that on film, it was cool to see that. Because I've always wondered what the hell I looked like, pitching. I hadn't seen *any* of it. I knew I pitched in the fourth game, the game we got beat. Pitched all right, and I was the only guy warming up in the bullpen the rest of the Series—nobody got in. Mayo played his cards right.

I didn't know who I'd be facing, when I came in. The object was just to come in and get them out. And I pitched well that day, I had pretty good stuff. It was just fun to get in, I wanted to get in and pitch. But, see there—I was trying to kick mud off my shoes, on the mound. Because when it's wet like that, it'd get in between your cleats, and you couldn't throw strikes. It'd screw up your pitching.

Your stride might not be—probably isn't the same length. So you're hitting on the edge of the hole. So you have to kind of dig it out, move over on the rubber, get away from that spot. Sometimes mine would be shorter, or a bit longer. So you have to kind of kick the dirt out of there, and try to find a different spot to land. Yeah, that could be a problem. When you first come in, you loosen up and if everything's fine, you're landing in the same hole. Otherwise, you've got to move a little dirt.

Yeah, I remember doing that quite often, in fact. But when it's wet, it's *miserable*. For everybody.

The fans were unhappy, I'm sure. And I think that's when we went down 3–1—we lost that game.

But—I was nervous for the first pitch... then it's gone. I remember when I came up, the first game against Baltimore. Pitching in Montgomery and Toledo, you know, you got *some* people in the stands but not many. But coming up to Detroit, being in the middle of the pennant race, place was *packed*. It's almost like your legs feel a little weak going out to the mound the first time. You throw the first pitch, and you're ready to go. And you just throw good pitches, hit spots. You make good pitches, you'll get guys out. If you don't, you're going to get hurt. You can't pitch to the middle of the plate in the big leagues; I don't give a damn how hard you throw. We had no scouting report—just *throw strikes*. Throw them to good spots. Hit the corners. Change speeds. Go right at them the way I usually pitch. You can tell if someone makes a bad swing on a pitch, you try and feed him some more.

But not so they can key in on something, you know? Just throwing them all fastballs, they'll key in on the fastball. Mix them up. When I was a pitching coach, I'd get pissed if a guy threw too many pitches the same speed—you have to have them changing speeds and mixing them up, that's how you pitch. That's why it's nice to have about three or four pitches.

I had Frank Robinson one night in Detroit, I had him 3-2. I think he was 1-for-7 off me in my career. And I threw him six curveballs in a row. And he's just ticking 'em, just ticking 'em, fouling them back. And I was getting frustrated, so finally, the seventh one I threw, he hit in the upper deck seats in left field! Mayo come out to the mound, he says, "Jesus Christ, why didn't you throw him a fastball? You had him set up for it!" And I said, "I didn't think I could throw it over the plate!" I was in the groove with the curveball. But I got one a little too much over the plate, and he hit it out on me.

Willie Horton:

See, me and Fred Lasher met each other my first year in baseball, up in Bismarck, North Dakota. He was with Pittsburgh, sinkerballer.

Mickey Stanley:

My first year or second year that I was at Duluth, I had to face that bastard, Lasher. He was in Minot. Or Bismarck, with the Twins organization. We were in the Northern League. So we traveled from Duluth to Bismarck, and had to face him. And man, he was *nasty*. You know, for a high school kid to see something like that… and he threw *hard* from down there. I didn't like that experience. And then he ended up being up on our team. I said, "Fred, boy am I glad you're on our side!"

He was no fun! I didn't like facing him. No way. It was his delivery, that sidearm—it wasn't him. But shit, he was one of the meekest guys on the mound. He never threw at a hitter in his life, I don't think. You know, he didn't brush anybody back, it was just a wicked delivery and he threw hard. Big breaking ball. He was probably the worst guy I had to face in the minor leagues.

Fred Lasher:

They were playing for Duluth, I was playing for Bismarck. Mickey tells a great story, when we were in the minor leagues, he says, "When you guys were coming to town, and you were pitching, I tried to get lost on the bench." They didn't like facing me—Willie didn't either. I pitched *sixteen* innings against those guys, one game. I came on in the first inning or something, and I think—pretty damn sure it was sixteen. Sixty-two, in Duluth.

Northrup was always saying, "I used to eat you up for lunch!" And I said, "Yeah, that's why my ERA was under 1.00, because you hit me so *good.*"

Dick Tracewski:

Lasher was a strikeout sidearmer. I mean, he was nasty. Lasher was the kind of guy who would come in and strike out the side, that's the kind of pitcher he was. I remember one time in Boston, in particular, in a big game—he struck out the side with the bases loaded. Struck out Conigliaro and Yastrzemski and everything. He was that kind of pitcher. He had great stuff.

Tom Matchick:

Lasher had one of the best arms on the club. He threw from down *here*. I think he got in Mayo's doghouse one day and that was it for a while. But he threw a ball, I seen Lasher throw a baseball from the left-field corner to the right-field corner, up into the stands. At Tiger Stadium, just throwing the ball. He had an *arm*. Nobody liked to hit off him in batting practice, because he came from down *here*.

Fred Lasher:

Well naturally, you hold a two-seamer, and when you throw a sidearm the ball just naturally sinks, the way it's released on your hand. I was trying to work on a sidearm curveball, too, that would actually rise—and I was starting to get it, a little bit.

I kind of wish we had radar guns back then, because I'd like to see what the hell I was throwing!

I'd developed that because, as a kid, I'd skip stones across the water. I played one year of high school ball, my senior year, that's all. And the guys I played sandlot ball with—our star pitcher for the high school team was hurt, he hurt his arm—and they told me, "Why don't you go out and pitch? Gosh, you'd do *great.*" I didn't want to at first, and then I did, and I was 7–0 with a no-hitter. And a guy came from the Washington Senators, Joe Cole was his name. He said, "Do you wanna play pro ball?" I said, "Hell, yeah." Kid out of Poughkeepsie. And I went to the rookie league, it was unbelievable how many guys came and went. The competition was amazing.

And then one time, before that, I went with the Dutchess County All-Stars, and played the prison team. In Ossining. We went there to play a game against them, and I remember going through the front gate of that place—it was *scary!* We got in there, and inmates are betting cigarettes on the game and everything else, rooting against your team of course. I think I pitched two or three innings and struck out about eight.

Jon Warden:

Lasher was sort of off the charts a little bit, he was a sidearmer. But very competitive. He came down to fantasy camp one year. And I had this girl on my team, and she would bat like *this*. Terrible. And so Lasher's pitching—and he's *bringin' it*. We're sitting there saying, "Fred, this is a *fantasy camp!* Just lay it up there." Well a lot of the guys can't do it, just can't take anything off. And he's whipping one in there, and he hit her right there—and broke her arm. Broke her arm! They had to take her to the hospital, I said, "Fred, what are you doing!?"

Then also, at the fantasy camp, there was a close play at the plate. We've got local high school umpires, you know, and they're getting fifty bucks for a game. And there was a close play and then he called the guy safe at home, and Fred's in there arguing, getting in his face, telling the umpire, "You suck!" and we're like, "Oh my God—Fred, you can't do that!" I guess if you want the experience, here it is, we're gonna have arguments and kick dirt on the plate and everything.

Dick Tracewski:

We had a *great* bullpen. Jeez, we had Don McMahon, we had Fred Lasher. We had John Hiller, and Pat Dobson. And Hiller threw *bullets*. Pat Dobson went on to be a 20-game winner. But McMahon was our closer. And McMahon was strange, he was the senior guy, we got him late, and he was a big strapping kind of a guy, and a very aggressive pitcher—he threw almost exclusive fastballs. But he had very good command of his fastball. If he wanted to throw his fastball inside, he'd throw it inside. And if he wanted it outside, he had good command.

I would say that McMahon is gonna close your game. Because when he got on the mound, the game was over. His stuff, I didn't think it was great. But he did it, you know, and he was the closer when the Braves won two World Series—he was their closer. He played with Eddie Mathews. Our bullpen was *loaded*.

	1	2	3	4	5	6	7	8	9	R	H	E
Cardinals	2	0	2	2	0	0	0	4	0	**10**	13	0
Tigers	0	0	0	1	0	0	0	0	0	**1**	5	4

Fred Lasher:

You know, when we were down 3–1 after that game, and we knew Bob Gibson was going to pitch another game... we were out in the bullpen, figuring how much we were gonna make from the World Series.

What the *losers'* share was gonna be.

HOW RUNS WERE SCORED

Cardinals first:	Brock homered	Cardinals 1, Tigers 0
	Shannon singled, Maris scored	Cardinals 2, Tigers 0
Cardinals third:	McCarver tripled, Flood scored	Cardinals 3, Tigers 0
	Shannon doubled, McCarver scored	Cardinals 4, Tigers 0
Cardinals fourth:	Gibson homered	Cardinals 5, Tigers 0
	Maris grounded out, Brock scored	Cardinals 6, Tigers 0
Tigers fourth:	Northrup homered	Cardinals 6, Tigers 1
Cardinals eighth:	Gibson walked, Shannon scored	Cardinals 7, Tigers 1
	Brock doubled, Javier, Maxvill, and Gibson scored	Cardinals 10, Tigers 1

GAME FIVE

Tiger Stadium | October 7, 1968

José Feliciano:[49]

Well, I don't know how he heard of me, but Ernie Harwell invited me to do the national anthem.

And for the anthem I always noticed that baseball crowds always wanted it to be over and done with, you know? So they could get back to their popcorn and the game. And this, to me, was a very sad state of affairs, because ever since I was a little boy I always was taught to pledge allegiance to the flag, and when doing the anthem, to do it willingly, and not like, "Oh, shit—I've gotta sing this thing." And so I came in with a soulful rendition. A rendition with *soul,* as opposed to singing it the way Robert Merrill would sing it, or any of the opera singers, you know.

And Ernie didn't know about my rendition, beforehand. I didn't tell *anybody*—because I felt that if I told anybody, they wouldn't let me do it. So I just took it upon myself to, you know, try and steal second when somebody was hitting, you might say. I just took a dare, I took a challenge. "José, this is your chance to make something great out of the anthem."

And I feel bad every now and then, because the man almost lost his job with the radio station.

Jon Warden:

When José Feliciano sang the National Anthem… oh my God, that was—we're standing there and we're like, "Are you kidding me?… holy shit." He came and he started out, "Wooah sayyy can you see… bythedawn's *early* liiight…" And we're going, "Whoa, OK—sing it José!" But he just drug that out and drug it out and drug it out. It lasted for like *five* minutes, it seemed like! Even the Cardinal guys are looking over at us and we're looking at each other like, "Wow… what's going on!?" We're on the third-base line, and they're on the first-base line. And he starts, and we're looking down the line at each other, and sort of look over across the way, like "Wow." Everybody was just shocked, it was rumbling in the stands, people were booing.

Tom Matchick:

A lot of people didn't like that. It was different, but he didn't sing it the way it should've been sung. A lot of people came down on him for that, even the press and that stuff, you know. But it was a *lot* better than what's her name that sang it one year. Movie star, what was her name? Years back, I don't know how many years back. Roseanne Barr! Did you hear that one? Oh my God. "Ooooh sa-yyyy, can you see-heee!"

Orlando Cepeda:

Well, a couple guys from the Cardinals, you know, they were from the South. Like Billy Muffett, our pitching coach. He was really upset about it. Very upset. Right there when Feliciano was singing it, he was very upset. "That's not the way to sing it, arrhh!" But I enjoyed it, I liked it.

Tony Kubek:

I knew that NBC was getting a lot of phone calls saying the anthem was almost disrespectful. And I remember talking to Ernie about it, and Ernie must've been right down there with José Feliciano on the field, and I know there were some people with instruments as I recall. And I was down on the field at the time, I wasn't doing much work at the booth, because they were using George Kell and Harry Caray before the game. But I can remember saying something to José Feliciano, it may have just been, "Hey, good going," or something, I'm not sure.

And also, I remember about four or five years before all that...

When José Feliciano was a very young kid, we saw him perform in Chicago, when I was with the Yankees. I don't remember the name of the place, but right on Rush Street. He lived upstairs for a while, and would travel a lot around the country, to New York, and he'd got to Canada and so forth. And a few of us were going to eat, it must've been a warm summer day, '63 or '64, I'm not sure. But there were a bunch of us on that team, and we went in, and there was the young man, with his sunglasses on, on a little stage, with his dog lying down in front of him, playing his guitar and singing. And this was *way* before José Feliciano had really a lot of acclaim, so to speak.

So I can remember that, and I remember during the Series when he came and played.

José Feliciano:

I really didn't think I was doing anything...*bad*, let's say—or what I didn't think was bad. It was all off the cuff—I didn't prepare anything, I was too busy working in Vegas. I didn't even know that there was a band that was going to accompany me. But I'm *glad* that I did it with my guitar, because the band was ho-hum! They were surprised too, but I just did it with my guitar. My guitar was my band, you know. So I felt very alone when I started playing, because I couldn't hear the guitar very well. Sound systems in ballparks, you know how they are. And I mean, it was a large audience—the World Series is always big. So I felt kind of alone, and then when I started getting into it, I did what I had to do.

And then when I heard the audience, I heard some applause, but a lot of boos. It shocked me. It *shocked* me. I said, "What did I do wrong? What's going on here?" Because I heard a lot of boos. If you listen to the playback, you can hear them too. And so when Tony Kubek and some of the announcers came to me after and said, "You know you've just caused a riot on the switchboard? Veterans threw their shoes at the television…" it made me kind of sad. I said, "*Really?*"

Because the thing was, in '68 we'd just gone through so many *bad* things. Like Martin Luther King being shot. Bobby Kennedy being assassinated. I mean, the '60s didn't have a lot of *good* in them. You know, and they started off, in '63 with the assassination of the president, you know? And things got worse in the late '60s. And I guess they thought, "Ah, here comes this young hippie." They wanted to deport me from the United States, but they couldn't. I had to go through a lot of things, but, it's funny, pioneers get the stones thrown at them, and then everybody that follows, it's acceptable. But at least I gave people the freedom to do the anthem in whatever way they felt it, and that was a good thing. And that's what I tried to be, a pioneer.

And you know, none of the players—it was almost as if I'd been pitching a perfect game, and they didn't want to jinx me. Nobody would talk to me! Like, "Oh shit—what'd I *do?*" Willie Horton was one of the first ones to come up to me and tell me how great it was, because, you know, he being African-American, it *hit* him—that I did it with *soul.* Because Marvin Gaye had done it before me, but Marvin stuck to the regular way. And I took a step forward.

And then, after, they took me to the airport. I had to leave as soon as possible, because I had to get back to Vegas and continue my show. At that time I lived in Vegas, I was on the bill in Vegas with Bobbie Gentry. You remember her, don't you? "Ode to Billie Joe"?

So I did it in my own way, and it was *never* my intention to defame the anthem in any way—I was just very proud, and I still am, of being a Puerto Rican–American, and so that was my crux. And this way, I think it made it *different.* And now, people can listen to it themselves and judge it, and then they'll see that I didn't do anything defamatory to our anthem.

Jon Warden:

José, he came to our 45th reunion, four years ago. And he sang it again, at Comerica. They invited him back. And he and his handler, companion, were sitting over here, where there was sort of a railing. And all the '68s and their wives, we were all over here. And there were two seats open, and I said, "José, get over here with us—you're part of our '68 mystique, man, you're part of that, you're part of the history!" "Really?" "Yeah!" So he and his buddy came over. And they were talking—you know, he was born blind—about how all he wanted to do was become a baseball player. So I said, "Well, José, you'd make a great umpire." Our whole table, everyone, got laughing! Even Hal Naragon got laughing, and he's real straitlaced.

And José goes, "Hey—that's a good idea, that's a good thought, I *would* make a good umpire! I could just walk out with my stick and go, 'That sounded like ball one!'"

Hal Naragon:

All of them just roared when Warden said that. Especially José, he thought that was good. And I want to tell you, I'd had the wrong opinion of José Feliciano. He is really a nice guy. I'm ashamed of myself. He is really a nice guy, José.

José Feliciano:

You know, Detroit did a lot of good things for me. I paid my dues there playing at The Retort—which was a coffeehouse located in the Mt. Royal Hotel on Woodward Avenue, and I played there for quite a while. And I got my first guide dog at Leader Dogs.

And of course I met my wife in Detroit.

But I have to tell you, the anthem gave me a different type of fame… for a while my career was on the skids because of my rendition. Radio stations stopped playing my records, and it was tough. It was tough for a few years, for me. So when I came back there in 2006, and everybody gave me a standing ovation, I said, "José, this is what it's all about." And

I saw Ernie Harwell again, who I think was one of the best play-by-play announcers on the planet. There's nobody like Ernie—he was one of a kind. He was a wonderful human being, and I'm sad that the Lord took him from us—but he and his wife were really good people, and I knew him. And as I say, I *love* Detroit, you know?

I did what I had to do, and I owe Detroit a lot. I owe the Tigers a lot. And I love the Tigers.

I hope that soon they'll be winning a pennant.

	1	2	3	4	5	6	7	8	9	R	H	E
Cardinals	3									3	3	0
Tigers										0	0	0

GEORGE KELL: The 3-2 count to Cepeda... and he hits a *high* drive, to deep left—that one is sailing back, going, and it is... *in* the seats, for a home run!

And these Cardinal bats continue to *boom* at Tiger Stadium...

Orlando Cepeda:

In the first inning, Lolich, he threw me a 3-2 slider. He made a hell of a pitch. Three-two slider, low and inside. That was a good pitch; it was a hell of a pitch. But, well, you know—sometimes you're there.

I thought, "We got 'em!"

Willie Horton:

When we were down, we never thought we were down—because we'd trained our minds, that we were never out of the game till the last strike. And we'd been involved in forty-six or forty-seven games where we came back and won, that year.

I remember that year playing against the Cardinals, and we're sitting in the clubhouse laughing—we said, "Well how'd they pick St.

Louis over *us?*" And what they did is, they won it the year before, so that's how they did it. You know, everybody picked St. Louis to win. And so, I said, "Hell, we won 103 games!"

Jim Price:

It's interesting, we always had that confidence, that we could do it—*anything*.

I would say the locker room was pretty loose, and we had a good starting lineup.

We were loaded. I mean, we could hit. We could all hit, knew how to play the game. We always felt we were in the game, you know, we always felt we could do anything. Because we lost in September the last game of the season in '67, then rolled right through in '68. We had a lot of good players, *a lot* of good players.

And we were such a loose team. Dick Tracewski says—and he played with the Dodgers a couple World Series—he said, and he meant it the right way, that we were the most out-of-control great team he's ever been around. We had fun, we enjoyed ourselves. And we knew we were going to do what we could do.

Al Kaline:

You know, we always thought that we were good enough to win. But losing a game, we weren't depressed or anything like that, or down. We knew we had a good team and we were capable of bouncing back and winning. We were a team that always rallied, late-inning rallies, always scored a lot of runs late.

John Hiller:

We won so many games from the seventh inning on, and in the World Series it was the same idea—we just had an idea that we were gonna win. We came from behind all year. And so we always just had that gut feeling. And I think, you know, if we were all honest with each other, we'd probably sit down and say, "Ah maybe St. Louis had a better team than us, overall." But, we just had that feeling—that we were going to do it. You can't explain those things, but it was just a little intuition.

Tom Matchick:

We just kept the same attitude. Like we can come back. We came back all year—there was over, what, forty some games that we were tied or behind from the seventh inning on that we won? So, we could score runs. We could come from behind. And if you walked in our clubhouse, you would've thought we were *up* three games to one. Their attitudes were just, you know—it seemed like *nothing* bothered them. Nothing bothered them at all, the guys.

Down three games to one, you would've thought we were *up* three games to one. Those guys were nuts!

Fred Lasher:

Hopeful, it was hopeful.

Dick Tracewski:

The atmosphere was always, "We could *win* this game."

All we did was we had a good time, we enjoyed each other, and if we were gonna lose, we were gonna lose. But we were gonna lose fighting. And we were gonna be tough to beat. Because there's no definition of *coming back*. When you're down in the major leagues, you're gonna lose most of the time. But somehow or other, we came back a lot…

Jon Warden:

Before Game Five, Norm Cash was in the locker room walking around, bat on his shoulders, saying: "Hey guys—*they're* the ones that can't get a BB up their ass. They're the ones that should be nervous. All the pressure's on them, they gotta win this one to clinch it. Let's just go out and win one for the fans—have *fun*."

He was casually walking around, just sort of bantering, you know. The other guys would pop off and say something: "Hell yeah, let's go, let's kick their ass, come on—keep 'em close, we'll beat 'em." We were that type of team anyway, we'd come from behind all year. It's just another game, let's start right now, give our fans a win.

We were 0–2 at home, let's go out and give them a win.

CURT GOWDY: Mickey Stanley starts it off for the Tigers, in the last of the fourth inning.

Ball one—and Briles *fell* down. That's an unusual sight. Very rarely see a pitcher fall flat on his face like that…

The 2-2 pitch to Stanley… there's a drive down the right-field line, it's a *fair* ball! Stanley has a *triple!*

Mickey Stanley:

You know how I was talking about triples? Who the hell was it off, Briles? It was kind of a—looper to right field, or something. And I remember it, that it wasn't one to be proud of.

Probably, on a triple behind me, I'm looking at Cuccinello, yes. If it was in left-center or down the left-field line, no. I'm a better coach than the coaches, on the bases. No, I'd be looking at the third-base coach, but I'd have a pretty damn good idea if I had a chance or not by what I saw when I got halfway to second. If I'm halfway to second, I'm looking, taking a peek. Probably know I can make it, but probably looking. You don't hear anything. You don't—it's kind of just a blur, you know. You're so into the game that it doesn't mean much.

And I came home on a sac fly [by Cash], I think. I know I didn't have to run very hard, I know that. It was deep enough to where there wasn't going to be a play.

CURT GOWDY: They're playing Horton deep.

Fly ball… and that ball is going to be bounding around out there! The Tigers trying to battle back, and their fans are *roaring* here.

Willie Horton:

That triple? I hit that *good*—hit it off the fence. That was the deepest part of the park; I think it was 445 feet out there in center.

I didn't think about it much, I just hit the ball—and when I hit it, I thought I hit it hard enough to get out, but then I knew it wasn't gonna go, and so you *run*. And I thought about a triple. If I saw the outfielders pull up, I would've known it was gone, because I hit that ball hard. When you run, you see all of that. And then I knew how he was running at the ball, so I had to turn into second gear, and I started thinking *triple!* I looked over to third base to see if the coach was putting the stop on me, but he never put his hands up. You always pick up the coaches. And then he told me to slide. You can't hear him, but he gets down with you.

Bill Haller:

You know, there was a play in that fifth game, when the ball went like *this*! I remember that. It hit… something! This is the fifth game of the Series, the Cardinals are winning the Series three games to one, they're winning this game, 3–1. Routine ground ball to Javier, and Javier probably never made an error in ten years, and the ball goes *over* his head..

It had to hit something… it was just a *freak* thing!

	1	2	3	4	5	6	7	8	9	R	H	E
Cardinals	3	0	0	0						3	4	0
Tigers	0	0	0	2						2	4	1

Julián Javier:

That was a hit—they didn't give an error I don't think. But it was a *strange* ball—it hit some rock or something in front of me. It bounced real high, there.

If it was a little lower, I would've gotten it—but it went too high! So it hit me right in the end of the glove. The ball must've hit a little rock, a little hole in the dirt there. It shot up, and I wasn't expecting that big bounce. Today, the infields look better than before—every park you go to. I don't know what kind of dirt they use now.

I didn't feel bad, I couldn't do nothing about it. But you can tell it was high because I even *jumped* up to get it—and my hat fell off.

Dick Tracewski:

Maybe somebody stepped and there was a little hole or something, and the ball hit it. But the field in Detroit was quite good, it was good. And it was an old ballpark. It goes back to—it was the first ballpark built. And they had a drainage system there; they had three drains in the outfield. When it rained, everything would go into these drains and then out. And sometimes the outfield would get muddy. But by and large, it was a pretty good field. But nowadays, when I went back to Detroit and I went to Comerica Park, Holy Christ, it's like a pool table. It's beautiful.

Willie Horton:

That ball did hit a rock or something, but I was gonna score anyway. He might've *tried* to throw me out, but he wouldn't have gotten me. I was going on contact there, I'm just coming home. I think it must've been two outs.

CURT GOWDY: Top of the fifth inning. Brock on second, one out. Javier, in the batter's box with a .353 Series average.
Line drive into left…

Willie Horton:

At that point in the game, we were losing. It was the fifth inning, and I know Lolich had kind of decided to close up the park by then. You always want to set up one or two plays in your head. Think ahead. So we closed the park up, and I had ten feet either way—coming like a seesaw at the ball, going towards home plate. If the ball comes at me, either way, I can go ten feet either way, *slanted*. And knowing who was batting, Javier, and knowing how Lolich was going to pitch him, I said, "He's not gonna pull that ball. If he hits it my way, it's gonna be ten feet on either side." He's not gonna pull it hard, but it might go to left-center, in the air.

I was in the right spot, knowing who's hitting, and which way he hits the ball off of Lolich, and who was running.

But also, I thought about the score of the game, and I thought in my mind about reading the reports before the Series, how we saw that since the All-Star break, Brock had picked up bad habits from being successful. What he did, we noticed that from first base, he used to go around second and drift into third. The same way that when he was at second, he'd go around third base and drift into home. He'd break his stride, and just drift. Because nobody would even *attempt* to throw him out. Our scouts picked up on how when Brock was running, the National League outfielders would just lob the ball back to the second baseman or the shortstop. So with him being so successful, he got lazy.

Before that play, I was thinking, "Well, Freehan knows the same thing."

Julián Javier:

I was at bat, and I got the base hit on Lolich, to left field. He used to throw a lot of balls inside, and I think he threw me a fastball inside. When left-handers threw me balls inside, I hit them good. I used to hit them well, even Lolich. Every time we faced them—spring training, and so on.

So I hit it, and I ran to first—and then I was running to second base after they threw home, so I was turning around, watching the play. When I got to first base, I turned a little bit, and I was looking at it.

CURT GOWDY: Horton's up with it... Brock's being waved around, the throw from Horton, and he is... *safe. Out! OUT!!* They called him *out* at the plate!

Julián Javier:

I tell you... I don't know what happened to Brock! I didn't know why he didn't slide into home plate! I think maybe he tried to go back to second, because I hit the ball real hard, it was a line drive. He must have gone back to second base—and that's why they got him at home plate.

Willie Horton:

When I was going at the ball, my mind was... I didn't care about anything, I didn't see Brock run, I didn't see nobody. Everything was blocked out, except that *field*. I just thought about hitting Coyote right on the *nose*. The third baseman, the cutoff. Coyote is my guideline throwing a guy out at home—and I don't think they do that now, they just throw the ball. For us, the third baseman being there, it was like a plane landing. If he'd hit the ball to right field, Kaline would've thrown the ball at Cash's nose, probably. Same thing.

So I didn't think about how to throw it or anything—I think about *Coyote.* That's it. See, if you think about anything else, you'll mess up. I'm not thinking about Freehan, I'm not even thinking about the runner. I'm only thinking about Coyote. Once I know what I've got to do, it's up to Freehan—he can cut it off if he thinks we don't have the runner. You're just taught to get rid of the ball. I just get it and I react, because if you start thinking about throwing it all the way, you might make a bad throw. That's where you mess up. If you think, you'll mess up. It's just like landing a plane. Hit the cutoff man on the nose—he lines you right up.

So Coyote would listen to Freehan, and this time, Bill had seen Brock break his stride. And so he said, "Let it come through."

We knew he was gonna come in standing up, because he did that! And we knew we were gonna get him. So the ball came through, and it was a little high. It came over Coyote's head. I made the throw, he didn't slide, and we got him. I did my job. It's as simple as that.

But it was a wonder Brock didn't break his leg. You know, Freehan's a big man.

Don Wert:

I was playing third base. Brock never touched the plate. And it's pretty much a normal thing when there's a play at home, to make the attempt at cutting off a ball and not cutting it off, and I think I did the good thing there and Brock never slid. I think Freehan did yell, "Let it go!" Because he normally said something when we had a play at home—that's the normal thing that you do, to throw to second base if a guy's running, when you cut it off there. So I would've thrown it to second if he said otherwise. But it was my judgment, you know, what I should do, and it was a good throw. Willie had it right on the button.

People I talk to say that my faking the catch at third base, that meant the difference. Because he never slid, you know, so I guess it was pretty good. If I didn't put that fake on, the way I did—I faked that I was gonna catch the ball and throw to second—and if he saw that, he wouldn't slide. Brock figured that he had home plate made, you know. With the speed he has, he probably never thought he was gonna get caught. And he almost didn't, if he'd have touched the base. So if I didn't fake that catch, at third, he would've slid. I was about even with the pitcher's mound, so his sight would've been able to see me.

Different guys told me that's what happened, and that's what changed the Series.

Mickey Stanley:

I don't think that had anything to do with it—I say Wert's full of shit, call him and tell him!

Willie Horton:

Well Wert didn't do a fake, he had his hand up—that was for guiding the ball. And if he didn't hear Freehan, he would've caught it and gone to second base, to keep Javier from reaching.

Julián Javier:

Look. That was a close play. But you know what happened in there? He didn't slide! The throw was right in there, so if he slid, he would've been over there—the catcher wouldn't have been able to go down and get him. However he slid, he would've gotten in there! Look. See? See where he touched? It was a close play, too—if he slid, he would've been safe, easy!

As I said, when I hit it, I saw Brock going back to second—maybe he thought the shortstop was going to get the line drive, but the line drive was high.

But, nobody said anything about that after. Because he *knows* he had to slide home!

Mickey Stanley:

See that? Isn't that neat, that the camera got that—me kind of ducking behind him at second base?

No one mentioned to do that—but I'd seen shortstops a million times before do that, in front of me. When you're playing center field, you see everything, you know? You see everything. Or, you know, maybe the coaches told me to do it. They didn't have to, though. It doesn't take any genius. I guess if a guy was lazy he wouldn't do it, but—we were afraid of him stealing third! You know, third's just as easy as second for him. Some say it's maybe even easier. And another reason for it is to make it harder for him to score.

Tony Kubek:

Wherever I was standing, I always had a monitor that I could look at, so I could see it. And I would say this on that: chances are pretty good, and I'd have to see it again, that Freehan *might* have decoyed him. The third-base coach sends him in, or maybe he ran through the sign, but I think he was probably sent in. But, Brock then had his back to the left fielder—so he's not looking over his shoulder seeing the throw. So there's a chance that Freehan might've decoyed him a little bit. And then the fact that Freehan planted his foot right on the corner of the plate on the foul line—and sliding into that. That's a ploy that's perfectly legal, the catcher can put his foot there, and you try to slide and if you don't dislodge it, you won't hit home plate, so he kind of hit his foot that's planted there. So Brock may have thought, "Hey, the best way for me to do it is to come in full speed."

And the Cardinals probably figured, based on the scouting report, "OK, when the ball's hit to this guy, we're going to take chances—because his arm might not be accurate, or he takes too long to get rid of it."

John Hiller:

I remember Willie charging the ball—he always played aggressively, and he was a little better than average left fielder. Accurate arm, but not real strong all the time. He got a good jump, and so I remember him charging that ball, and him coming up and throwing—and I almost made a comment in the bullpen, saying, "He'll never get him." Because that was Brock who was running, you know? And I do remember him not sliding—but I still thought he was safe, from our vantage point. And then the umpire called him out, and it was just like, "OK—we got a chance."

Jim Price:

Willie had a good arm, he didn't get the credit as a defensive player that he should have, in left field, because he was such a hitter. And he made a *perfect* throw. One-hop throw and it was probably belt high. And for some reason, Brock didn't slide. Now, I don't know if he'd have been safe if he slid, or Bill would've been able to block him easier if he slid.

But, he was definitely out!

That turned the Series—no question about it.

Tom Matchick:

Willie threw a pea. I mean, he didn't usually have a great throwing arm, but he got rid of it really quick. Charged it, and came up throwing. And Brock could *run*.

He was—*out.*

We were standing up, we weren't sitting down. Not on *that* play.

Bill Haller:

I think I was at first base in that game. I suppose Brock missed the black part of the plate—and he didn't have to do that. No one was close to him! If Brock scores, they win the game. They win the Series. But they didn't. That's what's so great about baseball.

Jon Warden:

Willie had the throw of his life. Freehan caught it chest high, right there. It was just catch, hit, boom, done. Simultaneous. Bam bam. It's almost like a play at first base. Big Ten was a stud, man, piece of granite.

And so then all hell breaks loose—here comes Schoendienst, and everybody's out there arguing. Brock makes a circle coming back towards the plate, and Freehan just reaches out and tags him again, like in the stomach.

Denny McLain:

Every camera you've ever looked at shows that he was out. Brock just made a mistake, you know, he didn't slide. Didn't think he had to, thought he could outrun Willie Horton. So did we. But Willie made, as I recall, it may have been the most perfect throw he's ever thrown in his career. One hop to Bill, and Bill blocked the plate. He could block anything, former football player at the U of M. Brock would've broken his leg had he slid.

It was like playing real baseball. Today, they play parts of it.

Pat Freehan:[50]

When you've caught as long as Bill had, I think that that's second nature, positioning himself. He played football, he played baseball for years and years and years, and... you know, Bill had concussions with his catching and that—so they don't know whether this disease is a result of that, but they're doing so much now with outlawing collisions at the plate. But I don't think Bill would've liked that. I think he *liked* standing his ground at the plate! I think it harkened back to Bill's football days—he liked standing there and letting Lou Brock run into him!

I'm so protective of Bill, and for a long time I couldn't even say "Alzheimer's" or "dementia." But, I mean, it's a fact of life now. It's nothing that he did—he didn't drink himself into oblivion, he didn't whatever, you know. We don't have it on the family on either side, this is just something that Bill has. He's here, and life whirls around him, and I'm thankful that I'm able to have him at home. We're in a pretty place—we're on a lake, and it's a nice, peaceful, wonderful area. And so, you know, that's how life is at this point.

John Hiller:

Bill Freehan was a great catcher, wonderful. Eleven-year All-Star, my goodness. It's too bad you won't be able to talk to him...

Denny McLain:

Bill Freehan was just... absolutely the best catcher I've ever seen.

Jim Price:

Bill was a tactician. And he knew what guys hit. You didn't have all the reports in those days, but you knew what guys hit. And he really knew what guys hit. Guys that, you know, would lean out over the plate, or guys that would back off the plate—he saw all those things. And I don't think pitchers shook him off very often, I don't think so. Because he knew the pitchers really well, and Bill was great at that. He had confidence, also, talking with the pitchers. If they're in trouble, he's out to the mound, he knew how to handle each pitcher, because they're all different personalities. You know, some different, strange, some jolly, you know what I mean.

John Hiller:

These catchers nowadays that sit so far outside—Bill Freehan was the type of catcher who, let's just say if it's a strikeout, he'd just as soon try to get you to strike the guy out in three pitches. He didn't sit this far outside. I mean, catchers nowadays, this far outside, this far inside— you get a strike on a guy, and then they move outside and it's a ball. Unless the batter's really swinging at a bad pitch. But Billy sat in the middle of the dish, almost. And as pitchers, I'd sit with my roommate and they'd say, "How do you do it?" "I throw for his shoulder—I don't have to throw to the *glove*." I need a target, for my eyes. And John Sain would say, "Aim for the middle! If it's got any movement, it's gonna hit a corner!" But Bill would just, he wouldn't get on the corners, outside. And I hardly ever shook him off.

Dick Tracewski:

One thing about Freehan, he was a *horse*. And he caught all the time. I don't know this for a fact, but I wouldn't be a bit surprised if he didn't catch doubleheaders once in a while. That's the kind of player he was. And he was a good hitter. But, like everybody else, one guy got into the World Series and didn't hit a lot. I think he got two hits in one of the games late in the Series. I remember the same thing happened when I was a kid, with Gil Hodges. And he got the same thing, and they were praying for him in church!

Al Kaline:

You know, I don't think we had one leader, but I think Bill Freehan was probably the biggest leader on our ballclub. And, that's another thing that I get a little—and I don't want to use this word, but—*pissed off* about. Bill Freehan was the best player I ever played with for a long period of time, on a team. And he made, I don't know, seven, eight, nine All-Star games, maybe more than that—and he never gets any recognition around here. And I get mad about that. Because, he was a leader, he was a horse behind the plate, he played when he was hurt, he got hit by a lot of pitches all the time, and he was a great leader, a great catcher, and got a lot of big hits for us, all the time. I mean, he was a *horse*, man. I remember one time, he had an irregular heartbeat. And he would have to lay on the floor—he was covered in sweat, and for whatever reason then all of a sudden it settles down. And he gets up and he goes to play! It was unbelievable.

But nobody ever talks about him, and I really get mad when I do things here in the stadium, and people don't bring up the name Bill Freehan. They bring up other players. Which, rightfully so, but Bill Freehan, in my mind—I don't know whether he deserves a statue out there or not, but certainly his name should be out there on the wall someplace.

And back in those days, the catcher called the game. They didn't get signs from the dugout like they do today, stuff like that. They didn't have video about every hitter, and scouts on the road telling them how to pitch certain hitters and everything. I mean, he had to do that by memory, and remembering each player, how he reacts at the plate. And he did that. He did it great.

Pat Freehan:

I met him in high school, in Florida—we met when we were fourteen. But having been born in Detroit, having gone through grade school there, and being a hometown boy, I think he might have felt more connected to the Tigers. And a lot of the Tigers adopted Michigan as their home, Al Kaline made that his offseason home for years.

And Bill did come back every summer and play summer ball up here, because the competition was better. And in Florida, black and white people didn't play on the same teams, and didn't play each other. I mean, we grew up with segregation in the south, in the '50s. And so,

Bill thought the caliber was better and so he'd come up and stay with his grandparents or whatever, and play in the Adray League. I think Adray Appliances or whatever, sponsored sandlot baseball. And I think Bill and a group of players from the Detroit area went in a group to the University of Michigan—there were about six of the guys, and the year Bill signed and went, they went on to win the College World Series— and I think that's the last time a northern team might've won the College World Series! This group of men came from Detroit sandlots, and they liked Don Lund, and they went up to Michigan and played college ball together. So he had a very definite connection to Detroit. His grandfather worked for General Motors, and his parents met in high school at St. Rita's.

So they played against each other, and you know if Bill's Adray team won whatever league, then they'd pick up Willie and some of the other better players from the league to go with them to Altoona, Pennsylvania. Then they went to the Hearst All-Star team, he played in Yankee Stadium when he was a high schooler!

Willie Horton:

Well, Freehan and I met not in high school—I met Freehan before that. Bill's about a year older than I am, I think. And I played in like three different leagues, you know, and one year they picked me up to go to Altoona, Pennsylvania—we won the Little League World Series, I mean the Babe Ruth League World Series. We beat Pete Rose, Eddie Brinkman, John Havlicek—the Hall of Fame basketball player. That's the kids from Cincinnati we beat, in '59. They beat Freehan and them the year before, but Bill and them picked me up to go, they picked up Dennis Ribant, and a couple of guys. That year I went with Bill and them, they picked me up. I was thirteen and Bill was about fourteen, something like that.

Tim McCarver:

I have always defended Lou. I think if Lou had tried to slide, he would've *definitely* been out. But I think he saw a little crevice, between the outstretched legs of Freehan—and went for that part of the plate. And I'm not too sure he wasn't safe to begin with, after all was said and done. I thought he might've been out, it was really close. He *might've* been safe.

Tony Kubek:

You can give a guy goat horns for that, but, you know, most guys don't make excuses. Some might. They called them "Alibi Ike" years ago.[51] You might make an excuse and say, "Ahh I did this or that, I fell down, I slipped…" Well, Alibi Ike would do that. But I don't think Brock nor Flood were those kinds of players. And most guys don't make excuses. They'd just say, "Yeah—that was my fault."

Ray Washburn:

I was in the dugout then, and I thought he was safe. But then when he didn't slide, well, that's what you live with. There was no replay challenge—whatever the call was, that was it! So the Tigers got the break they needed. And we just—Lolich was up to the task, he just had us. Our hitters were off stride against him that game, and all Series. It wasn't overpowering, but there was the movement, the location, and different pitches in the strike zone at different times.

Bobby Tolan:

A lot of people wanted to know why Lou Brock didn't slide at home plate… and Lou said that, you know, he couldn't get there—because Freehan had the plate blocked. So he came in trying to stand up, and a lot of people say that, you know, that could've been our downfall.

I don't believe that. I just believe that Willie Horton made a great throw from the outfield, and… it wasn't supposed to be!

Willie Horton:

I'll never forget, after I made that throw, I ran and hugged Stanley at shortstop—I said, "Thanks for all the hard work and long time you put in with me. All that work paid off."

So he helped me learn how to play the outfield. I always had a good strong arm, but I had to *learn* how to throw from the outfield. I'd been a catcher my whole life growing up, so I had to learn how to get the ball on *top*. You had to throw different. And I'll never forget the last thing he taught me: "Act like you're getting off a bus." So you get on top of the ball. Come right over top, and stay on top of the ball, and you'll have something on it. And you hold the ball across the seams—you learn how to do that in your hands. If you hold it *across* the seams, it won't go off line or anywhere else. I had to learn that, it took me a *long* time. And I think, the other important thing he taught me—you learn your pitching staff. And you learn to play your position. You learn to get the jump on the ball.

So I'd thrown out guys before then, but that one moment, in the biggest game in our life, it all came into play. That all comes from Mickey Stanley working with me. See, I didn't want to just be a regular outfielder. I mean, somebody that's just out there. And so I worked at it. That whole play came from going over things, studying things. I got credit for it, but it's *everybody*. And I remember telling Yaz the next year, down at Lindell, the sports club, I joked, "Well I don't take the back seat to Yaz no more!" That throw gave me the confidence that I could do that—and actually, I've got one of the major-league records, I think it's tied, 12 putouts. That record's still there.[52]

Mickey Stanley:

I don't think I really taught him anything on that. Willie threw overhand all the time!

But it was perfect. Everything was perfect there. Everything was perfect. Freehan had the plate kind of blocked with his left foot, I was darting behind Brock every once in a while at shortstop, to keep him close to the bag.

It was just perfect.

Pat Freehan:

Bill always said: "Willie, it was the *perfect* throw." I know it was *right* there, right where it was supposed to be. And it was a bang-bang play, as Bill would say. The ball got there, Lou got there, he held on to the ball, he spun Lou around… And everyone said, "Why didn't you slide?" That if he had slid, he might've been safe, or this or that, you don't know.

I can remember one time we were in Hawaii, and they had something called the Legends Game. Lordy, lordy, lordy, when would that have been? In the late '80s probably. And Lou Brock was there, and his wife, and they went to dinner with us. And Bill and Lou always joked about that. "Lou, why did you come back and touch the plate again, if you thought you'd touched it the first time?" I know Bill and Lou always talked and joked about that, and they would go back and forth and back and forth about that.

But in the pictures, it looks like Bill's leg or thigh has prevented Lou from touching the plate, that he's standing guard on the plate. Bill always said, "Lookit! You can see the *top* of home plate"—you know, it goes straight across, you don't see a shoe, you don't see anything breaking that straight line across the top of the plate. And so he always joked, "Hey Lou, if you thought you were safe, why'd you come back and touch the plate again!?" And Brock would go, "Well, I just wanted to touch it a second time!"

Willie Horton:

When Lou Brock was in town one time, he *still* thought he was safe. And my son was talking to him, so I said, "Well you tell him, your dad got the *ring*." And I said, "How are you safe—you didn't slide!" If he had slid, around this side, he would've gotten in there with his hand. And not discrediting him, he was very successful—he stole seven bases that year in the Series.

Julián Javier:

That play was why we lost the game. Because that would've gotten Lolich out of the game. They would've brought somebody in, he was ready to come out. If Brock scored, Lolich is going out—because they already had somebody in the bullpen. But then, he stayed in, and we didn't score any more runs.

And then they started hitting…

Johnny Edwards:

That was *the* big play of the game, you know. Before that, the Tigers were *dead*. I remember when Javier hit that ball, and Horton threw Brock out—only he wasn't out, he was *tripped*! And then Freehan catches the ball and runs back over and tags him.

And so that was the spark that got them going again.

	1	2	3	4	5	6	7	8	9	R	H	E
Cardinals	3	0	0	0	0					3	6	0
Tigers	0	0	0	2						2	4	1

Willie Horton:

We *knew* we were coming back. We knew it. The only way we weren't coming back was if the game was over with. And we couldn't help from thinking that way—because how many games we came back that year, forty-six? And some of those in the ninth inning. Some down to the last strikes.

So we felt it wasn't gonna change—we were always into the game. We always thought: until the last inning, until the last strike, we had more innings ahead, and we always believed that the guys were gonna come through for us. We always thought we were in *every* game we played, it didn't matter how many runs down we were. Because we won so many games doing that, so didn't ever think about being out of the game. And that's what makes you keep concentrating.

We *knew* we were coming back.

And that throw turned everything around for us.

Mike Shannon:

Let me tell you the key to that Series, why we lost. Everybody talks about Brock not sliding—that's bullshit. Safe or out, or whatever. Do you know why they beat us? Mickey Lolich. And it wasn't his pitching. It was when Mayo Smith let him *bat*! In Game number Five, when we were up three games to one, he let Lolich bat. And he got a base hit, if I'm not mistaken. Well that changes the whole goddamn atmosphere, all right. And the reason, in my mind, that Mayo Smith let him bat, was because every time we got to the bullpen, we lit that bullpen up. And Lolich was the only guy that was pitching well, so he just left him in there. Well, Lolich got a base hit, and once he got that base hit, the momentum just *rushed* into them. And they came back and beat us.

And that's the way I look at baseball, OK. I look at the psychological part of it. When Lolich got that base hit, it changed the momentum of the whole Series. They're sitting over there, saying, "Goddamn—if he can do it, why can't we?"

And first of all, the players knew that the only chance they had was Lolich. And here's Mayo Smith, he's got a chance to take him out of the game. Correct? And he doesn't take him out, he lets him hit. So when he let Lolich hit, and he got the base hit—psychologically that changed *everything*.

Tim McCarver:

The oddest thing in the world, down 3–2 in the seventh, and Mayo Smith let Lolich hit for himself. And he plopped that ball in front of Ron Davis in right field. That's one of those, not looking back, but had Roger Maris been playing, he played a shallow enough right field where he probably would've made that play.

But, it's just. . . one of those things. Destiny, and fate, who knows…

Bill Haller:

Who comes to bat, but Mickey Lolich! Well, you pinch-hit, don't you? But the reason Mayo didn't pinch-hit, because he didn't have anybody as good as Mickey in the bullpen. So he took a chance, he let Mickey hit! Mayo took a chance with Lolich, and it worked out for him.

Hal Naragon:

I think Mayo was thinking, he didn't want them to get any more runs. And Lolich wasn't pitching too bad! I think, stay with the pitcher. I know you could be criticized, that was probably a little gamble. But you just think about it a little bit: 3–2, and you've got a few bats left, you don't want them to get another run. And Lolich was a pretty tough pitcher. You know what Roger Maris told the Cardinals, he said that Lolich would be tougher to hit than McLain. And Roger and I are good friends, he was with the Indians.

Jon Warden:

In the bottom of the seventh, Lolich comes up, his turn to bat is going to come up in the bottom of the seventh. So Mayo, he lets Lolich hit. He's the *worst* hitter in the world! And Mayo's reply, it's on one of the tapes, he says, "Waall he's come this far and I was just gonna let him hit." What happens? Lolich duck farts one into right field that the right fielder dove for and just missed catching. So he's on first base. Then Stanley—*boom*. Base hit. Base hit, base hit, base hit. All of a sudden, we're up. But to let—how's the hell a manager let Mickey Lolich hit? But then he gets a base hit. That's how goofy his managing was. He would pinch-hit left-hander against a left-hander, and Northrup would get a hit, off a lefty. Game after game like that, something would happen. And Mayo would do something stupid, and it turned out great. He's like magic, man.

GEORGE KELL: Well you can hear the crowd coming alive here, at Tiger Stadium. A walk to Stanley loaded the bases, and here's the old pro, Al Kaline...

There's a *drive* into right-center... base hit for Kaline! A run is in... here's *another* one coming in—and the Tigers have taken the lead!

Al Kaline:

It was against Hoerner, Joe Hoerner. Their relief pitcher, or their closer. I don't think they used the word *closer* back in those days, but he was their best relief pitcher from what I understood. And I knew that he used to like to turn the ball over, and so I fouled a bunch of pitches off, and finally got the base hit to right-center field. And, it wasn't the hardest-hit ball I ever hit in my life, but it was one more people remember than the home run I hit or anything else. So I remember facing Joe, and anticipating that he's gonna turn the ball over, he's gonna keep the ball down and away, down and away. And had he busted me inside, he probably would've gotten me. That was my mindset, and that was what I was thinking. That he's gonna pitch me to my weakness, and I thought my weakness was low and away.

So, I basically knew how they were going to pitch me. Anybody that played as long as I did, you should know what your strengths and weaknesses are. And I knew they were going to try to pitch me away. And every once in a while, bust me off the plate and go back away again. So that was always my game plan, and that's how I got the big hit in the fifth game. It wasn't a big line drive, but it was a base hit. I fouled off a lot of pitches—but I knew in my mind that they were going to keep coming low and away, low and away, low and away, so I kept fouling it off, and finally I put one out there. Had they busted me inside, they probably would've gotten me, but I just always thought that they weren't going to pitch to my strength, they were going to pitch to my weakness. Especially in a big situation, a tight situation. They didn't want me to pull the ball to left field, because I was a good pull hitter, and they didn't want me to get one mistake, and maybe hit one out of the ballpark. So they were going to stay away.

Tony Kubek:

Ordinarily, I think they probably would've tried to pitch around Kaline a little bit more, because of what he'd done in the past—I mean, his record was outstanding, he was such a good player. But they maybe said, "OK, he didn't have a good year, so let's go ahead and pitch to him." But how many runs did Al drive in in that Series? Seven or eight in that Series? I've forgotten now. But he was such a complete ballplayer.

Al Kaline:

There were a lot of great moments and plays that helped the Tigers become world champions—and certainly you have to do those kind of things if you're going to become world champions.

	1	2	3	4	5	6	7	8	9	R	H	E
Cardinals	3	0	0	0	0	0	0			3	6	0
Tigers	0	0	0	2	0	0	2			4	8	1

Jon Warden:

After that happened, and we took that lead… We're like, "OK—we got McLain, we're going back to St. Louie, Game Six."

HOW RUNS WERE SCORED

Cardinals first:	Flood singled, Brock scored	Cardinals 1, Tigers 0
	Cepeda homered, Flood scored	Cardinals 3, Tigers 0
Bottom fourth:	Cash hit sacrifice fly, Stanley scored	Cardinals 3, Tigers 1
	Northrup singled, Horton scored	Cardinals 3, Tigers 2
Tigers seventh:	Kaline singled, Lolich and McAuliffe scored	Tigers 4, Cardinals 3
	Cash singled, Stanley scored	Tigers 5, Cardinals 3

GAME SIX

Busch Stadium | October 9, 1968

Tim McCarver:

It was hotter, in St. Louis. It was brighter, it was different. That's all I can say, from a batter's-eye standpoint—you never picked the ball up as well. And that's all you need to do is face Gibson, in Game One, and not being able to pick the ball up like you did at Tiger Stadium. It's a recipe for 17 strikeouts.

And that's why we had so much confidence going back there.

Dick Tracewski:

We had Denny McLain pitching, Denny won 31 games. Now that was unbelievable. He would pitch on the fourth day, I mean—it was unbelievable what he did. He did something that was really unprecedented.

Tony Kubek:

You can not discount what Denny McLain did. There's no Game Seven without him pitching a big Game Six for them—so he came through also. So when they got in those last two games after a long season—and I don't know if McLain got a cortisone shot or what he got, because he did have some tenderness, as I recall. And he may have resorted to a few more off-speed pitches.

Jim Price:

Denny, his arm was sore. But Denny had a year, boy, you've got to give it to him. *Great* year. Great couple of years.

Denny McLain:

As you can see, my arm was bothering me. I've got it up in the air the whole fuckin' game. I had an injection an hour before the game. And going into September, it was tough. I was taking more and more cortisone shots. I think I had sixteen or eighteen, and more than I think ten of them were after the All-Star break. *Every* game. During the World Series. I went out in the sixth game and I didn't even know I *had* an arm, that's how much fuckin' Xylocaine I had in my arm. I didn't know if I could *warm up*! I mean, I had no feeling at all in my right arm, *none*. I was all over the place warming up at first, and then a little bit of it wore off, a little bit.

I didn't think it was possible, to be honest with you.

And, you just got to get yourself settled quickly out there. And especially in a game like that, because you're playing sudden death. You know, you better be ready when you hit the mound. In the regular season, you normally have an inning or two to get into your tempo, get into your rhythm, but in that kind of a ballgame… you're *live*. You're live, first pitch. There's no timing, there's no set of time that you can get ready, to work your way up to your rhythm, up to your pace. And, that was the big thing. That's a big move for a pitcher.

But, you know, it's—I mean, the game's a funny game. Every once in a while, no matter *what* kind of stuff you have, you lose! And sometimes when you've got the worst stuff in the world, you win. But man,

I'll tell you—it was… I mean I didn't know *what* was gonna happen. And the good thing happened that was supposed to happen!

Jim Price:

Denny was a fastball pitcher. I don't know what his speed was, but I'd say low 90s.

He could throw any pitch at any time.

Dick Tracewski:

Denny threw the ball the same way, all the time. He was a beautiful thing to watch, because he had a great delivery, he threw a very light baseball—and by the same token, Mickey Lolich threw a ball that was, you would think it was *lead*!

Denny would lift his leg way up, point his toe… he was beautiful. He had great control, *great* control. If he walked a guy, he didn't care to walk him. But if a walk would hurt him, he'd never walk him. He'd throw strikes.

Tom Matchick:

Denny had the fastball that started down below your knees, and when it got to home plate, it was up by your armpits. And it was advantage, pitchers then—baseball was a pitcher's paradise. Now with the mounds being flatter, it's almost a hitter's paradise. They were looking *down* at you, throwing the ball. So it made a big difference.

And, plus he had the breaking ball…

Denny McLain:

It's a much bigger, difficult pitch. I mean, it's called the twelve-to-six pitch, and you start it at the head, and you hope that by the time it finishes, it's down around the feet. And in most cases, it would be. But it's a much slower speed, because nobody can throw it hard, a big curveball.

So you just gotta make sure you've got the same arm action on it as you do a fastball and a slider.

Mickey Stanley:

McLain's was a yellowhammer. Because it was over the top, it was slow, and it was just… off-speed. Something else to show them. It wasn't very effective. It was a horseshit yellowhammer. It was! But all McLain needed was that fastball… sometimes it would rise, sometimes it would run. Like Rivera, that reliever for the Yankees? His ball would run like that sometimes. They would rise, and sometimes it would run—it never sunk. McLain threw a changeup once in a while, but all he needed was that moving fastball.

Dick Tracewski:

Denny's big thing was—when he first came up, and I was watching him, it was very evident the first year I was there in '66, he was one of these guys with this big slow overhang curveball, like Carlton. And what happened was, that wasn't going to work. You had to have a harder breaking ball. You had to have something that you could rely on, being down in the count. What he did is—he still threw the slow curveball—he made it a slurvy curve, and he could get it over.

Tony Kubek:

Johnny Sain had a theory that he always brought in to his pitching staffs… He always taught guys, to Whitey Ford and a lot of the guys, he taught them what he called the "controlled breaking ball." Some people refer to it as a slurve. The overhand curve, which Whitey had, and Denny McLain had, can be very hard to control. But the slurve, you have a little more slack. It's not as hard as a slider, it's in between—but you can control it better.

And Johnny Sain's theory was, with all his pitchers: "If you can throw an off-speed pitch when you're behind in the count, especially to good hitters, you can win in the big leagues. So if a guy went 0-1 or 1-2, and if he could throw that slurve, you could get good hitters out. Because they're looking for fastballs! When a guy's behind in the count, you're going to look for a fastball. Not always, but almost all of the time. I think Mickey Lolich benefitted from that, and I'm sure McLain did too—he was straight overhand, great curveball, great change.

Hal Naragon:

In 1967, we're playing in Washington, and we got rained out. And they had an overhead, over in the bullpen, that you could go out to. And Denny McLain and Joe Sparma, we'd been working on this, John's hard curve, they'd say. And Denny was having a little trouble with it. And everybody else went back to the hotel, but Sparma and Denny and John and I stayed and went out there, and pitched. We were there a half hour or so. And Denny happened to throw the pitch, and he knew he had it. He *knew* he had it. And I had a log, and I went back and I picked it up and I wrote that. That Denny, I think, has that pitch. The hard curve. He had more of an overhand pitch before.

But anyhow, so about three years ago, there was a gentleman in Canton, he had a radio program. And he wanted to interview the old-timers, see. And he said, "Do you know of anybody that I can interview?" So I got to thinking, I thought: *Heck, yeah!* So I called, I don't think I called him first, but when I did call Denny McLain, the first thing he said to me was: "I will do anything you want me to do." He said, "You guys helped me, nobody else ever did that for me." He was including John when he said that. And he said to me, "Do you know that day, that I got that breaking ball, that hard curve? Do you know that day? We stayed late." And I said, "Denny, I got that down in writing." He says, "I have to see it." So he came in this area, Newcomerstown, the great Cy Young was from Newcomerstown. And Denny was the speaker. So I took those notes down and I showed it to him. He wanted to keep it, but I wouldn't give it to him!

Denny McLain:

Yeah, it was '67. Late '67. Well actually, it was during a rainout. There was a rain delay in the ballgame in Washington. It was during a rain delay. We had tremendous rain there in Washington one night. And most of this work got done while the field was being cleaned up. And so Johnny and I, and Hal, went out there. It had been a pitch I'd been working all year. I had the basics down but I just couldn't get the feel for it.

My slider would break away from a right-handed hitter, but for some reason, would go deeper down than it went sideways, which is a much better pitch because the velocity is still there. So that was the pitch that we really got control of that night, and all of a sudden I was throwing, you know, ten, twelve, fourteen, sixteen pitches in a row, and every one of them: *boom, boom, boom, boom, boom.* So after about literally an hour of that—shit, I pitched *two* games that night—after a good solid hour of that, I just looked at John, I said, "You know I think I fuckin' got it." He said, "So do I." He said, "I don't think you'll ever lose another game." Goddamn, he was almost right.

I mean, because I threw in the middle-high nineties, and the slider was in the low nineties, so it was great velocity on it, and I could throw it for a strike any time I wanted. That was the biggest thing, it was the strikeability. And the velocity had a lot to do with it, but it was a strike. No matter what count it was, I could throw this pitch.

John Hiller:

Johnny Sain was really the epitome of a pitching coach. He didn't show you much. It was up *here*, you know? He made you feel confident, but when you lost a ballgame he didn't make you feel inferior. He didn't have any ego. He'd see you and say, "How's the family, how are the kids? That's all that's important." I had other managers and coaches that would avoid you in the clubhouse the next day, if you blew a game. They'd walk around like you did something on purpose to them, you know?

But he would just build your confidence, and he would talk about movement on the baseball. He didn't talk about location, he didn't talk about velocity, or stuff—he said, "If the ball's moving a little bit, you can get by with pitches that are bad pitches."

And that way, he could teach everybody.

Hal Naragon:

Sometimes if a pitching staff had a bad slump, they would say to him, "Well, you don't run your pitchers." Well, he tells his pitchers you get yourself in shape, then just run enough to keep yourself in shape. Because what would happen is, this happened time and time again in my lifetime: they take a pitcher out, maybe he only pitched two or three innings, and the manager would say to the pitching coach, "Well his trouble is, you don't run him enough. Take him down, make sure he runs." Well why's that? He's not a sprinter, or anything. Why did they hit him? It's because that ball isn't moving! And if you're gonna improve, you've gotta throw the thing, you know? You just think about, now, if you tell the guys: "Go down, you gotta go run"—and you go run... still, what good is it?

"How much running do you have to do to pitch three innings?" That's what John would say. You don't have to do very much! I always told him, I'd say, "We're not coaching a track team, we're coaching a pitching team!"

And he knew his ideas were so successful that nobody was going to change him.

Fred Lasher:

Johnny used to work with us on how you hold different pitches, your fingers, and movement, and always working on movement on the ball. He didn't want us to throw a straight fastball—the *last* pitch you want to throw. Which made a lot of sense, because it was harder for a hitter to adjust to something that's moving, changing speeds. And he had this "spinner," he called it, to show us with.

It was on a stick, a ball on a stick, that you could spin. And he would put different pressure points on the ball, and spin it—and that would tell you how to throw a slider, try to throw a sinker, a changeup. He really believed in it. I never used it that much, to be honest with you. But he really believed in it, and I'm sure he helped a lot of people with their pitches. Throughout the year, he took guys down to the bullpen and guys would be working out, just loosening up, go down and working with them. He'd hold the handle, and you'd spin it with your pitching hand. Mickey used it I'm sure, most of the guys probably did. But I was so damn unorthodox, with my sidearm delivery...

Jim Price:

I wish I had one of those! I've talked about it on the air. What he did was, put his finger on the ball like he was throwing a slider, and then with a marker, and then he has that on the ball, so he doesn't forget. You could tell how to grip the ball, you know. If you want to throw a slider, you could move it over a little bit or whatever, knuckler, changeup.

I wish I had one, I've talked about it on the air. I wish I had one to show the guys, you know. Because Johnny Sain—he was the best pitching coach I've ever seen.

	1	2	3	4	5	6	7	8	9	R	H	E
Tigers	0	2								2	2	0
Cardinals	0									0	1	1

HARRY CARAY: Mike Shannon, the Cardinals' third baseman. In this Series, hitting .286. Out of play. One ball, one strike.

Denny McLain:

Who's that, Shannon? Well he's not getting a hit, I can tell you that. But we were surprised, he was a better hitter than we'd thought. Yeah, he was a better hitter than we'd thought. But see? See that high heater? Can't catch up to *that*.

Well it's just a good pitch. Little slider on the outside part of the plate, from sidearm. Sidearm slider. Exactly what he's supposed to hit—a ground ball to short, and a double play. See where the ball was? Down and away. That's the way it was drawn up, as they say.

I was saying to him there: "Just pay attention—I'll give you a lot of hints!"

HARRY CARAY: The Tigers now have runners at first and second, and Al Kaline coming up…

There's a smash—base hit! The run's going to score. Al Kaline coming up with his *ninth* hit of the series. As Billy Muffett comes out, that may be all for Ray Washburn.

Ray Washburn:

Pitching on the fourth day—I think normally I'd pitch every five days, so I was pitching a day earlier than I normally would've during the regular rotation. And so I guess I just didn't have as good of stuff as I did on other days. I didn't feel tired, but sometimes you don't quite have the movement, or the fine control. It's hard to say. That happened during the regular season, too. Sometimes you'd go out there and for no reason you just don't have as good of stuff that day.

But they probably felt that they wanted to try to stop them right there, and then go on and come back. And we had other pitchers— Jaster and Carlton, to come in and pitch. But as you can see, we always waited on the mound for the reliever to get there—it was just the way it was done back then, I guess. Sometimes how it evolves over a period of time, how it started to change I'm not sure, but that's just the way it basically was done.

Tim McCarver:

The pitching coach or the manager usually would release a pitcher when they didn't want him standing out there. But it's very important—you see, the pitcher's got the ball, so he would give the ball to Muffett, either at the last minute, or he'd hand the ball off to the pitcher. It's courtesy, common courtesy. Today, you don't do that.

Walking off the mound it used to be a way of showing a manager up. If you flipped him the ball and then walked off before the other pitcher got there. But, obviously, from a professional standpoint, you didn't do that.

HARRY CARAY: Larry Jaster, born in Midland, Michigan. The bases are loaded. And here is Jim Northrup. Who hit *two* grand slam homers in one game, earlier this year.

Well, they're loaded for him now.

There's a drive… it's going to be a… grand slam!!

Jon Warden:

The slam, we could see that, we said, "Whoa that baby's *gone*." That was his fifth one of the year—he had two in one game back to back in Cleveland. And the first time he was up that night, he struck out with the bases loaded. So he came to bat three times in a row with the bases loaded. And hit two balls out.

Mickey Stanley:

God, I remember rooming with Northrup and he hit two grand slams in Cleveland one night—the phone was ringing off the hook in the hotel room after that, with reporters.

Bill Haller:

Northrup hit a grand slam, I remember that. He was a big, strong kid. Left-hander. I never liked him as a person, I thought he was a pain in the ass. I didn't dislike him—I just thought he was a crybaby, which he probably thought I was, too.

Dick Tracewski:

Northrup was a hell of a player. He was the kind of guy that could play center field, he did play center field. And Northrup was a gritty guy that never had any respect for any pitcher or anything. He didn't respect anybody. He was a tough guy, and he played really well. They were durable guys.

Jon Warden:

Now, we were *really* fired up. And you could see the Cardinals, they're like "Ah shit…" Stressing a little bit, because they were all comfy, and should've been. They had plenty of reason to be pretty confident.

Julián Javier:

Detroit was hitting *good* that day. Looked like batting practice! I told you, they had that kind of hitting… they could do anything. And they woke up.

Al Kaline:

I remember, they were a cocky bunch, the Cardinals. Rightfully so, they were world champions. They would be around the batting cages when we were hitting, they're joking they're laughing, and then when we put up that ten-run inning, all of a sudden they weren't as happy anymore. Because they weren't used to seeing that.[53]

But that was our feeling, "Let's get 'em in the seventh game, and we'll go from there."

	1	2	3	4	5	6	7	8	9	R	H	E
Tigers	0	2	10							12	9	0
Cardinals	0	0								0	1	1

Denny McLain:

I didn't realize it until about the third, but I really had good stuff that day. The fact that I had good stuff that early. Normally when I have good stuff, I don't have it real early—I don't have it until about the third or fourth.

But see, you give me a two-run lead, I'm gonna beat you 99 percent of the time. And then it was the ten-run inning, and then it was over with. They should've applied the mercy rule.

Bill Haller:

Well, McLain got thirteen runs, so he didn't have to be *too* sharp. But he was. And that was the only game he pitched well in the Series. I don't know why, but it was. And Northrup hits the grand slam that broke the game open.

He had so many runs in his favor… but undoubtedly his stuff *was* good, he only gave up one run.

And I think the game's easier to umpire when one team's winning by nine hundred runs! Especially *that* game. You were apprehensive but you weren't too excited. I'd been in the league now over six years, so I'm still a rookie as far as the World Series goes, but I'd still got a few years in the league. I knew what the game was. You're so concentrated on what you're doing, you really don't think about that other stuff. You think I'm gonna umpire and worry about who's in the stands? I'm in trouble if I do that, you know.

But the World Series… it's the biggest. Especially as an umpire, your first one. You don't know what you're getting into. The thing is, see, I was a young umpire. Like Honochick, or Gorman, I mean they've been around for twenty years. It was different for them. This is *old school*. But I'm nervous. The first Series. And you listen. I learned very early going into the American League, you learn more by listening, and you do. A young umpire, if he's smart, won't even ask a question for five years. But he's learning—you're taking all the experiences that these old guys had: *How do you do this, how do you handle this?*

But, you know, I was familiar with McLain. I worked his 30th game, when he won.[54] He did not have a good game. In fact, the last part of the game, Detroit gets lucky. McLain is struggling, but they're going to keep him in the game to win the game. They come back. They were getting beat, and they go ahead. Then it was either the eighth or ninth inning. No, Oakland was ahead. Oakland was ahead. This must've been the seventh or eighth inning, when Detroit went ahead. Horton hit the ball off the fence, I think. Actually, the bases were loaded—Detroit had the bases loaded, I think it was one out. They hit a routine ground ball to Danny Cater at first, he throws the ball home and it's a wild throw. Detroit goes ahead, or at least ties. And Horton hits one off the left-field fence. That's about all I remember. But that was the inning McLain won his 30th game. And Oakland was not a very good ballclub, but they played them tough. And Danny was a real good player, he just made an error, that's all. Threw the ball wide, wide of the catcher. They would've gotten a double play—first to home to first. But when he threw it away, then it was dead. I remember *that*. I think I had maybe two or three of his games that year, and he was awfully good.

Jon Warden:

You ever see that picture, when Denny won his 30th? I think it was *Sports Illustrated*. You know why Al's helping him up? See how he's got his arm around him? The dugouts at Tiger Stadium are short, and when Horton hit the ball over Jim Gosger in left, Denny jumped up and hit his head dead right onto that cement, almost knocked him out. And so Al grabbed him, "You just won your 30th." Horton got the hit, the winning run scores, Denny's coming out, and so he jumped out and he smoked his head right on the top of that dugout. He's a little dazed there.

Denny McLain:

I sure did. Knocked myself out for a nano-second. The dugouts back then were all cement. And that's exactly what happened—I knocked myself out for a second.

Jim Price:

I'll tell you this—Al Kaline played there twenty-one years, never hit his head on the top of the dugout. I hit it like twenty times! I said, "You *never* hit your head?" He said, "Never hit my head." I said, "Geez, oh man…" *All* of us hit our heads on that dugout!

Mickey Stanley:

You know, McLain—McLain was funny. I loved playing behind him. He'd get through warming up, he'd come in the dugout, every time, he'd tell you how many runs he needed. He didn't tell you how many, he says, "Just give me one or two." And he'd stick it up their—shut 'em out. Then he'd come in another time, laughing, he'd say, "You better get me a bunch today, boys!" And he'd laugh about it. I mean, he was cool that way. And a lot of times we scored a lot of runs for him. And he gave up a lot of runs certain games, if you look through his record. But that was funny—he knew when he had it, and when he didn't. He'd come in and say, "Gimme a couple, boys." That was cool. And he never missed. I mean, if he said that, you knew you only needed a couple runs to win.

Denny McLain:

"Gimme one, gimme two, we're OK, let's go." That was it. Well, I kind of always had a pretty good feeling after I warmed up, especially based upon my breaking ball. If I had a good breaking ball warming up, I knew I was gonna be pretty good that day. So, that's where I would get the feeling for what I needed. And especially against a club you're playing against, because you've got to know who you're pitching against. With the different situations you have to be ready for. And Freehan would come down every time I'd pitch, and he'd warm me up. Once I got loose, Bill would spend five minutes down there warming me up. So we always had an idea.

John Hiller:

I remember McLain would beat you 2–1 or 13–12. We used to laugh, we'd say, "He pitches as good as he has to, maybe." He didn't do that, but that's what it appeared like.

Mickey Stanley:

One day playing shortstop, it was toward the end of those five games I had to prepare before the Series and we had already clinched. No pressure. It was somebody, I forget who the hell was on first, or second—didn't matter. Denny moved me over, in the hole at short. So I moved over. He moved me over.

Next pitch—ground ball right to me.

And I jogged in there and I says, "You're not that smart." He says, "Yes I am." I'll never forget it! The *next* pitch, a ground ball right to me. I mean, that had to be luck, too… But that was *funny*. He knew the hitter, he knew where he was going to throw the pitch. Moved me toward the hole, just a couple steps. Yeah, gave me one of these—*move over*—and a ground ball came right to me. That was funny. "You're not that smart." "Yes I am." Maybe it was when we went in the dugout. He said, "Yes I am." I'll never forget that…

Denny McLain:

We pitched guys a certain way, and if you pitch them a certain way, they're supposed to hit the ball over there, so… it's the law of averages. You know, you may pitch them ten times, and eight times they'll hit it there. I mean, just look at all the computers, now. We didn't have computers then, we had *memory*. And these guys have great computers and they're showing the same things that we saw fifty years ago.

Willie Horton:

You know… McLain, he didn't used to travel with us that much, he had his own plane—we'd only see him about every four days. Used to scare the shit out of me, man, he'd be playing with *our* plane. We called him "Sky King"—he'd be flying beside our team plane, and he'd be in *his* plane!

Hal Naragon:

I go play golf with him one time, and Jim Price, a few years ago. They would be saying something about a quarter or a half dollar or something. And then, "No no, the bet was this or the bet was that." And then Denny would say, "OK, I'll fly you home." You'd think, here they are talking about a quarter or a dollar about a golf bet. And then turn around and spend I don't know how much money on gas flying a guy so far away!

Willie Horton:

I remember in Cleveland one time, his wife Sharyn, she was sick, in the hospital on the east side, in Detroit.[55] And down by that Cleveland ballpark, they had a city airport. And they've got a city airport here, too, on the east side. And so, he had his plane by the ballpark, on the water. And it was the first time I'd seen a portable phone—it was kind of big, he had it in the dugout. He was talking to his wife, he said, "Well I'm gonna throw today, and if they give me a couple runs, shit, I figure I should see you by about five o'clock." And we had a game, a one o'clock game! I said, "*Five o'clock?*" The plane was about ten minutes away from us… and that man starts pitching, and we're out of that ballpark in about an hour and forty-five minutes! He was pitching against Steve Hargan, he said, "If *he's* throwing, just get me a run—I ain't giving up shit." And we won the game. I said, "Damn, man—he's *gone*." So we called him Sky King. He flew back to Detroit, saw his wife at the hospital!

And I remember we had a meeting one night, in Washington, DC. Fred Lasher was complaining, Jimmy was complaining. And so Mayo

Smith got out, and we had a team meeting out in Washington. They were saying, "That goddamn McLain…" Grey Fox [Northrup] said, "I don't give a damn if he travels with us, but if we've got a *team,* we should be together. But far as I care, I don't give a damn if he ever travels with us." And Lasher just said, "I'm just tired of this shit, too, Mayo!" And then I remember we were out in Oakland, and all us guys were about in two carloads, and we were late. So Lasher said, "Hell, you got in my ass, you got in Ratso's ass, you got in Dobson's ass, and you didn't say shit to Horton and Cash!" He said, "And McLain, he didn't even *show up!*" Mayo said, "God*damn,* Lasher, well you ain't winning a goddamn thing!" Then he said, "This man McLain, he's making money for *all* of us! That man's winning a game every time he's pitched." And Lasher said, "Goddamn, Mayo—I can't believe you'd say that."

Dick Tracewski:

Mayo let the players alone. Some of the guys would laugh at Mayo, because he would let Denny do anything he wanted! He won 31 games! Every time he'd go out there he'd win! So Mayo gave him a lot of room. And a lot of the guys didn't care for him.

Fred Lasher:

All the guys were fun. Denny, maybe the least fun. He kind of did what he wanted to do. He had fun—at the expense of other people.

Tom Matchick:

Denny was sort of on his own, he was on his own. He sort of kept to his self a little bit, you know. Denny was a little tough on the guys and that stuff, and everything he said and different things like that. He just rubbed a lot of the guys on the team the wrong way.

Jon Warden:

He was twenty-four and one. Just like Bonds.

They go:

"Oh, the Giants? Yeah they're twenty-four and one."

"What do you mean?"

"Twenty-four players, and then there's Barry Bonds."

There's the team of twenty-four, and then this guy gets to do what he wants.

Tom Matchick:

I think he went to Vegas—and he got $150,000 a week to play the organ in Vegas!

I remember the one time when he won 31 games, we were in Anaheim and Denny invited us up to the room, he was having a big party because he won 30. And what's-his-name was there. Oh, man, it'll take me a while. Country singer. Oh gosh. *Glen Campbell!* Glen Campbell come over with an entourage of his friends and that, up in the room and that stuff. He was there, too.[56] I guess everybody wanted to meet Denny, too. Thirty-game winner, you know. Hollywood. California. Big lights, you know.

Mickey Stanley:

Denny was just... God, he had the world by the ass. He *had* to be a big shooter. A bigger shooter than he was. He wanted to be a big shot—I'm not smart enough to figure out why.

But he sure screwed his life up, *God.* He never did a thing to hurt me, and I enjoyed playing when he pitched. It's just, I know he put the screws into some people, that, you know, had their pensions stolen—shit, that's bad stuff. And to lie about it.

The paint company, that's where it first started. That was the first thing. But I don't know if any ballplayers invested. But ballplayers are, you know, they're pretty honest people. Hard-working, you know, blue-collar people, for the most part. And—we're stupid!

Jon Warden:

After the season, when the World Series checks come out, Denny called me. He calls me and says, "Hey Warden, why don't you come up and spend the weekend?" I go, "Well, OK." So he had some celebrity group or whatever, because he was doing *Smothers Brothers* and the *Ed Sullivan Show*. So I went up on like a Friday, I was gonna come home on Sunday. So on Sunday, he says, "Before you leave, come back here in my office. What are you gonna do with your World Series share?" We'd just cleared, we got $10,936, and I think 66 cents. He says, "What are you gonna do with your share?" Because, being single, I cleared about eighty-five or eighty-six hundred. I said, "Denny, I dunno—hell, I'm from a single parent, my mom doesn't have much and she works her ass off every day, and I'll buy her a TV and some furniture and stuff." And he goes, "Well actually, see, I've got this paint company—and it's gonna go crazy. I've got Chrysler, I've got Ford, I got General Motors, contracts, we got it. And it's gonna go *crazy*." And I'm like, "Ah—I don't know…"

Because, I'll never forget, as I drove up there and then after he asked me about this, my mom, when I showed my mom that check for eighty-five hundred dollars, she said, "I worked all year to make that much." And I made that in ten days. And that stuck in my mind. And it still sticks in my mind, you know, the good decision I made. I said, "Well lemme think about it." I drive home, and thank God I didn't have the money with me. Or sign my check over to him, which would've been a real dumbass move. I said, "I dunno, Denny…" And he got some guys in it, he got some guys in it. And they were getting these false statements saying it's doing great, that we're going to start making payments back to you for your investment. So I guess some guys drove by where the address was, and it was just a burnt-out warehouse. He had no paint. I can't even believe he had a can of paint made up that way. But that's crazy. The paint company that everybody lost their ass on.

Dick Schofield:

He was a basket case, I guess. I didn't know him, but… I would play in the Old-Timers' Game, and he'd just come out of jail. He was funny. God, he was funny. He was telling stories about jail—I mean, he had guys laying on the floor crying, laughing.

I was with the Red Sox in 1970, and I remember when he threw the bucket of ice water on the sportswriter and was suspended for twelve days. We'd come to town, and that was his first day back, he pitched against us. And he walked out on the mound, they're booing him and everything, and I walk out and the second pitch, I hit a line drive for a home run. I'm running around the bases, and he's got his glove up, he's saying, "You *little* son of a bitch—these people hate me, and you hit a home run…" And I'm running around the bases with my hand over my face, I'm laughing! But he ended up beating us in the game.

I don't know what ever happened to him, but he never made too many good decisions, I don't think. But he was nasty when he pitched. He was really good.

Al Kaline:

Denny would be a Hall of Famer had he not gotten hurt. No question about it. I mean, he was a great guy to play behind—he got the ball and threw it. He threw strikes. And as a player, you're ready to go out and get the ball if they hit it. But guys that throw ball here, ball there, all of a sudden you get lax, and you don't get the great jump in the outfield. But, had Denny been able to go another two, three, four years, he'd have been a Hall of Famer, no question about it.

Willie Horton:

McLain used to talk about Lolich, he'd say, "Man if I had *your* arm, I'd win a hundred goddamn games!" But—*shit*, that man had game. When he won them 31 games, I bet you he *completed* 28 of them! And he hardly had people coming into even the games he *lost.* But that man, I tell the world, man, if he would've gave 10 or 15 percent to training, they would've seen something. In those five years, nobody could touch him.

I'll tell the world this. If McLain had worked out 10 percent of his ability, they would have seen something. He didn't work out, he didn't do shit to pitch. But he was the best I'd seen in five years. He was the best I'd seen. And he didn't believe in all that ol' warming up shit—he'd go out there, flip three or four, he'd say, "Let's go." And you know, like, in between innings, he'd be saying, "Get your ass on out there, let's *go*."

Denny McLain:

Of course, then I go out and I get hurt. Because if I stay healthy, we win it two years in a row.

I think I've told everybody this: everybody has got one pitch in their career that ends their career, no matter who you are. And it may not be the *day* you end a career, but it *starts* the end. You can feel a little bit of this, a little bit of that, and all of a sudden you know you've got a little bit of an issue. All we pray for is it doesn't happen until we're thirty to thirty-five years old. You know, that's all any of us can hope. It happened to me, for Chrissake, at twenty-two or twenty-three. That's when the end started. Despite the fact of winning 30 *after* that. But the *end* started two years earlier. Absolutely, at twenty-two. Game in Minnesota, that's when it started. I knew something bad had happened that day. But it didn't hurt so bad that I couldn't pitch. Now, had I been able to take a year like they do today, I may've pitched another ten years, but that wasn't the case. But it is what it is.

You know, there's only one thing—arm strength is the key. If you develop your arm strength, good things will happen. And one thing will *not* happen. You won't hurt yourself too early. So, there were a couple of things I did to make it through. There's a number of things I did in the winter of '67.

I was bowling a hundred lines a day.

At least a hundred lines a day, because then I'd bowl in two leagues every night at six o'clock and nine-thirty, and then bowl in pot games till two o'clock in the morning, till the bars closed. In Detroit, every night. Almost every night, except Sundays. Sharyn made me take Sundays off.

Different crews in different places. There were twenty different houses that we were bowling in. It was a great time, just a great time. And I made a lot of money bowling! You know, everybody wanted to beat the pitcher, well… no one knew the pitcher bowled a hundred lines a day. And if you do that, just like pitching in the rain on a Wednesday night in Washington, DC, if you do it enough and enough and enough and enough, something good *has* to happen.

Or you're gonna fuckin' kill yourself with your arm.

You know, and my dad was really a hell of a baseball player—and he played a great deal of influence in there. Growing up, you couldn't ask for any better parents than I had. They proved one thing, if you practice, you work hard, good things could happen. And lots of good things happened because of my parents.

And, you know, the biggest regrets I have in life all deal with my dad. I mean, obviously my daughter, God almighty.[57] But, the biggest regret I have with my baseball career is that my dad never saw me pitch. That's the one monster regret I have. I think about it often, especially when I see somebody with their mom and dad at the end of a ballgame, they just won a big ballgame or a pennant or a World Series—you wish you could've had that moment.

When I was a kid, Mount Carmel gave me a four-year scholarship, which my dad arranged. Father Austin, because my father had died, he had arranged for me to get some "walking-around money," as Father Austin would call it. You know, twenty, thirty, forty bucks a week once in a while. And that was a great thing, because my mother and I and my brother couldn't have made it without that kind of help.

Those are special schools, most of them are Catholic schools, with tremendous, tremendous athletics, but more importantly, tremendous discipline. Because if you fuck up, you ain't staying there very long. Unless you *win*. But the only disappointment I had in high school was when I graduated, nobody offered me a contract to hit! Because my junior year, I led the city of Chicago in hitting, I hit .601 I think it was. And nobody offered me a fuckin' contract, I was so pissed off. Everybody wanted me to pitch—so, I said, I guess I'm gonna pitch.

CURT GOWDY: Denny McLain's father was an insurance salesman, who got McLain interested in two things, as a youngster: playing the organ, and playing baseball. They're both paying off for him. McLain's father used to give organ lessons on the side.

And today, Denny is playing the right tune.

Denny McLain:

I was lucky, if it wasn't for Sharyn, years later… I would've quit baseball when the White Sox decided to do what they were going to do with me. I'm standing there waiting for the waiver wire to be concluded, and not knowing if I'd be picked up by anybody. I was picked up, I didn't know it, but I was picked up within three minutes by Detroit. Which would've made me feel a lot better had I known.

But I'd told Sharyn, I said, "If I'm not gonna be with Chicago, I'm gonna quit."

She says, "Don't call me."

Excuse me! So I said, "Well, I've gotta think about that."

She said, "Don't think very long."

So when I came down a few minutes later, Detroit had drafted me. And one of my two idols was Al Kaline—I mean, Jesus, what a gift from God. So there I was, on my way to Detroit.

And I remember this, a few years after that.

In the first major-league ballgame I ever played, I hit a home run. So I said, "Shit, this is easy!" But it wasn't so. Never hit another one. Hit a triple, a couple doubles… it's remarkable. It's a miracle, when you think about it. That was in '63, against the White Sox, the club that released me. My *first* game.

Al Lopez had said, "He'll never be a big-league pitcher, *never*. Listen to me, read my lips:

"He'll *never* be a major-league pitcher."

CURT GOWDY: Right now the Tigers are leading *thirteen* to nothing.

The last Tiger pitcher to pitch a World Series shutout was Bobo Newsom, old Bobo—1940, when he beat the Reds eight to nothing.[58]

Denny McLain:

I'll tell you, the most amazing thing was that we had a break in the game. It was raining—I don't know how long, but we had I think a forty-, fifty-minute break in the game. And the last thing in the world I was gonna do—I don't care what the score was—the last thing I was gonna do was go out of that game. So we went out there, and fortunately we still had good enough stuff to pitch the last inning or two. But, I was not gonna give up that ballgame. Had nothing to do with the complete game, it just had to do with the win. And at that point in time, I didn't trust anybody. And, you know, it worked out the way it was supposed to.

So, by the end, there was nobody there—it was all over with! And I don't blame 'em. Because it came down in *buckets*. Typically, a St. Louis, Missouri rain—it was unbelievable.

Julián Javier:

At the end of the game, I hit a single. To right field, I think. So I got to mess *everything* up! Breaking up this shutout, breaking up the no-hitter, in the '67 Series.[59]

And we said, "Well, we lost today, but we can win tomorrow." Like when you go 0-for-4. But sometimes the next day, you put your head down—and you go 0-for-4 again!

Jon Warden:

So, Denny finishes that game, and we end up beating them, 13–1, and—shit, we're all on cloud nine, man, we're in the clubhouse like we won it.

Denny McLain:

I was proud, that day. Proud, a little angry. Tired, too.

But boy, that pissed me off they got one run, I can't even tell you…

	1	2	3	4	5	6	7	8	9	R	H	E
Tigers	0	2	10	0	1	0	0	0	0	**13**	12	1
Cardinals	0	0	0	0	0	0	0	0	1	**1**	9	1

Al Kaline:

All we ever started saying was, "Let's get them into the seventh game. Let's take 'em to the seventh game, and whatever happens happens. Just don't get swept, you know." We said, "If we get in the seventh game, we'll see where it takes us." And that's all we talked about was, "Let's get 'em in the seventh game, and see how they hold up."

Tony Kubek:

I know this: it was hard to bet against Bob Gibson, pitching the next day. Even though at the time it didn't look like he would get to pitch Game Seven, because they were ahead—but again, it's the same thing, when we played in '58, it's crazy how even veteran players, after they have a 3–1 lead, they're not taking anything for granted, and all of a sudden it's now 3–3. You're still at home, but you say, "Uh-oh… uh-oh…" There might be a little doubt in the players' minds. I'm not saying there was doubt in Gibson's mind, because he was *something*. But there's something that creeps in that creates a little more tension.

I remember the '63 World Series, when the Dodgers beat us four straight—and of course, it was Koufax, and Drysdale and Podres. But Koufax was too much. I remember I talked to Sandy after, he said, "You know, after we had you down three games to nothing, I called a meeting along with Drysdale, and we said, "OK, we *know* what can happen in baseball, we *cannot* let them up." They had a meeting about it, saying anything can happen.

A player who's got that kind of class knows: *anything can happen.*

HOW RUNS WERE SCORED

Tigers second:	Horton doubled, Cash scored	Tigers 1, Cardinals 0
	Freehan singled, Horton scored	Tigers 2, Cardinals 0
Tigers third:	Kaline singled, McAuliffe scored	Tigers 3, Cardinals 0
	Cash singled, Stanley scored	Tigers 4, Cardinals 0
	Northrup homered, Kaline, Cash, and Horton scored	Tigers 8, Cardinals 0
	Kaline singled, Wert and McAuliffe scored	Tigers 10, Cardinals 0
	Cash singled, Stanley scored	Tigers 11, Cardinals 0
	Horton singled, Kaline scored	Tigers 12, Cardinals 0
Tigers fifth:	Kaline homered	Tigers 13, Cardinals 0
Cardinals ninth:	Javier singled, Maris scored	Tigers 13, Cardinals 1

GAME SEVEN

Busch Stadium | October 10, 1968

Dick Tracewski:

In '67, we had a riot in Detroit. And it was a bad riot, a lot of people were killed…

Don Wert:

We were playing a doubleheader in Detroit, on a Sunday, and that's when the riots started. The smoke was coming up over the stands in the outfield from the fires, during the game. And so after the game, we were taken straight to the airport.

Willie Horton:

I left the field in my uniform, after the game, and tried to bring peace. I was on top of the car in my uniform, trying to have peace. Right where it started, right there in that neighborhood where I used to have a paper route…

Al Kaline:

It was a terrible time, in '67.

But we have pride about 1968, because many people have said, even to this day, that with us getting off to a good start that year, it pulled everybody together, and they had one thing to root for together. Whether that's true or not, well I *hope* it is. And a lot of people say it is.

Fred Lasher:

The '67 season didn't end too well—even after those riots.

Boston came into town, it was a three-game series, and we had a one-game lead. The first night, Mayo brought me in in the eighth, and I was *tired*. I struck out the first two hitters I faced, then Yastrzemski came up. I hadn't given up a home run all year, in the minors or anywhere else, but I got behind him, 2-0. And I was always taught, "Make the guy hit the ball, don't walk him." So I made him hit it, and… he hit it in the upper deck in right field.

That tied up the game, 2–2. And they went ahead later and ended up winning, they swept the series.

And so that was it for us.

And the fans were kind of raucous, you might say, that last day of the year—tearing the seats up and everything else. *Raucous.* There were a lot of pissed off people. And George Cantor, who was a sportswriter, he blamed me for losing the pennant. He blamed it on *me.*

Al Kaline:

We had a very good team in '67, but we lost out on the last day of the season, against the Angels. A very fluke thing happened that game— Dick McAuliffe, who hadn't hit into a double play all year long, hit the ball *so* hard to second base, and they turned a double play for the final out.

Dick Tracewski:

In '67, when Mayo came over, we should've won. I always said, we should've won. We were the best team in the league. But it was one of the closest races in the history of the American League. It was the White Sox, the Tigers, the Minnesota club, and Boston.

We should've won. We got into the last weekend, and we had a four-game series with the Angels. And we got snowed out on Thursday and Friday, but we had to play a doubleheader on Saturday and Sunday. And in both those games we won the first game and we got beat in the second game.

Denny McLain:

I say this in all honesty—I think we had the best baseball team I have ever seen, for three or four years. In 1967, I got hurt the first of September, and I didn't pitch any more other than the last game of the season, I tried to start and could only go an inning or two. I had a bad foot. And that was *my* fault. Purely my fault. I kicked my foot—and my dog jumped up in the garage, and I jumped up, and jumped on my foot and sprained it. Jesus, I just couldn't believe what happened. But, of course, you believe that it's just something that's going to heal in two days. Well, thirty days later, I couldn't walk on it, still.[60]

So, we should've won it in '67—or at least should've been there. Sixty-eight, of course, we won it. Sixty-nine, you know, we won 90-some ballgames, and we're eight or ten games back, because Baltimore won over 100 games that year. So we had—we were so competitive and so good, at that point in time, but... it wasn't meant to be. You can be as good as you think you are, but, look at what happened with the Dodgers this year.

Willie Horton:

I'll never forget, Boston got to sit back and watch us beat ourselves, in '67. And George Scott called me—we were playing the worst team in baseball, the Angels, but they beat us two out of four. We should've beaten them, and went on to the World Series. But I remember George Scott called me from Boston, he said, "Thanks!" They sat back and watched us beat ourselves.

So, '67 was one of those years that I think was a learning experience—we *should've* won, best team in baseball. But I missed almost a month and a half, Kaline missed some time. I know we could've made the difference in one game.

But then, after that last game, we sat in that clubhouse a good two or three hours.

Jon Warden:

Johnny Podres, Larry Sherry, and Hank Aguirre were three of the pitchers that sort of didn't produce much down the stretch. And I remember, Bill Freehan used to tell this story. He came into the locker room, and those three guys were sitting by the lockers, drinking a beer and crying their eyes out. Bill was a young guy, been on the All-Star team, great catcher, and he goes, "Hey come on, guys, get your head up—we're gonna *win* this thing next year!"

And they said, "That's why we're crying… we know you're gonna win it, and none of us are gonna be here!" And none of them were. They released Podres and Sherry, and then Aguirre after spring training.

Hal Naragon:

Hank Aguirre knew that was his last year, and the older players—I don't know about Kaline, I didn't see him—but they had tears in their eyes, because they knew. Hank knew. It was something he always wanted, to pitch in the World Series, and then he was going to retire. Just needed one more year.

But I think, in a way, that had an effect on the players, because of their attitude when it came to spring training. It was: Hey—we're gonna win it this year. And they knew they had the ballclub to do it. I mean, they didn't go around telling everybody, but you could see that: *Hey, we can do it.*

Willie Horton:

We said, "Well, next year in spring training, let's get them used to it." And I think the majority of us came to spring training a month early. We said, "Let's get these guys ready, with what we gon' do this year." We just knew we had a great team.

Dick Tracewski:

We got to spring training in '68, and we *knew*. They can't beat us, nobody could beat us here. In '67, I don't think we knew.

But in '68, we *knew*.

Al Kaline:

In a way, that '67 season had a big influence on us going to spring training the next year. Because I think most of us thought we had the best team—and we lost, so we didn't get into the World Series. So I think everybody was determined, going into spring training, "What can I do better? What can I do to help the team?" What can I do to help the team get to the World Series? So, we played well in spring training, and everybody was focused, and...

It came about that we finally had a *chance*.

Jon Warden:

Well, we played the Cardinals the last weekend of spring training, in '68. And of course, they had won the world championship the year before, beat the Red Sox. We might've played them a few times, because they were pretty close—they were in St. Pete and we were in Lakeland.

And of course at that point, late in spring training, they've got most of their regulars playing over half the game, and some of the guys are still in there. You know, Brock or Flood, Maris, Cepeda. I mean, they had a great lineup. McCarver and Maxvill, Mike Shannon. They were stacked. And, you know, they were definitely favored to win, to beat us.

But in the bottom of the twelfth inning that day, Wayne Comer hit a home run to win the game.

And little did they know, at the end of the year we were gonna get them.

CURT GOWDY: An almost *perfect* day, here in St. Louis— 65 degrees, no humidity, just a slight breeze. A brilliant, bright fall afternoon. For Game Seven, with Lolich against Gibson.

Tim McCarver:

I remember before Game Seven, Bill Freehan and I were both asked by Sandy Koufax if we'd come to a studio and tape a small segment. Well this was before the game, you know. And were on as the catchers, opposing catchers. And, you know, we kind of muddled our way through the show, and I think that was Sandy's last year. Could have lasted maybe another year or two. He just didn't like it, you know, you could almost tell. But he'd retired after the '66 season. When he won *twenty-seven* his last year. It's kind of ridiculous, you know! Win twenty-seven, and you retire? I think he was thirty years old, when he retired. But anyway, he had asked Bill and me to come and interview, and so we did! In St. Louis. And, no prognostications or anything like that, but it was interesting. And I was just a little tired, it was a hard thing to do, to go by there—because, you know, you're getting there about an hour and a half early normally, and so it's tough. It was tough. If it had been anybody but Sandy, I don't know whether we'd have done it.

Mike Shannon:

Did Denny McLain say something in the papers about us?[61] If he ever did, I don't remember it, I don't know anything about it, and I wouldn't have paid any attention to it that much. Because I'd figure it came from some writer. And let me tell you something. In 1967, the seventh game of the World Series, you know what they had on the front of the *Boston*

Globe? Big headline, big headlines. Four-inch headline: "Lonborg and Champagne." Now *that* pissed me off.

All that trash talking, and all that b.s. and so forth and so on, 99 percent of it comes from the writers. Correct? And that's the thing—their manager at the time, somebody came in and he said, "Well, who's your second pitcher?" He said, "Lonborg and Champagne." So they plastered that all over, in four-inch black letters on the front of the *Boston Globe,* well, that gets your attention. And that backfired.

John Hiller:

I remember the second trip to St. Louis, the night before the last game, there were about three or four of us in the bar about two in the morning—and it was a *day* game the next day. We were just down there, and I said, "Why change? We did this all year—so all of a sudden we're going to change?" It was Willie, and Northrup and Pat Dobson and myself. We did it all year, so what's the difference, you know? Chances are, I wasn't going to be in there, and Dobson wasn't going to be in there, and Gates, well, he could pinch-hit so it didn't matter. And Willie was going to play, sure, but—well, why change things?

We weren't focused, in those days you didn't focus. Guys might tell you they're focused, but we were there to have fun. I was, at least.

Dick Tracewski:

In St. Louis, nobody expected us—and we went in there and when we went to the ballpark, we weren't feeling great. Mickey Lolich beat them twice already, and here comes Gibson again, you know…

I'll never forget, Mayo Smith in our meeting before the seventh game, he had a meeting. And he didn't say a whole lot as a manager. But, he did say one thing that got everybody laughing. He says, "Now listen guys, our pitcher is pitchin' well, and this guy that's pitchin' against us, don't forget this—he's not Superman." And Cash says, "Mayo, I just saw him dressin' in a phone booth!" So everybody busts out laughing, and then we went and we played. But he was, at that time, he was *awesome*.

Gibson was in a class by himself. And he was kind of a scary guy. Because he was a monster, on the mound. You're never comfortable against Gibson, he was nasty. He was even nasty to his catcher! McCarver told me a number of times, McCarver would go out, he'd look in and he'd get a sign from the bench. "Go out to the mound and slow him down a little bit, you know?" And he would get up and he would go the mound, and Gibson would look around and he says, "What are you doing here!?" He says, "The only thing you know about pitching is that you can't hit it!"

Orlando Cepeda:

We were thinking of pitching Bob in St. Louis for Game Six, but they changed their mind, because they figured, "We're gonna win anyway." He was the guy.

Al Kaline:

We were still upbeat, even though we were facing one of the great pitchers of all time. But, the third time we faced Gibson, he didn't throw quite as hard. And I think he only had, what, a few days' rest? So the last game, he wasn't quite as strong—although he pitched well. He wasn't, like any pitcher would be, throwing as hard as he did the first time.

Willie Horton:

He was the same, it was just his location was off. I just saw it and hit it.

Tony Kubek:

I think you might've been able to say that Gibson was a little tired that game. That he might've started trying to spot the ball a little bit more than he would've liked. Because we're talking about a long season, with pennant races and so forth, and guys get an inning build-up of—I'd have to look again, but I'm sure Gibson had 300 innings, and 30 starts or more... And you look at Lolich and look at McLain, they were probably close to 40 starts. Guys don't get that anymore.

So I would guess that at the end of a long season, with his innings pitched and so forth, and when you strike out *that* many in the first game... that isn't something you can get over in one or two or three days, at that time in the season. As *strong* as Gibby was, and as *good* as he was, when you're striking out 17, plus the number of balls you threw, you're talking a *lot* of pitches. And there are very few pitchers in baseball that can stand that. Gibson wouldn't admit it, but I would bet that it took him a while to come back. He already completed the first two games, now he's looking to win the *third* complete game.

Bobby Tolan:

We pretty much felt that it was a lock that we were going to win. I mean, we knew we had Bob Gibson on there, so... we weren't nervous.

We felt confident.

Tim McCarver:

As a matter of fact, and this might be revisionist thinking, and I think it is, but in looking back over that series, the fact that we had Gibson going in Game Seven, even if we were destroyed in Games Five and Six, we knew we had Gibson. And I'm not too sure we let up—we weren't the type of team to let up at all. We were ruthlessly competitive and intelligent, and I was very proud to be on that team, as a result. But if there *was* a let-up, it was certainly understandable, with Bob going in Game Seven. We knew he was our ace in the hole. And what better ace to have? The Dodgers had Koufax, and we had Gibson.

I know Kaline, for one, said after the Series that he was the best pitcher they'd ever faced. And that's credibility, when a guy like Al Kaline says that about somebody.

We were back home, and you know that expression—*playing with house money*? We were. And what better insurance policy did teams have than Bob Gibson? You'll take that all day every day, and you'd win nine out of ten times.

But, we couldn't score off of Lolich.

Jon Warden:

Well, after Game Five, they talked to Lolich, and they said, "Mick, can you pitch in Game Seven?" He said, "Yeah, I'll go down to the bullpen with the guys, and get loose."

And Mayo goes, "No, we want you to *start* the game." Two days' rest. "Well if you want me to, I will, yeah. I'll be ready."

So we go to Game Seven, and Mayo goes, "Just see what you can give me."

And Lolich goes out there, and he and Gibson are in a *head-knocker*.

Ray Washburn:

Who really stepped up and made the difference in the Series wasn't McLain but Lolich—he turned out to be the whole difference in the Series.

Julián Javier:

Lolich was, how do you call it—a *sneaky* guy. You know how hard he was to hit—because the pitches, they come in, and out. They come in, and you're waiting for the other one… and he comes in, and he's got you. And then, you look in, and he comes out. You have to be waiting for where he's going to throw—and if you're looking for the one inside, you're going to get caught.

So, I was hitting loose, and I got a couple base hits against him—but no luck, for us.

Jim Price:

Well, I caught all the guys, and McLain was unbelievable. And his arm was sore in the World Series.

But Lolo… he was a *freak*.

Lolo never had a bad arm, you know, he could warm up probably in twelve or thirteen pitches. And Bill would come down and catch a few—like I would, if I'm starting, I'd go down and catch a little bit just to see how the fastball is. But warming up Lolich, you had to be ready, because his stuff was *nasty*.

Hal Naragon:

He was strong. Mickey had good natural stuff. He really did, that ball would come in *hard*. And he developed a little breaking ball. John was interested in improving the players, that's what he wanted.

Dick Tracewski:

Lolich threw a heavy sinker. And he got a lot of ground balls. You had to pay attention because he had great stuff. So if he's throwing really good, right-handed hitters are not gonna pull him. So you gotta play them straight up instead of shading them, you gotta pay attention to how he's throwing. If he's throwing the ball well, you gotta take that into consideration, where you're going to play defense.

Mickey Stanley:

Lolich threw a lot more ground balls, because he turned the ball over a little bit. Denny gave up a lot more fly balls than Lolich ever would. But Mickey would throw that little cutter, a lot of cutters. If they hit it, which, you know, he didn't care. Ground ball, and bring up the next guy. He liked striking guys out, but he also liked fast games. We played fast games then—this game's in trouble now. What was it, a five-hour, no—four-hour-and-nineteen-minute game the Tigers had the other day? A nine-inning game. Four hours and nineteen minutes. Shit, if we had a three-hour game, we were pissed. There's never a less-than-three-hour game hardly anymore, is there? Especially on getaway day…

John Hiller:

All I remember of Mickey is his ball was just explosive. And down here on the knees. He threw two pitches—slider, fastball, basically. And just hard to hit, it was a heavy, heavy ball. Just hard to hit—you didn't want to play catch with him, you know, you'd hurt your hands. A heavy ball.

And he probably came into his own in the World Series, it all came together. He threw great. He never looked like he had an off-day, to me. Evidently, he did because he was in the bullpen some in '68, but he just didn't look like he had that off-day—he seemed pretty consistent.

Jim Price:

I mean, just, his stuff was so good.

Lolo was nasty. His stuff was filthy, let me tell ya.

It was hard to catch him. Because he had Bill and I split the outside part of the plate, and he threw the knees and shoulders. So here we are in Yankee Stadium, two miles behind us is the backstop, right—in the old days. So I remember catching a game there with him, and I'm out *there,* and he's throwing this slider, down and in, like 95 miles an hour down and in to a right-handed hitter—and you're out *there.* I mean, it wasn't easy. But that's the way it was. That's the way it was.

Heavy ball. He threw a heavy ball. Where McLain threw a light ball. More rotation, faster. And McLain threw a four-seamer, with a little riding action. You know, Denny was easy to catch—it was like plucking cherries, you know. He could throw any pitch at any time.

But Lolich, he kept the ball *down.*

Denny McLain:

He was a low-ball pitcher. I mean, we were two opposite pitchers. He was a low-ball pitcher, I was a high-ball pitcher. I mean, if I ever started throwing the ball below the waist, I was in trouble. Because my fastball below the waist didn't do much. My fastball above the waist did *a lot.* You don't hear that about many pitchers, I mean, that you can afford to pitch up. But that's what my strength was. And then I developed that slider. But he was absolutely a down-low fastball pitcher.

And Lolich didn't have much of a breaking ball, either, but what he had was, it was one of those great big sweeping things, whatever the fuck you called it—and when he had it going, at times, he had great velocity with it, also. And that's the difference of winning and losing. And I'm talking about the velocity, with a curveball or a slider. If you've got a good curveball or slider, and you can throw it for a strike with velocity, you're gonna win a lot of ballgames. And he learned how to do that.

But I don't think Johnny Sain had anything to do with that. He and Johnny didn't see eye to eye on very many things, and to be honest with you, Johnny just thought he was wasting his career, Johnny really thought that.

You know, you had to remember—Lolich was a non-entity most of the year. I mean, he was in the bullpen four, five, six weeks, couldn't get anybody out. He had all kinds of problems during the season—I mean, he couldn't get *anybody* out. But, Johnny Sain, and Hal Naragon, they kept working with him and working with him, we kept pulling for him and pulling for him, and lo and behold, he got his rhythm, and got *everything* going, just in time. Late August, the first of September. And all of a sudden—I don't know what pill he took—but all of a sudden, he was *pitching* again. And we all knew he had good stuff, we all knew it. We *saw* it. He had as good of stuff as anybody I've ever seen, when he was consistent. Late August, here he comes—here's he comes again. And, because everybody was pissed off as hell at him, up until that.

But of course, you know, in '67 he had a lot of interruptions in his life, with the riots, and he was a soldier for a couple of weeks. He still owes me money for the fuckin' gas. I flew him down in my airplane about three or four times. But we knew he had the talent, we certainly did. And against the St. Louis Cardinals, it really equalized that ball-club—because McCarver and Maris, neither one of them fucking guys are gonna hit him. And I don't know if either one of them did.

He was *terrific,* just absolutely terrific, in the World Series. And I can tell you, shit—if you're a left-handed hitter, you're in trouble against Lolich.

CURT GOWDY: Lolich's sinker is working, because the last seven batters have hit balls to the infield.

And he continues to match Bob Gibson in goose eggs here. Three up, three down.

	1	2	3	4	5	6	7	8	9	R	H	E
Tigers	0	0	0	0						0	1	0
Cardinals	0	0	0	**0**						0	1	0

Tony Kubek:

Mickey, if I recall, he was a little tired for that last game. I think he admitted he might've been a little tired, or didn't have the right rhythm—and so he threw a lot more sinkerballs. He had a good hard fastball that ran away from guys, and on occasion he would've kept it down if he went with a two-seam fastball, and he would sink the ball a little bit. And so I think in that last game he pitched, he probably threw more sinkers as far as I could tell.

Tom Matchick:

He was a money pitcher, he was tough. And the tireder he got, the more his ball *sank*—he was harder to hit.

Hal Naragon:

The main thing was, *keep getting those hitters out.* He was strong, Mickey wanted to stay in there, he didn't want out of there.

Dick Tracewski:

He was never in a lot of trouble, you know. He matched Gibson, and he was ahead of hitters. And I bet you he didn't throw a hundred pitches. Of course, they count pitches—they didn't count pitches then. They'd take you out when your arm fell off.

We just went in there and we played one inning at a time. And next thing you know, Lolich was matching him, pitch for pitch.

Tony Kubek:

You know, if you're the Tigers, with Gibson, as that seventh game went on, you say, "Uh oh…" But, Gibson pitched in 1964 the seventh game against the New York Yankees, and even though he won it—I think he was the MVP—he still gave up a bunch of runs. So if you're the Tigers you go to your guys like Kaline, the guys who produce runs.

Dick Tracewski:

We were sitting there watching that game, and then all of a sudden… Northrup hit that ball over Flood's head.

HARRY CARAY: The Tigers now make *their* first threat… Brings up the "Grand Slam Kid," Jim Northrup.
Fly ball…
Flood, *hey*—he almost… oh, he misjudged it! Over his head! Two runs are gonna score!

	1	2	3	4	5	6	7	8	9	R	H	E
Tigers	0	0	0	0	0	0	2			2	4	0
Cardinals	0	0	0	0	0	0				0	4	0

Willie Horton:

The ball that Jimmy hit, shit—when he hit it, I *knew* he hit it. And I took off running. Jimmy hit the ball past Flood. And he hesitated, but that ball was hit over his head anyway. That ball was getting *up*, that Jimmy hit. You listen to the sound of the bat, to tell you that ball was hit *hard*.

John Hiller:

We're in the bullpen, and we thought it was sort of routine. Maybe a routine catch, for the outfielder. And then all of a sudden we saw that hesitation. He took a step in, and then knew it was going to drop. That's why we all say, "It was meant to be." I think if you watch enough World Series and that, you can see things happening, and it's almost like. . . I don't know if it's pre-ordained, but it almost looks that way.

Fred Lasher:

The reaction was jubilation when he misplayed that fly ball. Because we scored a run off *Gibson*! He didn't give up too many.

Mickey Stanley:

I know he hit the *hell* out of it.

Flood didn't trip on that ball, he came in a couple steps, and then had to go back, on the triple. If he goes back to begin with, does he catch it? Yes. But it's a hard play. He hit the shit out of the ball. If he goes back immediately, I think he catches the ball, but it's not easy to make the correct move every time—especially on a line drive.

Dick Tracewski:

I remember I was sitting in the bullpen. And the bullpen at Busch Stadium was elevated, so I was sitting just above the fence, in left field.

And I was looking right at Curt Flood when that ball went over his head. He wasn't gonna catch that ball, that's what I think.

That ball was in there. That ball was in there even though Flood stumbled a little bit. You know, because it rained, and it was a little wet, and the ball was hit—he *scorched* it. He scorched the ball, and Flood did stumble, just a moment. But the ball was well over his head, he wasn't gonna catch that ball.

Hal Naragon:

It was a nice park, and I liked that the bullpens kind of sat up high a little bit where you could still see the game. And so we saw that play where that ball went over the head of Curt Flood. We had a good view of it, and it looked like to us, I think most of the players in the bullpen that were watching would think that he couldn't catch the ball anyhow, you know. That was a *big* break.

Tony Kubek:

If you see some of these real big tall stadiums back then, when you get late in the ballgame, playing day baseball—the shadow comes over the batter's box, and the pitcher's in the sun, and behind him there are guys in white shirts, it's a little bit more difficult to hit. Now, when they play night games, you've got much better lighting, and you can see the ball better, you're not hitting the ball against white shirts or a glaring sun. Same with fielding a baseball.

So I can't say, because I don't remember what the conditions were when Curt Flood lost that ball in center field, but there might be a chance that there was some sun in his eyes. Because the way ballparks are made, and the sun setting right behind the first-base side, maybe even shining at a center fielder if he looks into that—that can affect what happens to him when the ball comes off the bat. I'm not sure if that's what happened to Flood, but... I also know that the field was a little bit wet.

Jon Warden:

I could tell when Northrup hit the ball—see, he's a left-handed hitter, and he swung inside-out on the ball, and it was going *away* from Flood, and it was coming towards left-center more than it was straight at him. But, see, back then, back in the day, everybody wore white shirts and a tie or they had a hat on. Well, a white ball coming out of this white background, Flood lost it. He took about two steps in, and when he turned to go back, his foot slid. You can see a little bit of the sod come up, because they'd played a football game there that Sunday and they'd gotten a little water. And you can see when he goes, you can see it. Now, I've had some Cardinal fans go, "Well, you know, tell you what, if Flood hadn't fallen down…" I went, "Stop right there, stop right there—he never fell. And you probably weren't even at the game, so you don't know. He did not fall down. He slipped, but he did not fall down. And he was not gonna catch that ball. Once he took that step or step and a half in, he was toast. It was hit *well*. Hit hard, it was *whoosh!*—it was one of those.

Maybe if it was AstroTurf, he wouldn't have slipped.[62] Could've misjudged it, but he wouldn't have slipped. He might've taken that step or two steps in, but he would've had a lot better chance to regroup and go get it. He might've gotten it; he was a hell of an outfielder.

Tom Matchick:

I don't know if he would've caught that ball or not, he said he lost it in the crowd, but—when I would see that rerun, I don't know if he would've caught that ball. You know, the one that got by Flood in center field. I don't think he would've caught it, personally.

Don Wert:

He really misjudged it, went over his head. I remember him tripping. Northrup hit the ball pretty well, I don't know if Flood would've caught it anyway, it was pretty far over his head, almost to the wall.

Bill Haller:

In the seventh game, because of my whiskers—I didn't have any—so as a young umpire I ended up in right field. You answer me this: the game-winning hit, I'm in right field and I know Northrup hit it. And he hit it, I mean he hit it *hard*. But where I'm standing, I can't tell where the ball's going. Did Flood misplay the ball?

I know, from my position—I'm way over here and the play's way over there, and it's going that way—I have no angle. But I know the ball's hit like a *shot*. And I think, if I remember correctly, I saw Flood come *in*, a step or two steps, whatever it was. Then, all of a sudden, it's a base hit. Did Flood misjudge the ball?

Dick Schofield:

Flood just didn't see the ball. He broke, he thought he'd seen it and he didn't, he lost it in the shadows. Which is very possible. Because he was one of the best center fielders ever.

Johnny Edwards:

You know, we had an outstanding outfield—Brock, Flood, Maris. But who was it hit the line drive that Flood lost in the shirts, and that cost us the seventh game…

Ray Washburn:

Flood was underrated as a center fielder, because he was overshadowed by so many other great center fielders in that same era. But he was good defensively—and he also got several seasons with two hundred hits.

Dick Schofield:

He was a different type of cat—he was a little different. I think he had a lot of stuff on his mind, you know. And he was a good artist.[63] There was one time on a trip, we used to play cards on the airplane, and the stewardesses were coming around saying, "C'mon guys, you've got to get in your seats, we're landing!" And of course, we never did, we just kept dealing them out, you know. And so Flood—I don't know who's got that picture, what I've seen was just about like *so*—he did just a hand-drawn picture, with the plane landing and crashing, parts flying all over, and four guys are still playing cards in the middle of the crash! It was pretty good.

And that whole deal when Marvin Miller made the Flood thing happen and all that—that's when it started. It changed after that. Marvin Miller should be in the Hall of Fame. I mean, he did all this for these guys.[64]

Tony Kubek:

We hear this thing, this "mojo," this "momentum"… Well, one swing of the bat, or one good pitch or one bad pitch could change the game. Curt Flood was involved in that play, you know. It was a very muddy field—I think there was at least one rainout, because I was in the stands interviewing people during that rainout, they sent me down. Interviewing people like—Hubert Humphrey was there, and some other people… I forget them all.[65] And it was a wet field. The infield is always dry, but the outfield in some of those old ballparks, you get the drainage systems which weren't as good, and—whether or not he could've caught the ball, I think that's an old controversy about whether he could've. Flood was an important figure in baseball, obviously, with what he did about the reserve clause. But, he was also a great outfielder, and a darn good hitter, and a good baserunner and everything else.

So there were so many things from play to play, pitch to pitch, game to game, that changed the tide of the games. Which I think is the real fascination with baseball, you know, the little nuances, the shifting in defenses. And how from game to game, and from inning to inning, there are so many subtle changes defensively. It's almost like a boxing match, a punch and a counter punch. It's just the rhythm of the game, that's so different from any other game. You know, you watch a football game and there's twenty-two guys in the middle of the field piled up… You're not exposing weaknesses like you might. And they're not as magnified—if a guy missed a block on the interior of the line, until they review the film the next day. But in baseball, Curt Flood gets a lot of heat because, he might have caught that ball, and all of a sudden he becomes a goat, you know?

Bobby Tolan:

Well, I never talked to Curt about it, but I'm sure reporters asked him about it. And, knowing Curt like I know him, reading the statements that were in the paper, whether he said it or not… I *believe* Curt. He admitted to reporters that he had slipped on the wet grass. And Curt, you know, was a great outfielder, so I believe that.

Julián Javier:

I don't know what happened to Flood with that ball. It was raining in Game Six, you know—so it was a little wet. They say he slipped a little bit—it looked like he came a little bit in front, and then went back, and when he tried to go back he slipped a little bit. But, that thing can happen to anybody. Because Flood, he was one of the best center fielders, after Willie Mays. But—something like that can happen in baseball.

I turned around, to wait for the throw—I was the cutoff man. And what happened was, they scored a few runs.

But, somebody had to win. We lost. So—what are we going to do? Anything can happen in baseball. Like I told you:

"*La bola es redonda—pero viene en una caja cuadrada.*"

	1	2	3	4	5	6	7	8	9	R	H	E
Tigers	0	0	0	0	0	0	3	0		3	5	1
Cardinals	0	0	0	0	0	0	0	0		0	4	0

Dick Tracewski:

In the ninth inning, I was sitting there, and I wasn't thinking about getting in a game situation. All of a sudden, the phone rang, and somebody on the bench told me I was gonna pinch-run for Willie Horton if he got on base.

So Horton got on base, the call came, I ran in there from the bullpen, got my helmet, and when I got to first base, Wally told me about how many outs there were. And that was it, you know. And then Northrup, he hit a ball up the middle. It was a base hit all the way, and I had no trouble. I remember I was close to second base when the ball went by, and it was very easy for me to go to third base. And that was it.

Willie Horton:

I got into it with Mayo for that, I think this was in the ninth inning—I guess he switched around the outfield or something. And I told him, "Well we *should* win it with our regular outfield. Put Stanley back in center, and Northrup back in right." He took me out, and I said, "Wait a minute, I just *saved* a game in Detroit, throwing a guy out!" But I understood what he did, I understand it perfect. But I just said, "We ain't saving me for tomorrow—there *ain't* no tomorrow." Because I wanted to be on the field when we won, because you're part of that.

Mickey Stanley:

Late in those games, the four games we were winning, Oyler would come in at short, I'd go to center, and Northrup would go to left. And I think that's when Willie came out.[66]

It was easier when Oyler came in. Hell *yes!*

Dick Tracewski:

I was on third base. And Cuccinello says, "You're going on a ground ball, and you're going back on a fly ball."

And then Werty got the base hit.

All I know is I know Werty, and he doesn't give an inch, and the ball was out over the plate and up a little bit, and he served it into right-center field, base hit. That was it.

Don Wert:

It was I think a slider, and I hit it back over through second base, scored him.

Oh yeah I do remember that, I hit it over second base.

Dick Tracewski:

Werty, he was a very, very good fundamental hitter. That hit, that was him. He stayed back on that, and the pitch was a little bit out over the plate, and he hit it to right-center field. And that's the kind of guy he was. He hit good pitching. We always used to laugh about him—I remember one time we were playing against Luis Tiant, and Luis Tiant was throwing *bullets*. Nasty man, you know? And he pitched, and we're in the first game of a doubleheader, and we got a couple of men on base, and Werty walked up and hit one out of the ballpark, and won the game for us! And he's the guy we'd always used to say, "Werty will hit good pitching." And that's what he did.

Also, I remember in that game, Doug Harvey—you know what he did? After the World Series was over, you'll see in the pictures I didn't have a hat on. He wanted my hat!

After I scored that last run, I went into the dugout. And he told me when I was going by, he said, "I want your hat, after this is over." I said "OK, you can have it." So, I went out, and he took my hat. Or I think maybe it was at the start of the ninth inning when he was down the left-field line, and I was going out from the bullpen to pinch-run. He said, "When this is over, would you give me a souvenir?" I said "Sure!" That's why I gave him my hat. Because in that picture, I didn't have a hat on, you know. Doug Harvey took it!

Back then, the umpires wanted your hat for a souvenir.

Jon Warden:

Tracewski, because he'd been around a while, had actually been asked by the umpires, "Hey, can I have your hat?" So Tracewski asked me for *my* hat, when we were in the bullpen. We're getting ready to break out from the pen to jump in the celebration. Tracewski asked me for my hat, and I gave him mine.

I figured, "What do I care, I'm a young twenty-two year old kid, big deal, fuckin' hat!"

Now, I wish a had it here!

Tom Matchick:

A lot of them kept souvenirs like that. That's what they'd do, they run on the field and they just grab a glove and that.

Julián Javier:

After we won it in '67… you know Augie Donatelli? We went around the home plate, you know, so it was there—he said, "I gon' take your hat!" I said, "OK!" He said something about, "Hoolie!" And then he got my cap. Well, I didn't say, "OK"—he *took* it, you know what I mean?

I don't think that he stole it, but some of the guys, they like to keep something from the World Series, you know? So, yeah—he got it!

But, you know, I saw him later, in St. Petersburg. He had a bar, you know. And he said, "I got your hat, in my bar." I said, "Oh, good!"[67]

Bill Haller:

Doug Harvey was a very good umpire. But let me put it this way: Augie Donatelli was a veteran that was captured in the Bulge. If you're playing, Augie takes your hat, you say, "Ahh, OK Augie, what you've been through—keep it!" Harvey takes the cap, you're gonna get a little pissed off! I think that's just human nature.

	1	2	3	4	5	6	7	8	9	R	H	E
Tigers	0	0	0	0	0	0	3	0	1	4	8	1
Cardinals	0	0	0	0	0	0	0	0		0	4	0

HARRY CARAY: Lolich, going into the bottom of the ninth, has a four-to-nothing lead. He now has pitched sixteen straight scoreless innings.

Denny McLain:

Who do you think was warming up in the bullpen, in that seventh game? That was *me*. I couldn't wipe my ass, but I'm out there warming up!

Hal Naragon:

Denny was warming up, though he won the sixth game—in the seventh game he was warming up in the bullpen. Just in case they were needed. I forget who the other fellow was, I think it may have been Patterson. But Denny was throwing in the bullpen that game, even though he pitched the day before. He did get up and throw a little bit. That was all planned ahead of time. Can you go an inning? But it didn't happen. And Lolich took care of *that*.

Fred Lasher:

Denny? I don't remember—he might've, early on. I don't recall him being in the bullpen, I don't recall him being down there. I think I warmed up, didn't get in.

Denny kind of did what he wanted to do. He was going to be the big star of the Series, and it turned out he wasn't. Mickey was the better man. Which made me happy, and a lot of people happy. Happy for Mickey.

He pitched his little heart out.

Tom Matchick:

Denny, from what I heard from Mickey, Denny offered Mickey a check for ten thousand to pitch that last game. Mickey told him to stick it up his ass.

I'm glad Mickey pitched!

Denny McLain:

That's bullshit. I mean, that's absolute bullshit. But listen, lemme give you some insight.

In the seventh game, I was warming up. I was the number one pitcher they were going to, in the seventh inning, when Mickey got into a little bit of trouble. They got me up again. I'd just pitched nine innings the day before, that's number one.

And number two, Mayo Smith had asked me before the ballgame could I pitch an inning or two, if I needed to? I said, "Sure, of course." But I thought, "Well, I lost the first game. And I lost the next time Gibson came out there. How the hell are we gonna pick me to throw me out there?" But Mayo said, he says, "I think you're still warm—from the sixth game!" And I'm sure that's probably true, because you get that adrenaline going, at that point in time, all of a sudden you've got a whole lot more going for you than you thought. And, you know, after the ballgame Mayo paid me the greatest compliment of my life. Him and Johnny that day. I said, "Why did you think that I could've pitched another inning?" He says, "Who else did I have?"

And those were the days when… hell, we never thought about anything other than to *win one for the Gipper*—right? That's what it was all about. And, lo and behold, Lolich got into just a hair of trouble in the seventh inning, or Mayo was concerned that he was getting a little tired. And Mayo says, "Why don't you go out and get warmed up?" He says, "I'll go to you if we get in any trouble here." And that was the drama for me in the seventh game.

And then, the ninth inning, I was warming up the entire inning. I was ready to come in, in the ninth inning. Oh, I would've loved to come in for the ninth inning—I would've *loved* to come in. I just wanted to win. That's all I wanted to do, to make sure we won. And I just never ever believed the ball was in anybody's hands better than mine. And if you don't feel that way, you shouldn't be out there. Whether you're Mickey Lolich or Joe Sparma, or whomever, but if you feel good that day, you've got a chance.

But I was very very happy that he got everybody out—I can tell you that.

Mickey Stanley:

Mickey Lolich didn't want *anybody* pitching his games. He knew he was better than whoever was down there. Other than Hiller—he was tough. He had a great attitude. He didn't care, just, "Here it is—hit it! If you can." He wasn't scared of *anybody*.

Dick Tracewski:

Lolich was never coming out of that game. Nobody warmed up, in the seventh game. If they were, it wasn't a serious thing. He was gonna pitch. And that's the way it was, then. You know, you *pitched*. I remember when I was playing with the Dodgers and Sandy Koufax would be pitching, and Walter Alston would come to the mound and he says "Sandy, how d'you feel?" He said, "I don't feel worth a damn, but I'm better than that guy warming up." I remember him saying that. So Lolich was going to be *it*. And I don't remember anybody warming up.

Even in the ninth inning, we didn't warm up anybody. Nobody was warm. Otherwise, if they were warming up two guys, I would've been catching for one of them in the bullpen—and I wouldn't have been able see the field, because you'd be down.

But I watched everything, I had the best seat in the house.

And so did everybody in the bullpen.

John Hiller:

A lot of games we didn't watch, being in the bullpen, but we were intent on that game. Most of the time we were down there, I'd play gin with Pat Dobson, or we'd dig holes in the ground with our bats. And just something to do, you know.

But we watched every pitch of that World Series.

We *definitely* watched Lolich.

The only other guy I watched was Fidrych, years later. That's the only guy I watched every pitch he threw, because he was just fun to watch.[68]

Jon Warden:

After five innings, Mayo goes, "How ya feel? Can you give me one more?" And Mickey goes, "Yep—I can go another one." And after the sixth inning, "Can you give me another one?" He goes, "Yep." And at one point, after the seventh inning, he goes over to Mickey again…

And he goes, "Mayo, I'm finishing this game—you're not taking me out."

Tim McCarver:

In Game Seven, if that were a tie game, he'd have been the pitcher in the tenth. No doubt.

Al Kaline:

I remember Mayo saying, "Mickey, can you give us a couple innings?" And Mickey said, "Oh sure!" And then all of a sudden, "Can you give us a couple more?" "Oh sure!" And then all of a sudden, Mickey says, "I'm finishing this game."

And he did.

Jim Price:

You're just counting the pitches, you're counting the outs. It all started in the eighth inning, up in the bullpen, after we took that lead. And we were ready to go. We were all ready to go.

You're looking at Lolo, and he's running away with the game, knocking them away. And those balls weren't hit hard off of him. And so we got to the ninth inning, and we said, "Guys—we're gonna win. We're gonna *win* this thing."

Then Lolich pitches probably like a 95-mile-an-hour fastball…

HARRY CARAY: Tiger fans who are here on their *feet*. And I imagine bedlam will break loose, when this final out is completed.

CURT GOWDY: There'll be some automobile horns squawking in the Motor City…

Jim Price:

McCarver hits a little popup straight up in the air…

And Bill's calling for it, "Get away from me!"

He makes the catch of course, and then he hugs and *catches* Lolo—and Lolo is a big man! He just dragged him all over the place.

Pat Freehan:

Bill and Norm had a few collisions that year, and he wasn't going to let Norm *anywhere* near that ball. And so he said he was yelling, "I got it! I got it! I got it!" he was yelling at the top of his lungs. *Nobody* was going to get the ball but him. He would just say that as a joke: "Norman wasn't gonna get *near* that ball!" Because they'd had a couple of "I got it," "No, you take it" moments during the year, and that would irritate the devil—especially if it meant something. And of course this would mean something enormous if that ball had not been caught!

And Bill, he always used to say, his back hasn't been the same since! But that was just a joke he had. That after Mickey leaped on him, he said, "My back has never been the same!" But actually Bill had had surgery, spinal fusion, in 1969—the year *after* the World Series, but he always told Mickey that that leap was what done him in.

And, you know, a little woodworker down in Detroit carved that pose. And I think he carved one for Mickey, too. Ours was in Bill's office for years, of Mickey leaping on Billy. That's a good memory, that's a *great* memory.

So he was just proud, relieved, excited. When you go down three games to one and you come *back,* your chances are *against* you. Astronomical numbers against you doing that! And he was not having a good offensive series, I think he was 0-for-22 or 23 before he ever got a hit. And so, he was so concentrating on the running game, and I think the defense just really was in his mind.

So, to catch the final out, that was something that you'd dreamed for, wished for, hoped for, prayed for—it had to be the best feeling in the world!

We were screaming and yelling and hollering, all of the wives…

And St. Louis was sitting there *stunned.*

John Hiller:

I remember Mickey jumping up into Freehan's arms… I remember *that*, oh yes.

Willie Horton:

I don't have the words to really say the joy and happiness I had from that.

I thought about all the work and time my coaches put in with me as a kid, and I thanked God and was grateful to him to have put the people in my life to help me do something, and bring a smile to people's faces. That's what I thought about. Enjoyment not only for me, but them too.

It was unbelievable.

Don Wert:

After Freehan caught the ball, that was it. I was there, I was right there. I had to be there, because I wanted to catch the ball! It was about halfway between home and first, when he caught the ball. I came in from third automatically.

Jim Price:

Once Bill caught that little popup, we were out there, we were *gone*, man, no one could stop us. We opened the bullpen door, and ran out just like a herd of cattle. I remember coming toward the dugout, jumping right on top of the pile of players—you'll see number 12, right on top.

Fred Lasher:

We all got to run in from the bullpen, and that was exciting as hell. Because we figured we were gonna get beat! Gibson pitching, and he just had phenomenal stuff.

Tom Matchick:

We're running out there, and in the picture I see myself, number 2, running out there, jumping on somebody. And I remember Lolich jumping into Freehan's arms, you know. Then after that, everybody just wanted to get back in the clubhouse!

We didn't want anybody getting hurt, you know, a lot of times people get hurt doing crazy things. And in St. Louis, we didn't want to get bombarded with bottles and stuff, you never know. St. Louis is a great baseball town, but still, you know, somebody's going to throw something at you. Go in there and beat the Cardinals after they had a 3–1 lead?

Pat Freehan:

It probably would've been more fun for them to win it at home... We were in somebody else's place, you're in enemy territory! And I think they were stunned. I do think St. Louis was stunned. Because I can remember—where were we that I saw the St. Louis players?—but they were kind of cocky, because they had us three to one. And so then we had to win one to get back to St. Louis. And I remember them kind of, not being condescending, but going, "Oh well, that's the way the ball bounces, we'll take care of you soon—three to one we got ya down!" And I don't know where I got that little feeling, but... they'd won it the year before, and I guess they just thought, they were going to do it again. But, well, we had a surprise for them, right? Yes we did!

Jon Warden:

You can see me in that film when Game Seven was over... I come jumping in on the pile. When I was teaching school, I'd take this video in at the end of the quarter or whatever, and I'd say, "Hey, let's watch the Tigers World Series." They'd go, "Huh... OK..." I'd say, "I'm in this thing, man, come on, cut me some slack!" So Game One, Game Two, Game Three, "When are getting in!?" I tell them, "Hold on." Game Four, Five, Six, Seven. "You didn't play!" I said, "Hold on! Hold on... OK, right *now*!" Then, here I come from the bullpen, we're all running out, I jump on the pile and you can see my number 39.

Dick Tracewski:

Everybody ran out, but it wasn't like it is now. See, and that's another thing about the modern player. They go on, they jump on each other, they knock each other down—*that* didn't happen! We went out, there was a brief hug. A brief hug. Just a minute. We were off the field in a minute, maybe thirty-five seconds. Everybody went, they slapped each other and hugged or something like that. And into the clubhouse, into the clubhouse! Now, they get on the field, they rip their clothes off and... *Jesus Christ*! It's hilarious.

Denny McLain:

We did it. We *did* it.

We did a quick celebration on the field, and wanted out of there. Everybody ran in the clubhouse, took a shower, did all the media interviews that we could do within a few minutes, and *boom*—we were on the bus to the airport.

But they're taking celebrating to a whole new level today.

I mean, I've been a Cub fan all my life. Jesus… these motherfuckers killed me the first seventy-two years of my life! Unbelievable, wasn't it? It was great. It was great. Just great.

There wasn't a lot of excitement on the field, but I think we pretty much looked tired. But it was a great time, it was a great moment, it was a great time in Detroit history. Perhaps that was the biggest win for the city, than anything else. It made a *big* difference in the city's attitude for a long time—five, six, seven, ten years. Of course, then it went to hell again… but it was a good time to be in Detroit, it really was.

	1	2	3	4	5	6	7	8	9	R	H	E
Tigers	0	0	0	0	0	0	3	0	1	**4**	8	1
Cardinals	0	0	0	0	0	0	0	0	1	**1**	5	0

Hal Naragon:

What Mickey Lolich did in the World Series was just spectacular. I mean, that's quite an accomplishment. And I'm always upset when they talk about some of the pitchers today—someone pitches a game and then goes in for relief the next day, and they don't remember Mickey Lolich pitching three games in the World Series and winning it. And hitting a home run, too. Three complete games.

Jon Warden:

He was the last guy to win three complete games, *winning* games. Randy Johnson had three wins, but one was in relief.

Gibby would've had it instead, if he'd have won—but he didn't win!

Tim McCarver:

Think about Bob—he pitched *twenty-seven* innings that series, and gave up runs in just three of the innings. I just thought of that. They scored five runs in just three different innings.

Mickey Stanley:

I saw Tim McCarver, he was in the broadcast booth at Comerica Park visiting, and he said that Bob Gibson won—I think this is the exact number—251 games, and he had 255 *complete games.* He completed games that he lost. So just think of that. He completed more games than he won! And I looked it up on the Internet—it's true!

Just think of that. Warren Spahn pitched 380 complete games. These guys now… I think Verlander doesn't have much over thirty complete games in his career. Mickey had *twenty-nine* in one year!

These days if they pitch a complete game, they break out the champagne!

Hal Naragon:

Mickey Lolich pitching three complete games, who thinks of that? You think, *oh my goodness…* well he did it. He did it.

Tony Kubek:

When you look at what Lolich did—you know, you expect the 31-game winner McLain to be the key guy—but it's Lolich that has three complete games, and some on short rest. And I think that was really because of Johnny Sain. Johnny Sain kind of revolutionized pitching, as far as what they did. And you've got to believe that Sain had a little impact on the Tigers, just because his pitchers would stay fresh later in the season.

And if there's a parallel, all you've got to do if you want to talk about the '68 World Series, just look back at the '58 World Series, ten years prior to that. In the '58 World Series, Bob Turley pitched in the last *three* games.[69] He pitched the fifth game, and then the sixth and the seventh game. Of course, everybody said, "Well, Whitey Ford's gonna be the guy that's gonna dominate." You know, Whitey got beat one game, and then Bob Turley pitched in the last three games, which was unheard of. And you look at Lolich pitching on short rest, I mean that was quite an accomplishment.

The parallels to the '58 Series ten years before that were… the way the games were played, and how the same thing happened which was so unique. You're down three games to one, as the Yankees were in '58, you go into the visiting city—which is a very comforting thing to be in baseball, to be in your home city.

And Red Schoendienst, he was in the '57 and '58 World Series also, now he's managing it. There were just so many things that were *kind of* the same.

Al Kaline:

I'm not taking anything away from Mr. Bumgarner, who won three games in the [2014] World Series. But he didn't *start* all three, and he didn't *finish* all three.

Mickey Lolich *started*, and *finished*, and *won* all three.

And not *one* word is ever brought up about Mickey Lolich, pitching from the beginning to the end, and for the win. And, I mean, you ought to get *some* recognition. If you're talking about somebody that wins three games in the World Series, to bring up somebody that did the *complete* thing! And again, I'm not taking anything away from Bumgarner, who's a great pitcher, but Mickey Lolich *started* and *finished* every game. And got all three wins. Wow. *Unbelievable.*

Hal Naragon:

One big reason that Mickey could do that really, was that John Sain pitched *nine* complete games in twenty-nine days.[70] And he *knew* that a pitcher could do it. And like he said, "Prove it to yourself, just go out and pitch nine innings." And, I'm sure, Mickey knew that, or at least heard about that, and I'm sure he got encouragement.

And he did it.

I always try to mention that when I'm out speaking, and let people know that Mickey Lolich was one heck of a pitcher.

Mickey Stanley:

After he won the World Series he became a *pitcher*. I still say that. Before that, he was a *thrower*. He won that MVP there, when he learned to pitch. I think he realized, at that time, that you're in the World Series, you've got to *pitch*.

And he *pitched*.

And he pitched ever since.

HOW RUNS WERE SCORED

Tigers seventh:	Northrup tripled, Cash and Horton scored	Tigers 2, Cardinals 0
	Freehan doubled, Northrup scored	Tigers 3, Cardinals 0
Tigers ninth:	Wert singled, Tracewski scored	Tigers 4, Cardinals 0
Cardinals ninth:	Shannon homered	Tigers 4, Cardinals 1

AFTER THE SERIES

Julián Javier:

We lost that game, I don't know how we lost those last three games...
I don't know.

Tim McCarver:

Particularly when you're up three games to one... That's what made
that so tough.

If we're behind three games to one, and then tied at six, 3–3, and
then lose in seven, it's not nearly as bad a pill to swallow as it is when
you're up three games to one with Gibson going, assured with rest, and
then losing it.

Mike Shannon:

Personal things didn't mean anything to me. What meant something
to me was the satisfaction of *winning*. And we *lost* that Series. I was in
three World Series, and that's the only one I lost—and I'm still lament-
ing it, OK?

Dick Schofield:

We should've won the World Series. If Brock would've slid home, it's all over.

I just thought we were gonna win. I was pretty sure we were gonna win. I didn't know that much about Detroit, and I just thought that Gibson would pitch, and that's three games for sure. And the Cardinals had just won the year before, so I think the other guys expected to win, too. I just really thought we were gonna win the stupid thing!

But, you can't say *too* much, because Lolich—we didn't hit him at *all.*

Julián Javier:

The thing is, we had a good team. But Detroit had another good team, too. They had Kaline, first-class hitter. They had the first baseman Norman Cash, they had Horton, Northrup—they had Lolich and McLain. But we also had a good team.

But… that was a good thing for Detroit. You know what saved Detroit? That World Series. They won, so they forgot about the fights for a little bit. We feel bad, you know, because we lose, but that was good for Detroit.

Bobby Tolan:

We were favored to win, you know, with the team that we had repeated from the year before. And we felt real confident going in—and then we jumped out to that three-to-one-game lead… I don't think we got complacent or anything like that, it's just that the Tigers made a few moves, and they came back and they beat us. We jumped out to that big lead, eventually three games to one. And then the roof fell in. And we ended up losing three in a row. So, I don't what else to say, but… we were glad to be there two years in a row.

Johnny Edwards:

I felt like we had a better team. It didn't turn out that way, but I thought we had a better team. So I was really, really disappointed that I didn't get a World Series championship ring. But the Cardinal organization is a wonderful organization—in my one year in St. Louis, the Busch family would take us out to dinner, we'd go to the Busch farm with the kids, it was enjoyable to play baseball there.

Dick Schofield:

The '68 Cardinals were guys that kind of stuck together. I mean, we were pretty good friends, I think, and even after baseball I'd see a lot of those guys, and we were still friends, you know.

Ray Washburn:

The one thing I can tell you about the '68 team was that we weren't just a close-knit team, but we were accountable to each other. For how you played the game.

We even had a mini fining system—by today's standards it'd be five or ten dollars, it wouldn't be anything. But it wasn't any of the coaches involved, the managers involved or anything, but amongst the players. If you didn't sacrifice successfully, you know. Or if you didn't advance the runner, like if there's a leadoff man on second and you didn't get him to third. Miss the cutoff man, or baserunning errors like going to third from second on a ball hit right in front of you. Or getting thrown out on the bases, other than stealing, with nobody out.

It was kind of led by Maris, Shannon, McCarver mostly. And everybody contributed, which is important for a team to win. You have your stars of course, but all your role players have to be contributors, and then you've got a winning team. So that was really important, in both '67 and '68.

Tim McCarver:

We were a very disciplined club, as I said, and very intelligent. And that's the one thing about that club, as a group of people, we were intelligent. Humorous. Funny as a group, funny individually. We enjoyed being around each other. And I can't say this about any other team that I was on, or really that many other teams that played—but I know that that Cardinal team, or those Cardinal teams, in the '60s, you enjoyed so much going to the ballpark. You enjoyed seeing your teammates, you enjoyed road trips, you enjoyed being around them.

They were *friends*.

In that World Series, I would be with other teammates and we went out, you know, your wives of course were traveling with us. We had *four* nights, because it was all day ball, of course. And we would go out to eat in style, every night, and dress, and that team—along with a great sense of humor and intelligence—we dressed better than anybody.

In fact, when we lost Game Seven, a writer named Bob Burns, who was the head of the *Globe-Democrat* at the time, came out with his column that said, "We were more concerned with our clothes than we were with winning."

That article was filled with such nonsense—insane, it was insane. Not right. He was wrong. And he was *so* wrong, it was, "How the hell'd you come up with *that*? Cared more about our clothes than we did about winning? What are you, nuts?"

Johnny Edwards

Yeah, that was Bob Burns. And that was a wrong statement. It wasn't right, and it wasn't true. I can tell you that. There wasn't any of that going on, not in the World Series. That was unfounded, you know— because we weren't that type of club!

Tim McCarver:

Totally, total ludicrous approach. And it pissed all of us off. I'll never forget it; I never forgave him for that. He turned into a jerk. I mean, to even—well number one, you're not giving the other team any credit. They beat *Gibson*! I mean, you beat the best pitcher in the land, at the time, and that's… you tip your cap to them. The Tigers deserve all the credit.

And then to even imply that we were more interested in our dress than in playing the game? We were a tough fucking outfit, believe me. It was a bunch of tough players who knew how to play. That's why we won, twice! And that was all the more reason for a guy like Bob Burns, who had no athletic experience whatsoever—*ever*—to make a comment like that. Nonsense.

I was on winning teams. And I consider myself a winner.

As I told you before, I'm not used to giving interviews on losing.

Jon Warden:

After we won, we were coming back on the plane—and Northrup's wife is like *nine* months pregnant. If we'd have been on a commercial flight they would have never let her on, but we flew private charters. So, I'm one of the few single guys, so I'm running up and down the aisle, I'm hanging, I'm grabbing the stewardesses, and we're drinking champagne and we're just fuckin' around and all, everybody's cheering. And so I go by Northrup, I say, "Jean, are you OK? Cause I grew up on a farm— if your water breaks, I've delivered pigs, I've delivered calves…" She's going, "Would you leave me alone? I'm fine!"

So then I went by Kaline, I said, "Al—oh my God! I've been waitin' my whole life for this." He said, "Fuck you! I waited sixteen years—and you get it in your first year, you get the World Series." I told him, I said, "Al, you know, I've been waitin' a *real* long time for this."

And his teams were close a couple times, back in the early '60s, and then lost by one game in '67. And so I tell him, I said, "Hey, if you guys would've called me up at the end of the season, I'd have won three or four games for ya, we'd have won the thing back to back, we'd would've won two years in a row!" And they're all laughing.

Jim Price:

Oh my God, we couldn't land at the airport—it was *packed*. People, maybe thirty thousand people were there. And we go to Willow Run,[71] and there's like, I don't know, *twenty* thousand people *there*. And I remember on the team bus, trying to get down Telegraph Road, we couldn't get down—cars were everywhere.

It was the greatest thing in the world, really. And that's why we're remembered so much, you know. In '67 we like to think we helped bring everybody back together, you know. And sometimes baseball can do those things.

Tom Matchick:

And when we come in to land, we couldn't land at Detroit Airport. They had people on the runway, we had to go to Willow Run! They said the pilot radioed back, "We can't land, because there's people all over the runway, waiting for the plane to come in." Then we had to go to Willow Run. There was some people are Willow Run, too, but they weren't all over the runway. I don't even know how they could've been on the runway. Well, back then, they probably didn't have the security that they got now, you know.

And everybody was just laughing, talking, you know. They had stuff for us to drink, eat, whatever we wanted, stuff like that there. I mean it was—I don't know, you have to *experience* it to actually express how it was. World Champs, going back to Detroit, after they had them riots, in '67?

You know, we brought that town back together, in '68.

Took their minds off that and everybody was coming to the ballpark to see the Tigers play. That was big, them riots were no fun.

Dick Tracewski:

The town of Detroit, when we landed, when we came home… People were out at Metro, from what I'd heard, when the airplane landed, and the people came up and it wasn't us! And the pilot's thinking, "What the hell's going on here?" And then they diverted us to Willow Run, and that's where we landed.

And then driving the way from Willow Run to downtown Detroit, Tiger Stadium actually... it had to be 35 miles. When we got on the bus, there were people all the way on Michigan Avenue. And what happened is, they brought the fire trucks and they surrounded Tiger Stadium and put the spotlights on it, and they were just blowing whistles and everything. We got there, we had no luggage, we couldn't get any luggage, we went into the clubhouse with our wives, thinking, *What are we gonna do?*

So what we did is, we stayed up and then there was a Holiday Inn about four blocks from Tiger Stadium, and we walked up there. Right through the crowd. Nobody—just walked through the crowd. And went to the Holiday Inn and spent the night there. It was unbelievable, the town of Detroit.

Fred Lasher:

Getting back to Detroit, and sneaking us into the ballpark, everybody getting in their cars and leaving. It was *wild*. I guess Detroit was just crazy. They were crazy the year before, when we *lost* it, and just as crazy when we won it.

Hal Naragon:

Of course it was a great celebration, and it was really nice because in 1967 they had the race riot up there—I remember that, I'll always remember that. And because October the tenth is our wedding anniversary, the day they won it!

So, to do what the Tigers did that year... in '68, they just turned the attitude around, you know. It was very different in '68. I think once people got their minds off of some things and followed the Tigers, you know? Which gives them something else, both black and white.

That year, the 1968 Tigers, we were the last really true champions. Because we beat every team in the league, and then you played the National League winner. Not like it is today.

Al Kaline:

Well, winning the World Series, everybody just went *bananas*. Everybody was so proud to be part of a World Championship, and we hadn't seen one around here for quite a while—I think since the Lions back in, what, '55?

Dick Tracewski:

It had been pretty long. The people in Detroit, I think they realized during the season, because we drew a lot of people, I think they realized that we were a good club and we were worth watching, it was a special club, it really was.

And one thing I remember about the World Series specifically, after we won it, and after it was all over—we got to the bus and we were all sitting there and kind of smirking to one another, and everybody had some champagne and all of that. And Jim Campbell came to me, and he says:

"What did the Dodgers do, for a party?"

I said, "Well, every time we won it, we had a party at the stadium club."

"Well we don't have a stadium club at Tiger Stadium."

I said, "But what happened is, everybody and the wives of course were invited. And they would have a party, a big party."

And he says all right, and so the Tigers had a party.

Al Kaline:

When we came back from St. Louis, after winning, we went to... I can't even think of the hotel. And there was a little party there, and—but anyhow, that's a long time ago, I can't remember that much about that!

But it was great. The parade, and the people having a good time... It was great to see, it really was.

Dick Tracewski:

They had that party for us at a Polynesian restaurant, on the Boulevard. Near the General Motors building, on Grand Boulevard. And that was after it was all over, a couple hours after, because everybody was exhausted by then. They had a party there at Mauna Loa, I want to say. It doesn't exist anymore, but there was a big Polynesian restaurant there. Everybody was invited, and everybody went pretty much. I didn't, because I was going home, you know.

Mickey Stanley:

Oh yeah we did, didn't we? Holy crap, that didn't last long. Mai Tais. It flopped. It didn't last very long, Mauna Loa. Why, what happened— did we get drunk?

Most of the stories that you'd want to hear, we probably shouldn't tell you.

Pat Freehan:

Mauna Loa? No, I think we just went to the Holiday Inn and the big circular restaurant on the top of it, and they just kind of had a big private room for us there, I don't know who had arranged all that.

Denny McLain:

We went somewhere, but I don't remember. I don't remember going to Mauna Loa. I think *we* went home. And I wound up going to Las Vegas about a week later, but... I don't think Sharyn and I went to Mauna Loa.

We had the kids at home, and also, when we got on the ground— because we only had payphones—and called home, the babysitter said,

"Somebody has to come here, the house is *surrounded.*" And it was a woman from Haiti that was babysitting for the five or six days we were gone. We didn't know what the hell she meant—"The house is surrounded." So we didn't know if somebody was trying to burn it down, or… So we quick jumped in the car and we went home, and God, it had to be *five thousand* people surrounding the house. It was great. It was *great!* Fans. Just fans. In Beverly Hills, Michigan. And ours was tee-peed a night or two later. So there had to be a St. Louis Cardinal fan in our fuckin' neighborhood somewhere.

Mickey Stanley:

Our neighborhood, our trees were covered with toilet paper. God, we felt so stressed, we bought a house—for thirty-nine thousand bucks! It was a nice house, I mean—shit, that's more than we ever had. Neither one of us came from any money, my dad was a truck driver.

Pat Freehan:

So I wish we'd been at home, but Detroit certainly welcomed us when we got back that night… We had to change airports! Because they had stormed the runway where we used to land, at the United freight area. So we had to go out to Willow Run, and then they kept us sitting on the plane, and we're going, "Why are we sitting on the plane?" Well, the mayor and the governor wanted to greet us. So they kept us on the plane so they could get from Metro Airport out to Willow Run—and then by that time, the fans had figured that out too! So it was wonderful. And then they sent cars out, took us to the Holiday Inn over on Telegraph Road, where we had our own private party. And then Ford Motor Company sent drivers to take us home to our houses, because the guys had all left their cars down at Tiger Stadium—and we couldn't get there that night, because people were celebrating and going crazy.

And when we got home, my Lord, our street was decorated and there was a bonfire… and everybody was celebrating! Our house had big signs, and with toilet paper and this and that. So it was exciting for everybody. I think it had been quite a long time, 1945, since the Tigers had won. And so it certainly was a citywide, statewide celebration. Everybody identified with the Tigers.

Mel Butsicaris:

They didn't actually come in to the bar that night, because it was too late by the time they got home and stuff like that. But I was tending bar, we were packed and people were watching the game. And we used to have—back in '68 we had two TVs in the bar, we had a small 19-inch TV in one corner of the bar up on the wall so if you're sitting at the bar you can see that one.

Don Wert:

Actually, the two of us didn't go back to Detroit, we never did—we came back to Lancaster through Baltimore. So we didn't get back to the hotel, even. After the last game, I packed up all my clothes and everything, and we came straight home. We flew back into Baltimore; we didn't get back to Detroit. We weren't up for that.

But from what I saw… it was wild—people hanging all those signs, all around downtown, it was crazy. They went wild!

Fred Lasher:

It was funny, we were going back home, we were living in Janesville, I think. I was really speeding going down the interstate. And a squad car, state trooper was parked, caught us, came up behind us.

Pulled us over, and said, "Driver's license and registration."

He looks at it a minute and he says, "Are you Fred Lasher, pitched for Detroit?"

I said, "Yeah."

He says, "Well, drive carefully."

Denny McLain:

Well, after the Series, Bob Gibson and I both went to New York for the *Ed Sullivan Show*.

They had us do a duet—Bob was a guitar player, allegedly, and he knew about four chords. So our group, which was a lot of good musicians, we decided that we would just use the four chords that he knew, and we would try to play behind him, which we did. But I thought he was gonna piss in his pants, that's how nervous he was... couldn't get his hands set.

So, we fooled everybody, and we got through that probably ninety seconds of music. And it sounded pretty good, I mean, no one would think that it was bizarre or anything. And this is without any rehearsal. We were following *him!*

I mean, here we were, having a lot of fun with it... And, you know, I've always had a lot of fun with Bob, despite the fact that he still doesn't think that they lost the World Series in '68. But that was a good time.

Ed Sullivan was a perfect gentleman. Told some of the worst jokes we'd ever heard in our life—you know, because they were so corny, they didn't use bad language back then. But it was a good time for a couple of days. It was a real good time.

And... I don't know if Gibson and I really ever chatted much, beyond that. We've been at a bunch of card shows together, and I would say we're friends. We respect each other, and as competitors, we were probably maybe in the history of the game the two most intense people that may have ever played the game. When I was on the mound, I hated everybody I played against, and I think he still hates us all—so it was a tremendous, great rivalry, and the best team won! That's all there is to it.

And I always have laughed, at all these functions I attended with Bob, and card shows and what have you, and people will walk up and say, "Yeah, well, Bob that year had so many shutouts and innings pitched and..." And I'd say, "Really?" "Yeah, he did. Isn't that great?" And I'd say, "Shit, anybody can win twenty-two. I think I had twenty-two in July!" And everybody gets a chuckle. But that's the truth! And my point was, anybody can win twenty, but it was the next ten that were the tough ones. Just like anything else in life. You know, there's always a mountain you want to get to, and then there's the *peak*. And I didn't realize I was going to win thirty. But I knew at the All-Star break, Ray Oyler asked me at the All-Star turn, he said, "You gonna win fuckin' thirty?" My roommate. And I said, "You're fuckin' right, I am." He says, "Are you serious?" I said, "Listen, you keep me healthy, I'll win thirty." Goddamn, it worked out pretty well.

It's like a night we had at a New York writers' dinner, when they were celebrating—I think it was the fortieth anniversary of our win, at this New York writers' dinner and both sides had got players to come to New York, and we were kind of going to debate each other onstage. Well, the Cardinals wouldn't go for it. And, but there were like ten or twelve Cardinals, and there were only four or five of us—hell, most of our guys are *dead*. And so I was picked to be the spokesman for our crew, and all I heard all night, before we got onstage, was, "Gibson did this, and Gibson did that, and Gibson did this and this and this," and everybody talking about the same guy. So I said, "Ladies and gentlemen, can I remind you of something? Do you realize that I won *twenty* by July, and *thirty* before 144 games were played?" And I got a standing ovation, which really made me feel good because I didn't know how it was gonna go over. But it was a funny line, you know, "Listen, I had twenty in *July*, he had to go all the way to end of September to get twenty-two. And who *won* the whole thing?" You know?

They *still* think they won.

But we won. No matter what, we won—fair and square.

Dick Schofield:

We went to Japan after the Series—it took us seventeen hours to get there, fourteen to get back. And we were there were thirty-five days, and played about eighteen, maybe twenty games. We must've played ten of them in Tokyo, but then we went to Nagasaki, Sapporo, Hiroshima, and I don't remember all the others. We'd play one game someplace, then we'd go someplace else to play a game. And we took the bullet train, we went from place to place in that.

But I know other teams had gone there, for a long time. There used to be a team that would go every year, I think.[72]

Ray Washburn:

Several teams had gone before, and teams have gone afterwards, it was a promotional thing. It was baseball-crazy back then. And the parks always dimension-wise seemed small—so I got in the record books over there, when I gave up a deep home run to Sadaharu Oh.

Julián Javier:

Well, after the World Series I said, "No I don't want to go to Japan—take somebody else, it's too far." Then when I come back, I'd have to play winter ball? No. Then you have to pay for your wife? No way—we didn't make that kind of money. So, pick Gagliano, pick somebody else.

Bobby Tolan:

I did go on the trip. The Reds were curious, and wanted to know why I was going, or why I wanted to go on a trip, since I no longer belonged to the Cardinals. But my feeling was, the reason why I wanted to go, was because it was from the '67 team. That, I was a part of the team then, and I wanted to go. And it's not often that you get a chance to go out of the country, and to a place like that.

So, yes, I did go. But they didn't play me a lot, because I guess they didn't want me to get hurt or anything like that. Because the Reds would be upset because of that.

Because, you know, before the trip, I'd been traded. But I was traded right *before* Game Seven. I do remember that, quite a few years ago, I was with the Cardinals at a reunion of some sort, and Red told me that he had started to pencil me in to play in Game Seven against

Mickey Lolich. But then he had to change his mind, because supposedly I was traded. *Before* the game.[73]

And, you know, in baseball, you can't upstage the World Series by making trade announcements and stuff. But he told me that about seven or eight years ago, that he had scheduled me to start in Game Seven, in place of Roger Maris. On the way to the ballpark that morning, I read in the newspaper that I was going to be traded to Houston. And then, after the game ended, the batboy called me in, and Lou Brock looked at me and he just nodded his head, like he knew I'd been traded. And then Red told me I'd been traded, and I said, "Yeah I know—Houston." He said, "No, Cincinnati."

In the World Series, a lot of players get kind of—not like left off the roster, but you don't play, because it's such a short series. I think I got in like 110 or 115 games that year, and I started a few games... and a lot of the games I'd come in for defense in right field behind Maris, or filling in for Cepeda at first base. But then, when you get to the World Series, a lot of your starting pitchers, your number four and five pitchers, don't get to pitch that much. They go to the bullpen, because, you know, Gibson's going to pitch three or four games, and I think Nellie Briles was going to pitch one or two, and so you don't get a chance to play as much in the World Series. Unless you get in there and you have a fantastic AB or two, and then he might start you, but...

I was still shocked to hear Red tell me, years ago, that he was going to start me—because Roger Maris didn't do that well in the World Series, and neither did the other outfielder, Ron Davis. And he was going to start me over both of those guys, but then he told me that I had been traded!

But, I did go on the trip. You know, we wanted to experience the thrill of being over there... and I went out, and had shirts and suits custom made, and things like that. And they were really nice. So it was an enjoyable experience for me, getting over there at that time. But again, I just wish that I could've played more for the Cardinals, but it wasn't meant to be. It was destined for me to go to Cincinnati.

Dick Schofield:

We went there when that Sadaharu Oh was there. We met him, but no one could really speak English, and we sure as hell couldn't speak Japanese. But we played them, and it was nice. They had good crowds, and Musial was naturally a popular man—of course, he was done playing by then.

But I don't think they beat us too many times. They had a pitcher, though, who was *really* good. His name was Mori, I think. M-O-R-I. And he was a short stocky left-handed pitcher, and we didn't do much with him. I think he pretty much had us.

A lot of times we'd play a team, and we played the Tokyo Giants the most. But then every once in a while, we'd play an all-star team. And they had some good players… on that Tokyo Giants team, they had a third baseman who was a good player. And they had a pitcher that was good, that had pitched for a long time.[74] But some of the guys they said were good I didn't think they were quite that good. But nowadays, I'd betcha they've got some guys that are doing pretty well.

Johnny Edwards:

Most of the time, we played an all-star team, made up of all the teams over there. We were given an itinerary when we got over there for the whole trip, and everything was in minutes. And they were *always* on time. It was unbelievable how orchestrated it was.

Musial had been our general manager at the time, and he was a legend over there. So, we went over there, and it's a long trip over there, and we get up the next day and play ball. And so I think we lost the first three or four ballgames in a row. I remember Stan coming in and talking to us, saying, "You know, you're representing American baseball." And then we won the next thirteen straight.

Oh, and I remember something—before we left at the airport here, Mike Shannon was stopped getting on the plane with a doggone crossbow. To go hunting!

Mike Shannon:

I'm a deer hunter, OK. And this guy sent me a crossbow. So anyway, I took it to Japan, I was going to hunt bear in the Sapporo! And of course, you can't have a gun in Japan, since World War II. It's against the law. That crossbow's not a gun, but it's got a trigger—and when that got to the airport, they saw that trigger, and they didn't know *what* the hell it was. But they knew it had a trigger. When they saw that trigger, it really baffled them. None of those people had seen guns, and they'd *never* seen a crossbow, unless they were looking at history.

We had to go through customs, and… Musial was with us—so Stan came aboard and he said, "What the hell's going on over here?" Because everybody was lined up, you know, and stopped. So, finally, you know, they asked this, that, and so forth… and that's when the guy said, "What's it for?"

I said, "It's for the Emperor."

Well, once I mentioned the Emperor, and I was going to give it as a gift, to the Emperor, they let me through with it! They said, "Oh! Fine, come on through."

But I never did go hunting in Sapporo.

Bobby Tolan:

You know, they wouldn't let him go through with *that*, now…

But they told him to put it away, put it in the closet or whatever it was. And, years later, I went to Japan. Played a year over there, and I had some stuff shipped over. And one of the things I had shipped over was a popcorn machine. One of those air poppers. And, they asked me, you know, "What is this here thing?" And I said, "It's like popcorn—it goes like *pop, pop, pop, pop!*" When I said that, they thought it was like a gun… they told me I couldn't have it!

Johnny Edwards:

There wasn't a whole lot of pressure or anything when we were playing in Japan, but I do remember the strike zone was so much different. We took Al Barlick with us, who was the only umpire that went, and when he was behind the plate it was the National League strike zone. But when they had the Japanese umpires, it was *their* strike zone. And it was a higher strike zone, just below the waist to the shoulders. Our pitchers *hated* that. They're used to pitching down low, at the knees. When you've got to come all the way up, a sinkerball pitcher's in trouble then.

And the fans were very, very good, although it was not very many women at the ballpark. It was mostly businessmen, and soldiers. And they were great baseball fans, they loved the game. They still do.

The wives were with us, but they had a separate itinerary for them. They visited all the shrines, and the pearl divers and all that stuff. The customs over there were quite a bit different than ours—the bowing when you meet somebody, you get on the elevator and it's always the men, the women aren't allowed to get on until all the men are on.

Dick Schofield:

We all bought pearls for our wives, which was a really good deal. And electronic equipment, music equipment, was outstanding. They had all the best stuff back then.

And going out to eat, we ate at some pretty nice places—that Italian place we ate at was just outstanding. And then we'd go to these places where they had that Kobe beef, and you'd have big ol' steaks and stuff like that. And all I know is, they served beer in big bottles, like a *quart.* And every time we went to eat, they'd already have beer sitting on the table. Well, you could drink that stuff, it wasn't like our beer, it was like 12 percent or something like that. I saw guys throwing up out of the window of the bus the next morning, and we had to go play—so it wasn't too exciting, then!

And I'll always remember, if you wanted like a sport coat or something, I remember we got this guy, his name was George. That's all I remember, *"George."* And he'd come in, he'd come to the hotel, he had it all down pat. He'd have a suitcase full of material, and you'd say, "I want a red sport coat, that material." He'd measure you, he'd come back the next day, he'd have the coat, and he'd have it basted to see if it would fit. And if it fit, the next day he'd take it, come back, it would look like it had just come off the store rack. And they were *cheap*. I remember I had a couple sport coats, a couple suits made—and they were lined, they'd have your name in them, and, I mean, if you had the same suit made nowadays it'd probably cost you two or three thousand dollars, seriously.

I remember we got dress shirts, too. You could get dress shirts with your initials on French cuffs—you could get a dozen shirts and they wouldn't cost you nothing. It was clothes, pearls, music equipment. Those are the three things that stick in my mind.

Johnny Edwards:

One of the days there that I'll never forget was in Hiroshima. One of the sportswriters up there asked several of us if we wanted to go on a deep-sea fishing trip. We said, "Oh hell *yes* we want to go on a deep sea fishing trip!" He said "OK, I'll pick you up at the hotel at six o'clock in the morning, you go out early."

And so he picks us up, we got down the dock, we get on a sampan boat. We've got to take our shoes off. We get there, and we go out onto the Sea of Japan or wherever we were, and it was *cold*. I remember how cold it was. And so we got out there and we said, "OK, we're ready for the poles." And hell, there's no poles! They had a bamboo thing you put a line through, and you put a clam on the hook, and then you'd hold the bamboo with the line, and then would reel it in by hand! And that was the deep-sea fishing trip.

On our other off-days we played golf, and we used to have girl caddies and they always had the girls out in front. And, you know, Japan is in a lot of mountains, and all their courses were in the mountains, and we were scattering the ball all over the place. You know how ballplayers hit it—they hit it far, but don't have any idea which way it's going. But it was considered an insult if they lost a ball, and boy, they had four caddies out there, looking like hell for our balls.

One of the other good times was, we went to play on the American Air Force base, which was the only course we'd been on that was flat. The commander took us to his house to eat afterwards, and they had hamburgers—and we hadn't had a hamburger since we'd been over there. We had a run on those damn things, he ran out of food in about ten minutes!

So, you know, I was real happy to go on that Japan trip. It kind of topped it off.

Dick Schofield:

It was a good trip, but I just wasn't that thrilled with the trip. You know, you can only see so many shrines, and all that. I think if you took a vote, I think most people would've voted not to go. It was a long trip, and we'd just gotten beat, you know.

But it was an experience.

I remember when I we came home, my wife and I, our kid says, "You guys *stink* so bad—get those clothes out of the house, wash 'em, do something, they stink so bad!" See back then, over in Japan I guess they didn't use deodorant too much. You get on the elevator and it was just like… seriously, you weren't used to something like that!

Denny McLain:

Well, it's easier to go when you win, it's sadder and a longer trip if you lose.

And I guess that must've been a real *long* trip.

Orlando Cepeda:

You know, I remember everything from back then.

I see people at the airport I played with in 1956, in the minor leagues—and I remember them. I don't remember what happened *today,* but I remember what happened *then.*

Tom Matchick:

You know what, some of it I can remember, some of it I can't remember. You're talking fifty years ago, you know? I mean, I can still think, but I'm just saying, that's a long time. It don't even seem like fifty years, though. It just don't seem that long ago.

Jon Warden:

What's ironic and what's interesting—you take twenty-five guys, you know the game you play, where you give me a word, and then you pass it around and by the time the word gets back to you, it's different. Like that "telephone" game? Some guys remember key things, and other guys don't remember. They'll go, "Well I don't remember that." It's not that I'm lying, or they're questioning it, but they're like, "Oh man, I didn't realize that." Because everybody's got their focus on certain things.

Orlando Cepeda:

It's funny, because when you play, you see them every day—but then when you retire, you don't see them anymore. But, actually, me and McCarver are better friends *now* than when we played. And Bob, I just saw Gibson in Cooperstown, in July. We got to see each other, spend two or three days together there. But you don't see the others too much.

How's Lou Brock doing? I heard that he's not doing too good. I talked to McCarver this morning. Great guy, Lou. All of them. McCarver, Washburn, Flood. I was close with Julián Javier, Bob Gibson, McCarver.

Although, we got together in May for the '67 team reunion. Very nice, *very* nice.

Mickey Stanley:

How many did you say were gone, of us players? Well, most of us are dead! Cash croaked. Oyler croaked. Mathews... So I'm pretty lucky I guess, health-wise.

But you know, I don't remember much, from back then. I don't live in the—a lot of the guys I played with, like Lolich and some of the others, they remember everything, and they, you know, put major-league alumni stuff on their cars. I'm so far from that. I just turned another page when I got through, you know, it was over. I don't brag about being a major leaguer... and a lot of guys don't. McAuliffe would never do that, Wert wouldn't. But some guys really dig it.

But, you see my ring? I never take it off! I play golf, never take it off. Shower. It never comes off. I have to take it off for my PET scans, when I go. I've turned the page, but—I do wear that ring! I'm proud of *that*. I am proud, but, I mean, I could care less if people recognize me, you know.

But it does happen, and that's fine. This morning I'm in the car repair shop, I took my truck in to get a new mirror—anyway, I'm sitting there in the waiting room, there's five or six people sitting there. And nobody that's sitting there, I didn't think, knew who I was. This one old fart did. "You're Mickey Stanley aren't ya!?" I was like, *At least whisper!* You know? So I blew my cover. People do, but I keep a low profile.

But you know what's funny? I'd rather talk about developing property and that—I do so many other things. Baseball is a big part of my life, but I like doing a lot of things. I loved it when I was doing it.

I just felt lucky to be there almost every year.

Al Kaline:

It was a great Series. We played against a great team. And we played against the toughest pitcher I ever faced, Bob Gibson.

But anyhow, we won—so that's the big thing.

And I am forever grateful to the players, in '68, that battled and got us there. I wasn't part of it, five weeks of it, but we were able to get in the World Series and I had a chance to play. And it was spectacular. I mean, just the emotion… and the concentration level was out of sight. I mean, you didn't think about *anything* else. I wish I could've done that my whole career. I was *so* focused on *every* pitch, *every* play, every-thing—and I wish I could've done it in my whole career!

So I can't emphasize how proud I am to have played with so many guys on that '68 team, that really gave me the chance to play in the World Series, because of my injury. I'll never forget that.

Because all I wanted to do was to play in a World Series.

APPENDIX

1968 WORLD SERIES STATISTICS

DETROIT TIGERS

Dick McAuliffe	6-27	1 HR	3 RBI	.222
Mickey Stanley	6-28			.214
Al Kaline	11-29	2 HR	8 RBI	.379
Norm Cash	10-26	1 HR	5 RBI	.385
Willie Horton	7-23	1 HR	3 RBI	.304
Jim Northrup	7-28	2 HR	8 RBI	.250
Bill Freehan	2-24		2 RBI	.083
Don Wert	2-17		2 RBI	.118

Mickey Lolich	27.0 IP	3–0	1.67 ERA
Denny McLain	16.2 IP	1–2	3.24 ERA
Earl Wilson	4.1 IP	0–1	6.23 ERA
Pat Dobson	4.2 IP		3.86 ERA

ST. LOUIS CARDINALS

Lou Brock	7 SB	13-28	2 HR	5 RBI	.464
Curt Flood	3 SB	8-28		2 RBI	.286
Roger Maris		3-19		1 RBI	.158
Orlando Cepeda		7-28	2 HR	6 RBI	.250
Tim McCarver		9-27	1 HR	4 RBI	.333
Mike Shannon		8-29	1 HR	4 RBI	.276
Julián Javier	1 SB	9-27		3 RBI	.333
Dal Maxvill		0-22			.000

Bob Gibson	27.0 IP	2–1	1.67 ERA
Nelson Briles	11.1 IP	0–1	5.56 ERA
Ray Washburn	7.1 IP	1–1	9.82 ERA
Joe Hoerner	4.2 IP	0–1	3.86 ERA

WORLD SERIES APPEARANCES

1946	*Cardinals vs.* Red Sox	*Schoendienst, Sisler,* Cuccinello
1948	*Indians vs.* Braves	Sain
1950	*Yankees vs.* Phillies	Sisler
1951	*Yankees vs.* Giants	*Sain*
1952	*Yankees vs.* Dodgers	*Sain*
1953	*Yankees vs.* Dodgers	*Sain,* Milliken
1954	*Giants vs.* Indians	Naragon, Cuccinello*
1957	*Braves vs.* Yankees	*Mathews, McMahon, Schoendienst*
1958	*Yankees vs.* Braves	Mathews, McMahon, Schoendienst
1959	*Dodgers vs.* White Sox	Cash, Cuccinello*
1960	*Pirates vs.* Yankees	*Schofield,* Maris
1961	*Yankees vs.* Reds	*Maris, Sain*, Moses*,* Edwards
1962	*Yankees vs.* Giants	*Maris, Sain*, Moses*,* Cepeda
1963	*Dodgers vs.* Yankees	*Tracewski,* Maris, Sain*
1964	*Cardinals vs.* Yankees	*Brock, Gibson, Flood, Javier, McCarver, Shannon, Maxvill, Schoendienst*, Schultz*,* Maris
1965	*Dodgers vs.* Twins	*Tracewski,* Sain*, Naragon*
1967	*Cardinals vs.* Red Sox	*Brock, Gibson, Cepeda, Flood, Javier, McCarver, Maris, Shannon, Maxvill, Tolan, Gagliano, Spiezio, Briles, Willis, Carlton, Hoerner, Hughes, Jaster, Washburn, Ricketts, Schoendienst*, Schultz*, Milliken*, Muffett*, Sisler**

- 1968 -

1970	*Orioles vs.* Reds	Tolan, Washburn, Granger
1971	*Pirates vs.* Orioles	*Briles, Ricketts*,* Dobson
1972	*Athletics vs.* Reds	Tolan, Javier
1974	*Athletics vs.* Dodgers	*Maxvill*
1980	*Phillies vs.* Royals	*Carlton*
1982	*Cardinals vs.* Brewers	*Schoendienst*, Ricketts**
1983	*Orioles vs.* Phillies	*Carlton*
1984	*Tigers vs.* Padres	*Tracewski*, Brown**
1985	*Royals vs.* Cardinals	Schoendienst*, Ricketts*, Maxvill**
1987	*Twins vs.* Cardinals	Schoendienst*, Ricketts*, Maxvill**

*As coach/manager

**As general manager

Note: Tim McCarver worked on 24 World Series broadcasts;
Tony Kubek worked on 12 World Series broadcasts, and played in six (winning three).

ENDNOTES

GAME ONE

1.   Mary Ann Peacock, born with cerebral palsy, was chosen to be the United Way Fund "Poster Girl" from 1968–69, when she was four years old. The interview was conducted over the phone in August 2017.

2.   During the Tigers' 1966 season, both manager Charlie Dressen and his replacement Bob Swift fell ill, left the team, and died later that year. Frank Skaff, one of the Tigers coaches, took over on July 14 as acting manager, and held the position until Mayo Smith was signed for the 1967 season.

3.   Tony Cuccinello, the Tigers' third-base coach in 1968, was selected for major-league baseball's first All-Star Game at Comiskey Park in 1933. Also, during the 1954 World Series, he was coaching at third base for the Indians when Willie Mays made his famous catch in center field.

4.   Tony Kubek did not play in the 1968 World Series, but worked as the field reporter for the NBC broadcast, alongside Harry Caray, Curt Gowdy, and George Kell. Kubek played for the Yankees from 1957 to 1965, most at shortstop, and played in six World Series (winning three). The interview was conducted over the phone, from his home in Wisconsin, in September 2017.

5.   Before the Series, Stanley was quoted in newspapers as saying: "Playing shortstop is a lot of fun. I might get to like it better than the outfield."

6.   From umpire Bill Haller's interview for this book (July, 2017):

> "We had a game in Minneapolis one night, and after the game we went back to the hotel, and we walked into a restaurant in the hotel to have something to eat. And Mayo was there with his coaches, so we all sat together. And I said, 'Mayo, do you work in the winter?' He said, 'Yeah, I go and buy land for developers.'

Well, in my first year of umpiring, in the Georgia-Florida League, we had an umpire that lived in Kissimmee, Florida. And we got talking about hunting quail. And I said, 'You hunt a lot?' 'Oh yeah.' 'Lot of quail?' 'All over, as far you can see.' I said, 'How 'bout land? How much is land?' He said, 'Bill, as far as you can see, ten dollars an acre.'

Ten years later, when I ask Mayo what he did, he said, 'Well, I was in Kissimmee. We went to this farmer, he had 90 acres, we wanted to buy it. And we asked how much you want for it?' So, a hundred and eighty thousand an acre, that's what Mayo was willing to pay. And the farmer said, 'Double it before you come back.' You know why? Disney was coming in. Disney was coming for the land. Can you imagine? Ten dollars an acre, and then ten years later you can't buy it. Three hundred thousand something dollars, an acre!"

7.   Bob Christian was called up from Triple-A Toledo in September 1968, and played three games for the Tigers before heading to the White Sox at the end of the month.

8.   In the 1967 World Series against the Boston Red Sox, Javier batted .360, with three doubles, a home run, and four RBIs.

9.   During the 1968 season, Don Drysdale pitched a scoreless-innings streak with the Dodgers—from May 14 to June 8 (58 2/3 innings). Partially during the same span, Bob Gibson began a streak of his own, lasting 47 scoreless innings. Orel Hershiser currently holds the record (59), set in final month of the Dodgers' world championship 1988 season.

10.   Gaylord Perry, a 300-game winner and member of the Baseball Hall of Fame, went 8–12 with a 4.19 ERA in 1965 with the San Francisco Giants.

11.   Tony Kubek led off that game for the Yankees in the bottom of the first, beginning with the first of five strikeouts in a row to open the game: Kubek, Richardson, Tresh, Mantle, Maris.

12.   Sherry Gaston-Caldwell (then Sherry Gaston) appeared in a brief interview with Tony Kubek on the NBC broadcast of the Series. She worked as an usherette at Busch Stadium in 1967 and 1968, while she was in college. The interview was conducted on the phone in August 2017.

GAME TWO

13. Lew Burdette, with the 1957 Milwaukee Braves, was the first pitcher to win three complete games in the World Series since Stan Coveleski, of the 1920 Cleveland Indians. In 1967, Bob Gibson duplicated that feat—and then Mickey Lolich in 1968.

14. The entire 1944 Series was played at Sportsman's Park, in St. Louis—the last time both World Series teams played on the same home field.

15. October 2, 1949: Bob Feller entered the game in the sixth inning, on one day's rest, relieving Bob Lemon. George Kell, the Tigers' third baseman, went 2-for-3 in the game, with a fly ball in the seventh inning in his at-bat against Feller, to just retain his lead over Ted Williams and win the American League batting title. Kell later became a longtime broadcaster for the Tigers, and paired with Curt Gowdy for Games Three, Four, and Five of the '68 Series on NBC. He was inducted into the National Baseball Hall of Fame in 1983.

16. After the 1968 season, a Major League rules panel voted to both lower the mound and shrink the strike zone, as well as check against the use of doctored baseballs. Offense jumped in 1969 from 6.84 runs per game to 8.14.

17. "Fat guys need idols, too," Lolich was once reported as having said.

18. In the sixth inning of Game Seven, Lolich picked off both Lou Brock and Curt Flood at first base, after giving up a base hit to each, with the game still scoreless at that point.

19. During the 1968 season, Mickey Lolich received an average of 3.79 runs a game from his offense, while Denny McLain received 5.23. Lolich won 17 games to McLain's 31.

20. Johnny Sain served as the Tigers' pitching coach from 1967 to 1969, when Denny McLain won his two Cy Young Awards and the Tigers team ERA went from 3.85 in 1966 to 3.32 and finally 2.71 in 1968. Sain first rose to baseball fame in the 1940s on the Boston Braves, as the subject of poem by Gerald V. Hern: "Spahn and Sain; then pray for rain."

21. Norm Cash played for the Tigers from 1960 to 1974—winning an American League batting title in 1961, making four All-Star Games, and hitting 377 career home runs.

22. As Bill James described it: "He tucked his right wrist under his chin and held his bat over his head, so it looked as if he were dodging the sword of Damocles in mid-descent. He pointed his left knee at the catcher and his right knee at the pitcher and spread the two as far apart as humanly possible."

23. It was later that Tommy John suffered the injury that led to the famed surgical operation, during the 1974 season.

24. Schofield played with 24 Hall of Famers, in all: Stan Musial, Red Schoendienst, Enos Slaughter, Hoyt Wilhelm, Roberto Clemente, Bill Mazeroski, Willie Stargell, Willie McCovey, Willie Mays, Orlando Cepeda, Gaylord Perry, Juan Marichal, Warren Spahn, Mickey Mantle, Whitey Ford, Sandy Koufax, Don Drysdale, Don Sutton, Lou Brock, Bob Gibson, Steve Carlton, Carl Yastrzemski, Carlton Fisk, Joe Torre (in as a manager).

25. Dennis Ribant, from Detroit, Michigan, pitched 24 1/3 innings for the Tigers in 1968 before being traded to the Chicago White Sox in late July. Lenny

Green, also from Detroit, played 12 seasons in the majors, and finished his career with the Tigers in 1967 and a short part of the 1968 season.

26. Kaline, brought to the Tigers by scout Ed Katalinas, bypassed the minor leagues and joined the team directly from high school at eighteen years old—as a "bonus baby," receiving $35,000 to sign with Detroit. The Bonus Rule lasted from 1947 to 1965, and required teams to keep a player on the 25-man roster for two full seasons if signed for more than $4,000.

27. On June 2, 1925, Lou Gehrig replaced Wally Pipp in the Yankees lineup because of an apparent headache—and went on to keep the spot for the rest of his Hall of Fame career (2,130 consecutive games).

28. On August 11, 1968, against the Red Sox at Tiger Stadium, Gates Brown hit a pinch-hit walk-off home run in the first game of a doubleheader, started the second game in left field, and hit a walk-off single to cap off a ninth inning rally that brought the Tigers back from a 5–2 deficit.

29. Gates Brown's average in 1968 (.370) was the eighth-best season ever for a pinch-hitter. In his career, he totaled 107 pinch hits, the most ever in the American League. [Note: Brown hit .450 as a pinch hitter, .370 overall]

30. Crestline High School (in Crestline, Ohio).

GAME THREE

31. The St. Louis Browns, now the Baltimore Orioles, played their final season in St. Louis the year Al Kaline made his major-league debut, at eighteen years old (1953).

32. Mel Butsicaris was a senior in high school in 1968, and worked at the legendary Lindell A.C. sports bar run by his father Johnny and uncle Jimmy—at the corner of Michigan and Cass, in Detroit.

33. Kaline won the American League batting title in 1955, at age twenty, with a season batting average of .340. He become the youngest player to win it since Ty Cobb in 1907.

34. Norm Cash hit 25 home runs in 1968, but broke the 40-mark once, in 1961—with 41 home runs and the American League batting title.

35. The 1964 Series featured brothers Ken Boyer (Cardinals) and Clete Boyer (Yankees), both of whom started at third base for their respective teams.

36. Bill Haller's brother, Tom, who played with Orlando Cepeda in San Francisco, joined the Detroit Tigers in his last season—leading to complaints of a conflict of interest one game in 1971, when Bill was umpiring behind home plate.

37. Bill Haller, a retired American League umpire, worked four World Series, with 1968 being his first. In 1980, Haller was captured on tape in a now-famous argument with Orioles' manager Earl Weaver, who said to Haller (among other

things): "You're here just to fuck us!" And, interesting to note: in the video of the incident, '68 Tigers' infielder Dick Tracewski can be seen coaching at first base.

38. Cal Hubbard was an American League umpire from 1936 to 1951, and later became the top supervisor of the league's umpiring crews, from 1954 to 1969.

39. John Sain was on the mound for Jackie Robinson's first at-bat in the major leagues.

40. Earl Wilson batted .227 in 1968, with seven home runs on the year (and 35 career).

41. George Crowe played first base for the Cardinals from 1959 to 1961. To note: During a game in 1958, he switched from first base to second and turned a double play wearing his larger first-baseman's mitt—which led to a rule change that requires first basemen to replace their mitts with a fielder's glove if switching positions.

42. McCarver drew 548 career walks to 422 strikeouts.

43. Amadee Wohlschlaeger was a sports cartoonist for the St. Louis Post-Dispatch, signing his cartoons "Amadee." He drew the Weatherbird cartoon for nearly five decades, and drew covers for the annual St. Louis Baseball Writers dinner.

44. After suffering a heart attack in 1971 and leaving baseball, John Hiller recorded 38 saves for the Tigers in 1973, a major-league record at the time. He stayed in baseball until 1980, the longest of the '68 World Series group, and his 545 games pitched remains a Tigers record.

GAME FOUR

45. While a regular-season game with five innings completed constitutes an official game, postseason games are left to the discretion of the Commissioner's Office. The first game in World Series history to be suspended occurred in 2008, when Game Five of the Phillies-Rays Series was stopped by rain and resumed two days later. Three games in World Series history have ended in a tie due to darkness: in 1907, 1912, and 1922.

46. September 17, 1968—a night game at home, Tiger Stadium.

47. Mathews played third base for the Braves over 15 seasons, spanning from their final year in Boston, their 13 years in Milwaukee, and their first year in Atlanta. He hit 512 home runs in his career, and was inducted into the Hall of Fame in 1978.

48. Edwards played against Maris in the 1961 World Series, when the Yankees beat the Reds in five games.

GAME FIVE

49. José Feliciano is a Puerto Rican guitarist and singer, who rose to fame in the 1960s for his cover of The Doors' "Light My Fire," and later his Christmas single, "Feliz Navidad." The interview was conducted over the phone in September 2017.

50. Bill Freehan was diagnosed with Alzheimer's disease about ten years ago, and was unable to sit for an interview. Pat Freehan, his wife of fifty-five years, kindly shared what she remembered of his playing days and the '68 Series over the phone in September 2017.

51. From a short story by Ring Lardner, "Alibi Ike," first published in the Saturday Evening Post on July 31, 1915.

52. The record for most putouts in a nine-inning game by a left fielder is held in a four-way tie for 11 between Dick Harley (1898), Topsy Hartsel (1901), Paul Lehner (1950), and Willie Horton (1969).

GAME SIX

53. The ten runs put up by the Tigers were the most scored in a World Series inning since 1929, when the Philadelphia Athletics (down 8–0 at the time) scored ten in the bottom of the seventh inning against the Chicago Cubs to win, 10–8, and take a 3–1 Series lead.

54. On September 14, 1968, Denny McLain won his 30th game with the help of a walk-off single by Willie Horton—a pitching feat that hadn't been done in 34 years, and hasn't been done since.

55. Denny McLain married Sharyn Boudreau in 1963, the daughter of Hall of Fame shortstop and manager Lou Boudreau.

56. Glen Campbell won the Grammy in 1968 for Album of the Year ("By the Time I Get to Phoenix"), and won the Country Music Association's top award as 1968 Entertainer of the Year.

57. Denny McLain's daughter was killed in a car accident caused by a drunk driver in 1992.

58. In Game Seven of the 1940 World Series, Bobo Newsom pitched a strong game in a losing effort, just two days after pitching a shutout in memory of his father, who died on his visit for the Series. Before pitching Game Five, Bobo said, "I'll win this for my daddy." Before Game Seven, Newsom told reporters, "I think I'll win this one for old Bobo."

59. In the second game of the the 1967 World Series, Julián Javier broke up Jim Lonborg's no-hit bid in the eighth inning with a double that amounted to the sole hit in a complete-game shutout. In the seventh game, Javier hit a three-run home run off Lonborg, ensuring the Cardinals' Series win.

GAME SEVEN & AFTER

60. In 1970, Sports Illustrated published an article on McLain's involvement in bookmaking, citing sources who alleged that the foot injury he suffered in '67 was caused by a mobster who stomped on McLain's foot for failing to make a payment.

61. "I'm sick of hearing what a great team the Cardinals are," said Denny McLain, the day before the Series began. "I don't want to just beat them. I want to demolish them."

62. Busch Stadium opened in 1966, and for a brief time featured a grass field, until replaced by AstroTurf in 1970 (lasting until 1995).

63. Flood became known during his career as a brilliant painter, composing portraits of teammates and others, such as Martin Luther King Jr.—but it was revealed in a 2011 HBO Documentary, *The Curious Case of Curt Flood*, that his art career had been a fraud, and the paintings were done by someone else.

64. Curt Flood's misplay in Game Seven led, ultimately, to his departure from baseball and the start to the biggest piece of his legacy—opening the door to the beginnings of free agency, after refusing a trade to the Phillies in 1969 and challenging Major League Baseball's reserve clause.

65. Over the course of the Series, on NBC's TV broadcasts, Tony Kubek interviewed: Stan Musial, Joe Cronin, Charlene Gibson and Renee Gibson, Casey Stengel, Warren Giles, Frank Sinatra, William Eckert, Eugene McCarthy, Dick Williams, Monte Irvin, John Fetzer, Bob Hope, Carl Erskine, Ralph Houk, Judge Roy Hofheinz, Sid Hartman, Ernie Banks, Gene Mauch, Bob Skinner, Dizzy Dean, Joe Black, Pat Maris, Ben Kerner, Don Davidson, Dick Young, and several fans in the crowd.

66. Oddly enough, Ray Oyler didn't make a single play at shortstop in any of the four games he entered in for fielding duty in the later innings. He caught one flip from second base for a force out in one of the games, but otherwise nothing was hit to him.

67. At the end of the 1967 World Series, as the Cardinal players mobbed Bob Gibson after his third complete-game win, umpire Augie Donatelli ran past the group and snagged Julián Javier's cap. The red cap ended up displayed for many years in the bar Donatelli ran in St. Petersburg, Florida—named, fittingly (but only coincidentally), "El Cap."

And during the 1984 World Series, when Dick Tracewski coached for the Tigers, an exchange near the end of the TV broadcast went like this: Joe Garagiola: "Johnny Grubb, preparing for the onslaught, took his cap off and put it in his shirt—and that's why most of them have their caps off, they'll be running out there, fans love to grab 'em." The broadcast camera pans across the Tigers dugout, showing a nearly bald Tracewski with his cap off, waiting with the rest of the team for the last out. "And Tracewski! He doesn't like to take his hat off, he doesn't got that much grass!"

68. Mark "The Bird" Fidrych pitched for the Tigers from 1976 to 1980, going 19–9 in his rookie season with a 2.34 ERA (when Mickey Stanley, Willie Horton, Bill Freehan, John Hiller were still on the team, out of the 1968 group).

69. Bob Turley started Game Two of the '58 Series without getting out of the first inning. With the Yankees on the brink of elimination, he threw a complete-game shutout in Game Five, recorded a save in the 10th inning of Game Six, and won his third game in four days after pitching from the bullpen in Game Seven.

70. In 1948, with the Boston Braves, Johnny Sain led the league in complete games (28), and started and completed nine games between August 24 and September 21 (winning seven).

71. The Detroit area's second airport, located about six miles to the west of Detroit Metro Airport.

72. By 1968, many major-league teams had taken a baseball tour of Japan, including the 1962 Detroit Tigers—a team that featured Al Kaline, Norm Cash, and Dick McAuliffe.

73. After the 1968 season, the league held an expansion draft—from which each of the twenty teams could protect fifteen players. The 1968–69 offseason thus brought a bevy of trades as teams reconfigured their rosters before the draft.

74. Likely, Schofield is referring to Shigeo Nagashima, 1968 MVP of the Central League, and Masaichi Kaneda, the only Japanese pitcher to have won 400 games.

ACKNOWLEDGMENTS

Thank you, forever, to each of the men interviewed,
and each of the others in this book.

Thanks to Mom, to Dad. Thanks to Papa. Thanks to Larry Donley, for joining along at Wayne State and the Detroit Public Library. Tom and Cindy Donley, for the stay at PLP. Mark and Diane Donley, for the stay in Cincinnati.

Thanks to John Gallo, for giving me a copy of *The Glory of Their Times*, at the end of a youth-league baseball season, circa 2004.

Thanks to Ken Samelson, Jason Katzman, and Skyhorse Publishing.

Thanks to Facebook, Wikipedia, Baseball-Reference, the SABR Bio Project. Thanks to my Zoom H1 audio recorder, and to Audacity. My computer.

Thanks to Ken Davidoff; Bob Rosen; Peggy Thompson; Jerry Lewis; Bill Dow; Ashley Powell-Rhodes; Will Leitch; Ben Boyd; Matt Crossman; Ben Hochman; Al Seeger; Jim Greenan. The handyman at Tony Kubek's cottage, in remote northern Michigan. Jeb Smail; Dr. Julián Javier; Linette Hiller; Ellen Stanley; Amy Mader; Patti Poppe; Dick Gabrys; George Mahoney; David Silverman and Tom Cross. The kind folks who built I-94, I-90, I-46, I-55, and the rest of the roads I traveled. Susan Feliciano and Helmuth Schaerf. Sharon Arend; Eliza Rothstein; Flora Esterly and Bettina Schrewe; Nick Mullendore; Joe West; Lee Butz; Melody Yount; Larry State; Chad Crunk; Fred Gibson; Mark Armour; Mark Pattison. Thank you to the rainbow, the beautiful *double* rainbow, that appeared over the highway near Black River Falls, Wisconsin. The late David Vincent; Nathan Kelber; Dan D'Addona; Tony Paul; Al Yellon; Jessica Harden; John Thorn; Tim Wendel;

Levi Stahl. Thank you to the rolling hills of Amish country around Lancaster, Pennsylvania, for appearing like heaven at the end of a long day. Thanks to John Henry at the Super 8 Motel in Iron Mountain, Michigan. Thanks to Don Marsh; Alex Heuer; Elizabeth Clemens; Scott Ferkovich; Katherine Walden; Cassidy Lent; Andy Strasberg; Julie Walker Altesleben; Tom Derry; Howard Cole; Pedro Gomez; Sammy Roth; Justin McGuire; Nathan Bierma; Louie Kamberovski; Jamie Edmonds; Nathan Hill; Lynn Henning. Thanks to everyone else who wished me luck.

And thanks, Lawrence S. Ritter, for writing the greatest of all baseball books.